M29

TREVI

Terrorism, ~~Radicalisation~~,
Radicalism, Extremism,
& Substantive Violence
(P M)

The Threat of
Terrorism

The Threat of
Terrorism

Edited by

Juliet Lodge
Senior Lecturer in Politics
University of Hull

WHEATSHEAF BOOKS

First published in Great Britain in 1988 by
WHEATSHEAF BOOKS LTD
A MEMBER OF THE HARVESTER PRESS PUBLISHING GROUP
Publisher: John Spiers
16 Ship Street, Brighton, Sussex

British Library Cataloguing in Publication Data
The Threat of terrorism
    1. Terrorism—Europe
    I. Lodge, Juliet
    322.4′2′094 HV6433.E85
    ISBN 0-7450-0328-1
    ISBN 0-7450-0329-X Pbk

Typeset in 11/12½ Times by
Quality Phototypesetting, Bristol

Printed and bound in Great Britain by
Biddles Ltd, Guildford and King's Lynn

THE HARVESTER PRESS PUBLISHING GROUP
The Harvester Group comprises The Harvester Press Limited
(chiefly publishing literature, fiction, women's studies, philosophy,
psychology, history and science and trade books), and Wheatsheaf
Books Limited (chiefly publishing economics, international politics,
women's studies, sociology, and related social sciences).

Contents

List of Contributors   vii
Preface   xi

1. Introduction—Terrorism and Europe: Some General
   Considerations   1
   Juliet Lodge

2. British Policy on Terrorism: An Assessment   29
   Paul Wilkinson

3. Terrorism in West Germany   57
   Eva Kolinsky

4. Terrorism in Italy   89
   Christopher Seton-Watson

5. Dictatorship, Democracy and Terrorism in Spain   119
   Benny Pollack & Graham Hunter

6. Politically-Motivated Violent Activists in the
   Netherlands in the 1980s   145
   Alex P. Schmid

7. The Evolution of Belgian Terrorism   179
   David Laufer

8. Terrorism in France   213
   Edward Moxon-Browne

9. The European Community and Terrorism: From
   Principles to Concerted Action   229
   Juliet Lodge

   Select Bibliography   265
   Index   273

The Contributors

Graham Hunter, former Tutor in Politics in the Department of Political Theory and Institutions, University of Liverpool, is undertaking doctoral research on 'Working-Class Resistance and Opposition under an Authoritarian Regime: The Workers Commissions of the Baix Llobregat (Barcelone) 1962-77'. His research interests centre on contemporary Spanish and Latin American politics.

Eva Kolinsky, Senior Lecturer in German and Director of German Studies at Aston University, is author of *Engagierter Expressionismus. Literatur zwischen Weltkrieg und Politik; Parties, Opposition and Society in West Germany;* and editor of *Opposition in Western Europe.* She has also published chapters and articles on various aspects of contemporary German politics and political culture.

David Laufer is the European research analyst at a political risk assessment firm in London. He has published articles in The Royal United Services Institute's *Newsbrief* and in *Prism.*

Juliet Lodge, Senior Lecturer in Politics and Research Director of the European Community Research Unit at the University of Hull, has published widely on European Community politics. She is author of *The European Community and New Zealand; The European Policy of the SDP;* co-author of *Direct Elections to the European Parliament: A Community Perspective; The European Parliament and the European*

Community; and editor of several books including: *Terrorism: A Challenge to the State; European Union: the European Community in Search of a Future;* and *Institutions and Policies of the European Community,* and is currently working on the political and economic implications of the Single European Act for the European Community's internal and external policies.

Edward Moxon-Browne is Senior Lecturer in Political Science at the Queen's University of Belfast. He is author of *Nation, Class and Creed in Northern Ireland* and *Terrorism in France* and a number of articles on political violence. He is currently writing a book on Spanish politics.

Benny Pollack is Lecturer in Southern European and Latin American Politics, University of Liverpool. He was formerly at the Universities of Essex, Chile and London. A former political adviser to the Chilean Foreign Office and a delegate to the General Assembly of the UN, he has published widely on Portuguese and Latin American politics. He is author of *The Paradox of Spanish Foreign Policy;* and *Revolutionary Social Democracy: The Chilean Socialist Party.* His research interests centre on Spanish and Latin American politics with special reference to the transition from authoritarianism to democracy, and to Chilean politics.

Christopher Seton-Watson retired in 1983 from his Fellowship and Lectureship in Politics at Oriel College, Oxford. His chief publication is *Italy from Liberalism to Fascism.* He is currently working on Italy's political development since 1943. He is chairman of the Association for the Study of Modern Italy.

Alex P. Schmid is Associate Professor of International Relations at the Department of Political Science, Leiden University, the Netherlands. He is also Senior Research Fellow at the Center for the Study of Social Conflicts, and Visiting Scholar at the Program on Nonviolent Sanctions in Conflict and Defence at Harvard's Center for International Affairs.

His publications include: *Political Terrorism: A Research Guide to Concepts, Theories, Data Bases and Literature; Violence as Communication: Insurgent Terrorism and the Western News Media;* and *Soviet Military Interventions Since 1945.* He is currently preparing a new *Guide to Actors and Authors in the Field of Political Terrorism.*

Paul Wilkinson is Professor of International Relations at the University of Aberdeen. An expert on terrorism, he has published extensively on the topic in leading international journals. He is Associate Editor of *Terrorism: An International Journal,* and author of numerous learned papers, articles and books. Among his best known books are *Political Terrorism, Terrorism and the Liberal State* (revd. edn 1986), *The New Fascists, The Defence of the West,* and *Social Movement.* He has co-authored or edited many other books including *Terrorism, Theory and Practice, British Perspectives on Terrorism,* and *Contemporary Research on Terrorism.* He is Special Consultant on terrorism to CBS (America) and ITN, and Chairman of Trustees of the Research Foundation for the Study of Terrorism.

Preface

Western European governments' responses to terrorism during the 1980s continue to reflect a commitment to the maintenance of liberal democratic values and practices. It is true that internal security, police and specialist terrorist task forces have been refined since the spate of indigenous terrorism during the 1970s. However, this has been coupled with growing awareness of the importance of not sacrificing liberal democratic values for the sake of tighter security control measures. There are, of course, some people who would contend that terrorism does not really pose a serious threat to Western Europe; that its incidence has declined. Others offer contrary evidence and highlight the fact that terrorism is practised not simply by groups on the left, but also and increasingly in Western Europe by neo-fascist groups on the right. Such groups are not prepared to use the usual channels of political persuasion in order to attain their goals. Indeed, in some cases, their goals may be illegal and be proscribed for good reason. While there are indications of different trends in indigenous terrorism in some, but not all, West European states, in many older trends persist. They have also been supplemented by new trends and more intense international terrorist activity.

How several West European governments have responded to terrorism perpetrated on their territories or against their citizens abroad is the concern of the essays in this book. The states investigated are all members of the European

Community and the Community's response to international terrorism is examined in a concluding chapter. All the authors start from the premise that terrorism is an illegitimate means of conflict resolution in Western Europe. As will become apparent, there is no common policy on, let alone solution to, combatting terrorism. Instead, government action reflects different political traditions; it is also often fashioned in response to the type, goals, incidence and origin of terrorist attacks against states or others on their territory. Nevertheless, qualified consensus has emerged over the view that a laws-of-war framework is inadequate and that terrorist acts constitute criminal rather than political offences and should be prosecuted as such. Thus 'political' justifications for terrorist acts (particularly those endangering life) are not to be held defensible and warranting exemption from prosecution.

Various conventions giving expression to this idea are replete with qualifications and caveats, and no commonly accepted definition of terrorism exists. For our purposes, however, terrorism is the resort to violence for political ends by non-governmental actors in breach of accepted codes of behaviour regarding the expression of dissatisfaction with, dissent from or opposition to political goals endorsed by the legitimate government authorities of the state. The fact that indigenous terrorism seems entrenched in divided states in Western Europe where the legitimacy of government authorities can be questioned in relation to divisions and to the oppression of specific regions does not help appreciably to account for the form, frequency or intensity of terrorism. However, the way in which some states choose to deal with the activities of indigenous and international terrorists operating within their territory does help to explain the relative success or failure of existing national, international and European conventions designed to suppress terrorism.

Each of the essays adopts a case study approach with a view to illuminating the nature, incidence and persistence of terrorist activity in the state in question. The targets of both indigenous and international terrorists are examined along with international links that indigenous and foreign terrorist groups may have. Government responses to terrorist activity originating both within and outside its territory by indigenous and international terrorist groups are scrutinised. The aim of the essays is to produce a snapshot of terrorism over the last decade in the particular state in question. We are not concerned with attempting to devise a comparative theory of terrorism. The case study approach has been chosen to facilitate an analysis of terrorism within specific national settings. The European response is briefly surveyed to indicate that while terrorism is primarily dealt with by national instruments, far from successful but nonetheless potentially significant and increasingly important attempts have been made to inject a degree of consistency and predictability into West European government responses to limited terrorism-related matters (such as extradition).

National legislation designed to combat terrorism remains highly contentious. Even members of the European Community seem sceptical that their partners will honour obligations in respect of extradition and so on. It is very difficult to reconcile different national practices with one another. Moreover, as the chapters show, many states see anti-terrorist legislation as being invoked in exceptional circumstances only. MPs and the public often doubt the effectiveness of political controls and demand that such legislation be revoked as soon as possible. Clearly, however, anti-terrorist legislation and special forces are deemed necessary. But the emphasis is on keeping such measures within the realm, where possible, of civil rather than military control. The temptation to use force against foreign assassins operating within Western Europe and against international state-sponsored terrorism is growing. Moreover, the problems posed by maritime terrorism inevitably mean that states' naval forces are drawn into the counter-terrorism process. Their operating conditions are clearly different and the dividing line between terrorism and war is even less distinct. Indeed, international state-sponsored terrorism is now regarded as surrogate warfare. In this respect, terrorism becomes, as Wilkinson and others argue, a method of struggle.

The possibility of spillover into warfare has to be avoided. Western Europe states generally look to de-escalating confrontations. This is difficult to do under any circumstances. It becomes even harder to achieve under extreme provocation. Moreover, military forces will tend to seek military solutions to problems and any suggestions of joint military action, even justifiable defensive action, by a group of West European states (operating within the context of WEU or an international task force) can be construed as bellicose escalation of tension by the instigator of the crisis and supporter of international state-sponsored terrorism. Overreaction by the latter with dire results for peace has to be averted if possible. This highlights the need for cool heads and maximum coordination and cooperation among those threatened by terrorism. The targets cannot capitulate to blackmail. The targets may not even have envisaged close co-operation of the type that international state-sponsored terrorism behoves them to contemplate. An external threat acts as a kind of federalisator.

In such situations West European states (including those not in the EC) are likely to deploy all sorts of measures short of military intervention whenever possible. A combination of legal, political, diplomatic and economic packages has to be deployed. At the same time, numerous gaps in individual states' arrangements for countering terrorism may be revealed and repaired.

It is easy to criticise the West European states' apparent inability or unwillingness to employ unified responses to both indigenous and more particularly international state-sponsored terrorism. Loose, ad hoc cooperation coupled with intensified intelligence exchanges is giving way to continuous interaction but the preferred response of individual West European states, both within and outside the EC, remains the politico-legal package.

Strategies based on such a package demand a high degree of internal, interdepartmental coordination within individual states, among the various authorities responsible for police matters, as well as among the other agencies and principal government departments involved. The problems associated with bureaucratic politics have to be overcome. Moreover, the problems of policy coordination at this level are magnified when the various departments are engaged in international and supranational efforts. However, states' international policy measures tend to grow out of their domestic arrangements. Without an appreciation of the conditions under which these arose and the political responses, criticisms and reservations they elicited, the difficulties that face policymakers trying to fashion international and supranational responses cannot be understood. Harmonising all aspects of counter-terrorist measures—even at the judicial level—seems desirable but a long way off, even within the EC. No EC member appreciates public criticism of its domestic measures by its partners (as British objections to the views of Members of the European Parliament over Northern Ireland show). However, the search for concerted responses to international state-sponsored terrorism perpetrated in and against Western Europe and on the high seas demands prompt and ongoing scrutiny and reassessment of national anti-terrorism measures.

1 Introduction—Terrorism and Europe: Some General Considerations

Juliet Lodge

Although terrorism is as old as the hills, the upsurge in indigenous and international terrorism in Western Europe since the late 1960s has been regarded as particularly threatening both to those who govern the liberal democratic states within which terrorism is perpetrated or against whom it is aimed, and to the populations at large.[1] It has been argued that terrorism challenges liberal democratic values and endangers the very states which, by their comparative openness, permit the discussion of potentially destabilising ideas on the one hand, and on the other, react to the commission of terrorist acts in a manner that might be interpreted as endangering the very essence of the values they purport to uphold. Indeed, this is a recurrent theme in much of the literature on terrorism. This introductory chapter will examine briefly some of the issues raised in the literature on terrorism and will then sketch in the background to regional attempts within Western Europe to combat terrorism.

PROBLEMS OF DEFINITION

There have been numerous attempts to define terrorism. For some, terrorism is a process comprising several phases.[2] For others, it is strategy; for others still, a form of political violence[3] approximating insurrection, rebellion, anarchy or political protest[4] or revolution.[5] Much has been made of the

1

idea that one man's terrorist is another man's freedom fighter. Some authors have tried to isolate precisely those characteristics of political violence in given societies that may be said to typify terrorism. Attention is afforded to the effects, psychology and behaviour of terrorists, their motives, ideologies (however crude), purposes, actual rather than aspirational goals, and their politics. Many authors point out that terrorism is a moral problem,[6] and highlight the fact that because terrorism is not the exclusive preserve of the politically motivated but may be used by criminals and psychopaths, the issue of defining and identifying terrorism is rendered more complicated.[7]

Behaviour, the type and scope of violent acts involved, the nature of their targets—whether specific or indiscriminate—and the purported objectives of those committing terrorist acts have all been investigated. People have deliberated on whether or not terrorism is perpetrated by anarchist groups, by 'out-groups' or by those claiming spurious legitimacy and having pretentions to act on behalf of the allegedly oppressed masses; on behalf of those not so much denied representation in the sense of being enfranchised but denied an effective voice in contemporary politics.[8] As Merkl observes, there are some groups who can legitimately claim to speak for an identifiably oppressed group—ethnic nationalists may be one such group. ETA could for a long time claim to represent the Basques' interests against the Spanish state, for example, whereas the Red Army Faction could not credibly do so in the Federal Republic of Germany. Ethnic nationalists are also believed to be distinguishable from other violent collectivities by the more precise nature of their targets—they aim at the state, its symbols and law enforcement agencies: representatives of industrial capitalism and civilians are secondary targets only.[9] Moreover, it seems that ethnic nationalism when combined with regionalism and the existence of competing national loyalties (for instance in Spain between the central state and the Basques) rather than coexisting national loyalties (as in France where Bretons may perceive themselves as both Breton and French) can indeed result in terrorist groups credibly claiming to speak on behalf of an identifiably repressed group unable to translate political demands and aspirations into action on an immediate and direct basis. The very logic behind such ideas is, however, questionable in Western democracies where representation is indirect and government is not simply about representing the interests of the masses (however they may be defined) but the attempt to organise and administer complex socio-political and economic entities in the face of competing demands and ideologies. Conspiracy theories may explain the operation of a part of the whole on occasion but it is often far more difficult for outgroups practising terrorism (or more precisely indiscriminate violence on a tactical and strategic basis) to persuade the public of the validity of their cause.

The apparent lack of public support for terrorist groups in Western Europe has been investigated by various authors including those who have argued that elitism within the terrorist groups themselves is alienating.[10] Whatever the reasons for the lack of willing public support for terrorist groups on the European continent, there can be little doubt that the terrorists themselves endeavour to render their causes legitimate by referring to themselves and their 'struggles' in terms that recall past battles between repressors and the repressed that the latter won. Hence the imagery of colonial warfare. However, some authors use the term colonial terrorism to mean colonial wars where the colonised use political violence to oust the foreign regime. The notion of 'struggle' is central to many analyses of terrorism. Thus, terrorism has been portrayed as surrogate class struggle.[11]

Terrorism has also been depicted as a major symptom of the dysfunctions of a socio-political system afflicted by immobilism, a Marxist sub-culture, weak institutions of authority, a decline in religious beliefs, and resurgent radical neo-fascism.[12] In this view, terrorism is symptomatic of social disorganisation associated with urbanisation and secularisation.[13] From this follows the argument that terrorism, especially that on the right, is undertaken by alienated, marginalised (predominantly male) under 25-year-olds predisposed towards violence. However, this use of demographic, socio-psychological attributes to identify terrorists is inadequate, as it quickly subsumes hooliganism and other forms of domestic violence (both political and non-political) whose incidence far exceeds the occurrence of politically motivated acts of indiscriminate violence associated with terrorist incidents in most Western democracies.[14]

Trying to differentiate terrorism from political violence in general presents analysts with numerous problems. For some, generalisations lead to the view that terrorism is simply 'extreme, deviant, political behaviour'.[15] Others see left-wing terrorism as being qualitatively different from right-wing terrorism inasmuch as, in Western Europe, the two tendencies may employ the same general method while selecting somewhat different targets and incurring different penalties from the authorities on occasion. For example, Italy is notorious for having agents of the state involved in right-wing terrorism. Generally, however, Merkl argues that the distinguishing feature of right-wing, neo-fascist terrorism is its racial target.[16]

While socio-psychological interpretations and explanations of the incidence of terrorism (notably indigenous terrorism) seem fashionable, they supplement rather than supplant other attempted explanations. Many authors have attempted to draft typologies of terrorism which also attempt to locate its contemporary manifestations on a historical matrix. Germane to such attempts is the initial question of state and non-state terrorism.

Several typologies of terrorism have been constructed: 'enforcement terror' has been described as typifying state terrorism, and 'agitational terror' non-state terrorism.[17] By contrast, Wilkinson isolates three main kinds of terrorism: revolutionary terrorism, sub-revolutionary terrorism, and repressive terrorism.[18] However, typologies over-generalise; they stress characteristics typical of some but not all groups. Some differentiate between internal terrorism perpetrated by the state (e.g. the Spanish Inquisition, vigilantism, the OAS) and that pursued by small groups in pursuit of 'revolution' (the

usual examples of this are the Tupamaros and the Red Army
Faction). A second category is international terrorism—under
which are confusingly subsumed by various authors
imperialism, colonialism, freedom fights motivated by
nationalism, wars of independence and state-sponsored
external terrorism. For the purposes of this book,
international terrorism refers to acts of terrorism which
transcend the boundaries of one state either by virtue of where,
against whom and by whom they were committed or
sponsored; or by virtue of the search for safe havens by fugitive
terrorists.

Attempts have also been made to distinguish terrorism types
by the nature of their goals: terrorism may, in such a view, be
seen simply as an end in itself or as a means to a given end. It
may equally have either a tactical or a strategic perspective.
Terrorism has a place among the means employed by extremist
Muslim fundamentalist factions but, as Capitanchik has
argued, what might loosely be termed 'Islamic' terrorism and
terrorism emanating from the Middle East (where extreme
violence is part of political intercourse) differ in their
ideological inspiration and in their ultimate goals.[19] The aims
of terrorists may be expressed clearly or incoherently by their
perpetrators but the resort to terrorist methods often means
that their goal is not seen as legitimate by the authorities, the
public and the international community. So long as terrorism
was seen principally as a means of securing publicity for
'causes', observers tended to argue that revenge and the
induction of fear were obvious leitmotifs. Terrorism produces
fear, and is intended both to destroy public confidence in the
authorities and to offend, since civilised societies aim to reject
the resort to violence as a means of settling disputes.

It is generally agreed by Western observers of terrorism that
terrorism is an abhorrent and unacceptable means of pursuing
political ends.[20] For those who are responsible for protecting
individuals against terrorism and for apprehending and/or
punishing its perpetrators, the various typologies of terrorism
and the multiplicity of terrorist goals are less important than
the need to devise a workable legal standard that 'will

distinguish between permissable revolutionary activity and prohibited criminality in public international law'.[21] This is no easy matter.

However, West European liberal democratic governments do equate terrorism with criminal violence against which legal remedies are to be invoked in the first instance. As will become clear, it is not without reason that the rule of law is given particular prominence in the Federal Republic of Germany, and by members of the European Community intent on devising and invoking legal remedies against terrorism—both that committed within its own boundaries (wherever it may originate) and that against its citizens abroad. How the various states respond to domestic, indigenous terrorism depends largely upon historical factors. These may lead a state to develop a battery of anti-terrorist instruments (and most West European states have GSG-9 type forces) that rely primarily on legal remedies and military and security provisions. These may be complemented by measures that stop short of repression but which potentially or actually curtail individual liberties, especially if abused. In liberal democracies the aim is to balance military-security anti-terrorism measures by judicial and political controls.[22]

Legislative provisions against terrorism may also be developed[23] which seek to curb its incidence and, at a minimum, ensure that members of the international community uniformly treat terrorism as a criminal activity that cannot be 'excused' by the 'political defence'. The emphasis then is on the apprehension and prosecution of those suspected of committing terrorist acts. A battery of associated legal provisions has been devised to facilitate this. Its attainment is fraught with difficulties even in the European Community where, arguably, the possibilities of concerted regional action have been tested and might, theoretically, be thought to stand the greatest chance of successful implementation. There is, of course, another legalistic response to potential indigenous terrorism which can complement existing international provisions and attempt to legislate away indigenous terrorism by somehow co-opting potentially violent dissent. As Schmid shows below, this tactic has been usefully employed by the Dutch authorities, who arguably have the most liberal way of reacting to groups that might have or seek to develop a terrorist potential (see Chapter 6). The state's rapid response to their existence is a way of directly responding to them by non-violent state means. Whereas the political culture of the Netherlands may facilitate the emasculation of potential sources of political violence and indigenous terrorism (which Wilkinson terms liberal democracy's Trojan Horse), it does not follow that this is possible in other West European states.[24]

This book is concerned with terrorism in West European liberal democratic states and with the way in which they react, as a group in the European Community, to international terrorism. All the contributors interpret terrorism as an illegitimate means of attempting to effect political change by the indiscriminate use of violence. This characteristic is shared both by the perpetrators of indigenous terrorist acts (for example, those who might be seen as ethnic nationalists)[25], those who are citizens of the state against which they use terrorism, and those who engage in and/or sponsor international terrorism. The CIA and others distinguish between state-sponsored terrorism and terrorism by autonomous groups across state boundaries: the acts of the former are labelled international terrorism; the latter transnational terrorism.[26]

In practice, this distinction is artificial. Indeed, disentangling transnational from international terrorism is no easy matter. Terrorist groups that mount attacks across nearby borders—for instance the Red Army Faction (RAF) and the IRA—have been variously categorised as domestic terrorists[27] or supra-indigenous terrorists[28]. The labels are perhaps less important than the fact that such groups aggravate terrorist threat levels in Western Europe in general and in specific states in particular. In this volume, we refer to groups that predominantly recruit their members from among their own citizens and attack their own governments and states and its symbols, and others within its confines, as indigenous terrorists. Naturally, indigenous terrorists are not isolated and their various international links are noted. International terrorism is identified both in terms of where it originates, its targets, and the possibility of invoking international and/or supranational responses against it. However, if a terrorist act is clearly defined as an example of international terrorism, then legal remedies at international law may exist and be applicable.[29]

However, in practice, it is obvious that it is not always possible or diplomatically expedient to identify the alleged sponsors of acts labelled 'international terrorism' if state sponsorship is suspected. On the other hand, if state sponsors of terrorism can be identified—privately and publicly—then the range of counter-terrorist instruments at the disposal of a target government(s) may be increased. This does not imply, of course, resort to military might by the target (except perhaps under extreme provocation) but it does mean, as the European Community example shows, that additional measures may be invoked by the target. These measures may very well not be seen as typical counter-terrorist measures but may simply be other foreign policy instruments that can be used against any state with whom one is in disagreement and upon whom one wishes to exert non-violent pressure: economic sanctions and limitations upon the movement of diplomatic personnel are a case in point.

When examining terrorism in Western Europe, typologies are not always useful in identifying precisely the type of terrorism involved. Many terrorist incidents in recent years may have Western Europe as a general target (with governments, state or NATO installations, or European citizens symbolising the state). But attacks are not always launched in West European states by groups originating within those states. Increasingly, what might be loosely labelled indigenous terrorism has been supplemented in some states by international terrorism originating in the Middle East. Moreover, Westerners resident in the Middle East—notably Lebanon and Iran—have increasingly become the target of such groups: hostage-taking on home territory has been shown to be an effective means of obtaining publicity both for terrorist 'causes' and for the purported reasons for attacking target governments, mainly via symbolic intermediaries.[30] This is coupled with maximum inconvenience to Western target governments who have been drawn into negotiating (often indirectly) with terrorists in spite of a general principle of 'non-negotiation' with terrorists. Wilkinson has isolated some basic ground rules which liberal democracies must observe if they wish to pursue credible, tough anti-terrorist policies. He insists that:

The government should not engage in dialogue and negotiation with groups which are actively engaged in promoting, committing, or supporting terrorism. To do so only lends the terrorists publicity, status, and, worst of all, a spurious respectability.[31]

However, as recent events show, it is difficult for governments to resist understandable public pressure to secure the release of hostages. Moreover, given the absence of generally agreed international guidelines on this matter and given governments' predisposition to invoke national provisions, international conventions designed to combat terrorism and hostage-taking may often seem no more than statements of principle devoid of practical effect. (Witness the fate of the UN Convention on the Taking of Hostages).[32]

If international anti-terrorist conventions are difficult to formulate and are undermined by tardy ratification and non-implementation, then it may be supposed that a regional grouping of liberal democracies may be better placed to effect supranational action. However, despite some important West European cooperative arrangements, aspirations and principles outstrip the ability or willingness of states to comply. Indeed, one of the reasons why the European Community has been seen as a suitable forum in which to pursue concerted European action lies in the binding nature of its decisions upon its member states. Yet, as will be shown in Chapter 9, much European Community-based activity is conducted under the auspices of European Political Cooperation (EPC).

Being primarily an intergovernmental arrangement, EPC preserves national autonomy in sensitive foreign affairs matters. The EC's member states aim not so much to formulate and implement a common Community foreign policy (even assuming one were feasible) as to minimise divergence among themselves over critical international issues that might lend themselves to exploitation by non-EC states. Nevertheless, the 1980s have seen some significant developments in EPC and the conclusion of the Single European Act has spurred on Community-based action against terrorism. There has been a shift from principles to action.

At the same time, it should also be realised that West European states' concern with devising anti-terrorist measures whilst preserving liberal democratic practices has led them to explore the possibilities of action through several European and Atlantic bodies. Parallel and complementary action is vital to this endeavour, and complements the *ad hoc* bilateral anti-terrorism assistance states offer one another. Steps taken within the Council of Europe and the European Community are supposed to be mutually reinforcing rather than competitive. Similarly the Western European Union (WEU) and NATO discuss anti-terrorist measures. NATO promotes information exchanges on terrorist weapons, personnel and techniques; joint training visits and exchanges occur between security personnel of European Community and NATO states; and a permanent structure of police cooperation between EC member states has been set up.[33]

Terrorism and the public

It is usually argued that central to terrorists' objectives is the induction of fear among the public. This is one of the reasons why terrorism has been variously described as 'theatre' or 'spectacle'.[34] Wilkinson has referred to it as 'coercive intimidation'.[35] It is also why various authors have argued that terrorists generally rely very heavily on the openness of liberal democratic states. If they follow Bentham's first rule of politics—maximise publicity—then a free press and independent media free from government censorship, and cautious about self-censorship are instrumental to publicising their various causes.

However, as will become clear from the various case studies, indigenous terrorists in Western Europe are becoming less interested in seeing their communiqués transmitted by the media, and more interested in maximising the potential for disaster, and killing or injuring people on an indiscriminate basis to guarantee widespread publicity.[36] Attacks against military installations have a dual purpose: on the one hand, they provide a useful target that different groups can claim to attack 'as a legitimate target' according to their own peculiar ideological blends. On the other hand, they alert the public and (assuming that interpretations of terrorism as coercive intimidation are correct) induce fear among the public, and presumably also the authorities, of the disastrous potential of terrorist attacks.

A key supposition here is that the greater the scale of disaster terrorists threaten to generate, the greater public fear is and the more likely it will be that an attitude change will occur. While Merari and Friedland suggest that attitude change does occur, the effect may not always be as terrorists intended even though *post hoc* rationalisation may lead to them arguing the contrary. Thus, the more stringent anti-terrorist measures a state introduces, the more terrorist groups may be able to claim (as did the Baader-Meinhof Group, for example) that such measures provide proof of the state's fascist (and hence reprehensible and illegitimate) intentions. Alternatively, terrorists can portray authorities who refuse to negotiate or to accede to other demands as impossibly intransigent; any subsequent decision by the authorities to bargain with the terrorists can then be construed as capitulation to terrorism, in which case terrorists can claim 'victory'.[37] This has led some authors to reason that government authorities are placed in a 'no-win' situation. Others have suggested that, therefore, governments have the upper hand: the response to a terrorist threat is what matters.[38] This reasoning is particularly compelling for some social psychologists. Merari and Friedland argue that 'anti-terrorist attitudes are likely to crystallise faster and the erosion of public resistance to terrorism is likely to be slower when the issue of conflict is vitally important to the target public than when it is less important'.[39]

The importance or salience of an issue to the public is central to an understanding of why publics will incline towards making concessions to terrorist demands or why they will demand and accept counter-terrorist measures that, if abused, could threaten their civil liberties. This has implications for the terminology terrorists employ: while they may purport to champion the causes of the oppressed, their arguments frequently fail to find a resonance among the public at large. The parallels drawn between terrorists' fights against allegedly repressive government machines in Western Europe and freedom fighters seeking to overturn imperial, colonial powers does not impress West European publics. There is, thus, a mismatch between the rhetoric terrorists employ to persuade the public of the alleged justness of their cause, and the public's experience of life. Moreover, increasingly, the primary aim of a terrorist act is obfuscated in the cycle of reprisals, hostage-taking to secure imprisoned terrorists' release, and other related activities.

However, some argue that it is important to see terrorism as a strategy embracing several purposes. The target is always a government: the ultimate aim being to challenge its authority and legitimacy and with them the legitimacy of acts and policies undertaken in its name.[40] However, Stohl suggests that the most successful terrorism is that practised by the state for creating, maintaining and imposing order.[41] State terrorism so conceived appears to be associated in many observers' minds with governments of a fascist, dictatorial, totalitarian, military or post-revolutionary character. Stohl suggests that this is a myth and that 'all types of governments export terror': dirty tricks, he suggests, can be seen as the covert export of governmental terror.[42]

This is not to say that, even if this view were to be accepted, the covert export of governmental terror is tolerable. But it does highlight one of the problems governments face when hard evidence for state sponsorship of terrorism is ambiguous. Counter-terrorist measures may then have to be less conspicuous or more limited in their ambit. Only when a state overtly announces its sponsorship of terrorism can its targets publicly adopt and enforce a wide range of sanctions against it.

If terrorism is practised in the public eye and if authorities' responses are equally public, then to be credible such responses must be shown to have some effect. A good deal of research into the role of the media and terrorism has been done. The need for news blackouts and secrecy has been investigated, for instance.[43] The symbiotic nature of the relationship has also been probed.[44] However, satellite television inevitably poses greater problems if informal codes of self-censorship by the media in one state can be readily transcended or broken by the media elsewhere.

There is, of course, a counterpoint to publicity: governments can use it to indicate their intentions both to terrorists and to the public at large. The media becomes instrumental to moral suasion and to recording governments' pledges to uphold and invoke the rule of law. Since legal provisions differ from state to state, it will be useful to consider briefly what collective attempts have been made by states within the West European region to bring their provisions on terrorism more in line with one another.

SUPPRESSING TERRORISM: SOME LEGAL CONSIDERATIONS FOR EUROPE

The legal basis for action against terrorism poses numerous problems concerning matters of jurisdiction.[45] Difficulties derive not simply from the nature of states' jurisdiction, but also from the provisions of international public law and international penal law.[46] The latter is, moreover, often seen as no more than an extension of sovereign states' domestic territorial jurisdiction. The problems posed have been examined in detail elsewhere, and space limits preclude discussion here. However, it is important to realise that new steps to improve European states' ability to combat terrorism involve a reappraisal of the possibilities of international penal law. More importantly, in the case of the European Community, the legal basis for common action to combat terrorism is not clear-cut. This may be one reason why EC member states have used existing European legal provisions formulated outside the supranational Community as a starting point for more concerted action among themselves.

The European Convention on the Suppression of Terrorism (ECST) originated within the Council of Europe, which has taken an active role in trying to combat terrorism. In 1973 it took the lead in working towards the adoption of anti-terrorist measures by its members. The Community, which had just been expanded to nine members through the accession of the United Kingdom, Ireland and Denmark, was to draw inspiration from the ECST but ministers were not to act decisively until 1976. Even then, securing agreement among the Nine before Greece's accession in 1981 and that of Spain and Portugal in 1986, was not to prove an easy matter.

There are numerous reasons for this. Political factors and different legal practices—such as those distinguishing the civil-law states like France from common-law states like the United Kingdom—compounded member states' anxieties about the implications for national sovereignty of the adoption of a common Community policy to combat terrorism. Their concern was real, moreover, since in all areas where the European Community has jurisdiction, its law is binding and assumes precedence over national law. Furthermore, while the drafting of a common policy to combat terrorism may seem superficially fairly straightforward, its effects extend beyond what might loosely be termed domestic civil law to criminal law. Harmonising penal codes would be far from easy and the transnational nature of much terrorist activity in Europe means that all manner of niceties concerning the role, rights, authority and answerability of any forces (national or regional) pursuing terrorists would have to be resolved.

Moreover, the relationship of any EC law in this matter to international law would have to clarified and, equally problematically, the exact nature of European Community jurisdiction in a high political domaine normally defined as an exclusive preserve of national governments would be brought into question. Again, this is no small consideration in view of the fact that the Treaty of Rome does not commit the member states to the pursuit of common foreign policies. Nor is there appropriate machinery to make this feasible even if desirable. Indeed, by the mid-1970s, the first tentative steps towards promoting greater exchanges of EC members' views on foreign policy matters had only just begun with the establishment of consultative arrangements outside the Treaty of Rome. These were to become known subsequently as European Political Cooperation procedures and have been refined with the ratification of the Single European Act which came into force on 1 July 1987.

It is important to distinguish between the adoption of a common policy to combat terrorism, and the adoption of an agreement to endeavour to promote cooperation in terrorist matters among EC states. In the event, as will be shown, the member states were to embrace a policy of gradualism which would enable the individual states to combine flexibility and pragmatism with the potential for developing more concerted, harmonised or even common measures to combat terrorism if circumstances (both domestic and international) allowed. Naturally, such a tentative approach is open to criticism but it must be seen against the background of important developments relating to the process of European integration and its increasing impact on all manner of spheres of activity where member governments were once independent.

The binding nature and direct effectiveness of EC legislation is also critical in this respect since there would have been no point in a verbal commitment from the Community to adopt a common policy to combat terrorism if it stood no chance of being implemented. Indeed, the difficulties that any anti-terrorist legislation would encounter were well enough appreciated for the French to caution against the usual EC compartmentalised approach to policy-making, and to advocate instead the creation of a common judicial area, the *espace judiciare européen*. That the others opposed this approach had much to do with its implications for sovereignty, and it is instructive that measures to combat terrorism have more recently slipped into regular Community discourse under the banner of the completion of the internal market. (See Chapter 9).

Securing agreement in the Council of Europe on the ECST had not been easy either. Past experience gave little grounds for optimism: international endeavours to suppress terrorism had been unsuccessful. The two conventions sponsored by the League of Nations in 1937 failed for want of ratification by sufficient members to permit their entry into force.[47] The Geneva Convention on the High Seas, the Tokyo Convention of 1963, the Hague Convention of 1970 and the Montreal Convention of 1971 needed to be supplemented by additional measures if terrorism and notably hijackings and related offences were to be combatted more systematically and effectively.[48] Attempts by the UN to combat terrorism have had a limited effect, and UN documents seem to contradict each other in prohibiting terrorism on the one hand but encouraging assistance to freedom fighters on the other.[49] Moreover, not only does agreement on the definition of terrorism elude the international community, but many states use and sponsor terrorism as a form of proxy war against targetted 'enemy' states[50] and 'enemies' more generally conceived.

Given that individual states' attitudes, policies and provisions on terrorism were (and generally remain) divergent, endeavours undertaken by a regionally more limited group sharing many ideals and attachment to broadly understood notions of liberal democracy seemed attractive. Even so, the past ten years shows how difficult it has been even for limited groups either to agree on a common definition of terrorism or to develop common policies against terrorism even when there have been indications of Euro-terrorist alliances operating in Western Europe against European, US and NATO targets.[51]

Indeed, although the Council of Europe was to lead the endeavour to develop a regional, European response to terrorism, it was not until the 1980s that the governments themselves seemed willing to commit themselves to honouring bilateral and multilateral agreements. Wilkinson shows how, in the European Community, the foreign Ministers' package of trade sanctions against Iran following the embassy siege was undermined by the British[52] but how, in 1984, sustained British pressure led to the subject of international terrorism being discussed at the London Economic summit, and again at the 1987 Venice summit. The examples of intentions being sometimes deliberately and sometimes unwittingly undermined by members of the same community are legion. The problem is that lack of consistency can erode the credibility of any Community-based anti-terrorist effort. Even so, such efforts and agreements must achieve something for governments to see them as worth bothering with in the first place and, in the second to seek additional action based on them in other international fora having limited membership. There is more to the European conventions than words.

The Council of Europe
The Council of Europe's approach to combatting terrorism rests on gradualism *faute de mieux*. Many of its proposals seem to reflect *ad hoc* responses to terrorism rather than the development of a consistent policy. This, at times misleading, impression seems to be reinforced by the Council's preoccupation with matters arising out of state-sponsored terrorism and with confronting the issue of common definitions and penalties against terrorism. However, earlier this decade the emphasis was on extradition. The so-called 'liberation' fights of much indigenous West European terrorism during the 1960s and 1970s, along with the problems of securing the prosecution of fugitive terrorists, led the Council's members to concentrate on drafting a convention that would ensure that terrorists would not be able to evade the law; that if apprehended, they could be sure of being tried. The idea was to prevent recourse to the 'political' defence argument being used by terrorists seeking to escape prosecution: thus, the principle of *aut dedere aut judicare* (loosely meaning extradite or try) means that if a state holding terrorists refuses to extradite them, then it will nevertheless try them

(providing—and this is an important qualification—they recognise the principle of jurisdiction upon which the requesting state has based a request for extradition).

The Council of Europe has adopted the approach of building on existing extradition arrangements between its members, including the 1960 European Convention on Extradition, which, by 1981, has been ratified by fourteen Council members only. (The UK was not a signatory to this convention). Since this convention excludes from extradition fugitives accused of a 'political offence' or 'an offence connected with a political offence' (neither of which was defined), devising steps and an agreement to include people laying claim to the 'political offence' was a priority. Moreover, not only does the onus of proof remain with the victim but national extradition laws vary considerably over the circumstances under which the 'political offence' is allowed as a defence.[53]

The spate of terrorism heralded by the late 1960s and 1970s did not lead the Council of Europe to draft a new policy. That did not mean that the process of securing agreement on what was to become the ECST was to be any the less fraught. What is perhaps surprising is that subsequently when an even more limited group of West European states (the European Community) simply sought to build on the ECST to develop a Community policy to suppress terrorism, the issues raised by applying the *aut dedere aut judicare* principle still proved so controversial that it was impossible to secure either signature or ratification by all states simultaneously, let alone within a few months of each other. Yet, against this unpropitious background, steps were still being examined to extend the EC members' instruments to deter terrorism and related offences.

Important as the ECST is, it must be remembered that it represents but a very small step towards an effective international instrument against terrorism. The principles it establishes are significant, but equally important is the fact that some states can and have used deportation as a 'disguised extradition'. If the extradite or try principle is to work as intended, then it seems necessary to harmonise or standardise key aspects of national criminal codes and to clarify exactly what is meant by the concept of the *espace judiciare européen*. It also becomes clear that enforcing this and the *aut dedere aut punire* principle is far from easy and that flexibility rather than rigidity is demanded. With such qualifications in mind, what then does the ECST seek to do?

The European Convention on the Suppression of Terrorism
The ECST's primary purpose is the establishment of the *aut dedere aut judicare* principle for alleged terrorist acts. Signatory states are required to supplement their existing extradition arrangements in order to deprive alleged terrorists of the chance of escaping extradition (and therefore possibly prosecution and penalties) by pleading the 'political defence'. A number of offences involving violence, firearms, explosives and so on are listed, and signatories to the ECST are supposed to reject the listed offences as 'political offences' or offences inspired by a 'political motive' in the event of extradition proceedings. Terrorists have been adept at exploiting national extradition laws and international extradition treaties that commonly exempt political and politically inspired offences.[54] Changing this poses numerous legal and political difficulties, since the right of political asylum may be affected. In France and Ireland major sensitivities are aroused by this. Indeed, in Eire, constitutional issues are raised. It is instructive that nearly ten years elapsed between the conclusion of the ECST in 1977 and Ireland's signature of it on 24 February 1986.

However, the ECST does accommodate political and constitutional problems. First, it allows a signatory state to refuse extradition if 'it has substantial grounds for believing that the request for extradition . . . has been made for the purpose of prosecuting or punishing a person on account of his race, religion, nationality or political opinion, or that a person's position may be prejudiced for any of these reasons' (Article 5 ECST). Indeed, extradition proceedings are usually tortuous. Second, the ECST permits states to enter a reservation under Article 13 to allow them to reject a request for extradition on the grounds that the offence is of a political

character, notwithstanding the fact that a listed offence is involved. This provision is seen as a major weakness in the ECST. It seems to negate the ECST's core proposition that terrorist offences be regarded as crimes and punished as such. Yet, any state invoking this reservation (and France, Italy and Norway all did so upon signature, while Sweden did upon ratification) is obliged to assess the character of the offence with reference to criteria that might be said to typify a terroristic act of violence.[55]

A further weakness of the ECST lies in the nature of the Council of Europe's ability to ensure the implementation of its recommendations, decisions and conventions, and so on. The Council of Europe's jurisdiction is far weaker than that of the European Community. In effect, decisions of the Council of Europe's Committee of Ministers often seem to amount to little more than guidelines and the presentation of laudable principles. In January 1974, when the Committee adopted a resolution (74)3 on international terrorism, it deliberately outlined principles to guide member states when faced with requests for extradition.[56] These were necessary since extradition is not mandatory, even under the ECST, although the ECST does establish an obligation to grant assistance in cases involving offences under Articles 1 and 2—assistance which may not be refused on the sole ground that the offence purports to be political in character. Jurisdictional problems remain, however, and render the conclusion of conventions difficult: the Committee of Ministers, for example, is unable to issue a recommendation to the Council of Europe's members unless is it unanimous. Even then, a recommendation lacks the binding character of EC regulations and directives. Furthermore, Council of Europe conventions bind only those states that ratify them.

The Council of Europe is, of course, aware of its limitations and has endeavoured to minimise such problems by involving Ministers of Justice and of the Interior in its deliberations. A Conference of European Justice Ministers in Obernai in 1975 stressed the need for coordinated action to combat terrorism. Their commitment to securing some form of European-wide action against terrorism had certainly been bolstered by the experience of the effects of *ad hoc* national action and the failures of the UN. Simultaneously, the European Committee on Crime Problems suggested to the Committee of Ministers the convening of a committee of government experts to con sider issues raised by new forms of concerted acts of violence. This was to lead to the ECST. It was opened for signature on 27 January 1977 when all Council members save Ireland and Malta signed it (some entering reservations as noted above). The ECST entered into force on 4 August 1978 after ratifica tion by Austria, Sweden and the Federal Republic of Germany, and subsequently by Denmark, Luxembourg and the United Kingdom.[57] Although the ECST has been widely criticised, it was to provide the basis for the first agreement among EC states to combat terrorism: the 1979 Dublin Agreement.

The Dublin Agreement

It is perhaps surprising that EC member states should even have contemplated combatting terrorism on a Community-wide basis in view of the Council of Europe's experience. However, frustration with the latter, coupled with growing pressure for Community action from within the EC—notably from within the European Parliament—combined with disappointment over international efforts, underlined the need for an even more regionally confined and more concerted effort. This was inevitably helped by several additional factors. These included: the existing degree of parallelism in the Community, where in 1976 Ministers began to consult earnestly on anti-terrorist measures; the broad support (criticism of the ideas behind the ECST notwithstanding) for the Council of Europe's—and later the ECST's—overall objective of denying the political defence in specified (and hence qualifiable) instances; the member governments' unwillingness to apply a range of economic and diplomatic sanctions against states believed to provide sponsorship and/or safe havens for terrorists; and the realisation that intergovernmental arrangements lacking the direct effect of EC regulations could be used.

In the first instance, European Community endeavours to combat terrorism were restricted to ensuring application among EC members of existing international provisions against terrorism. Above all, members sought to close loopholes left by the ECST. They wished to overcome a major problem of the ECST relating to the fact that even apprehended terrorists may escape prosecution and extradition if they are apprehended in or seek refuge in a state that is not party to the ECST or to various international and UN provisions, or that does not have reciprocal arrangements with members of the Council of Europe concerning the commission of terrorist offences within the regions of the Council of Europe.

The Community's first priority then was to ensure that the ECST should be applied uniformly among its members. Related but secondary priorities concerned the adoption of a common system of extradition; the creation of a common judicial area; scrutiny of problems associated with terrorism—notably state-sponsored terrorism—including the abuse of diplomatic bags; the promotion of firearms controls; police and security force cooperation; and wider diplomatic efforts in respect of the Middle East and Third World. As is shown in Chapter 9, attaining the first priority has been fraught and other issues have received increasing attention in response to terrorism in the mid-1980s.

The Dublin Agreement grew out of the efforts of a working party of senior officials set up as a result of undertakings by the European Council in December 1975 and July 1976 to cooperate in the prosecution or extradition of terrorists, particularly those involved in hostage-taking. The Rome European Council decided to set up the TREVI system of consultation to enable Ministers of the Interior or Justice (depending upon member states' constitutional practices) to meet 'to discuss matters coming within their competence, in particular with regard to law and order'. While TREVI's brief now encompasses intelligence gathering and exchange, at that time it concentrated (as its name, derived from the French acronym, suggests) on terrorism, radicalism, extremism and international violence. By April 1978, the priority was intensifying cooperation against terrorism, and in October 1978 the EC Council of Ministers of Justice and the Interior decided to open for signature an agreement—concluded via the intergovernmental mechanism of European Political Cooperation—to apply the ECST among Community states.[58] At this stage, Belgium, France, Italy, Luxembourg and the Netherlands had yet to ratify, and Ireland to sign, the ECST.

The Dublin Agreement basically seeks to ensure the application of the ECST without qualification and reservation in extradition proceedings between EC member states regardless of whether the states involved are party to the ECST. EC states wishing to maintain the political offence reservations under Article 13 ECST have to make a further declaration under Article 3 of the Dublin Agreement expressly refusing extradition of political offenders as do states not party to the ECST. Denmark, France and Italy retain their Article 13 ECST reservations, and Ireland made a reservation to Article 1 ECST on the understanding that it would try offenders domestically.[59] This is an important point, since extradition does not always guarantee prosecution. Extradition can be demanded by a state that has no intention of prosecuting the alleged terrorist if the terrorist is extradited. Similarly a state can refuse extradition and also refrain from prosecution.[60]

In theory, member states wish to honour the idea encapsulated in the ECST that those acts associated with terrorism are regarded as extraditable offences, as criminal acts which should be prosecuted as such. Thus, the political offence argument has to be put to one side because it has been used to circumvent the obligation to extradite or prosecute. Moreover, states do sometimes violate conventions and so undermine them, and observers have suggested that if prosecution is the real aim of extradition conventions, then emphasis should be placed on prosecution.[61] This, in turn, raises problems over judicial assistance, judicial discretion, uniform sentencing, common penalties, and common rules regarding what happens to prosecuted terrorists after the criminal process has been completed.

A major problem with the Dublin Agreement was that the majority of the then nine EC member states were not party to the ECST yet; for the Dublin Agreement to come into effect all nine had to ratify it. Numerous legal and political complications arose over another ill-fated draft agreement, prepared by the same working party, on Mutual Cooperation in Criminal Matters.[62] At the time of writing, the problem of extradition has still to be regulated satisfactorily among EC states as a group. Naturally, several bilateral extradition arrangements and treaties also exist. Adherence to a common set of agreed principles would, however, simplify matters within the Community. Yet many observers are wary of the whole endeavour, since some jurists see the establishment of anything approximating a common system of extradition as a backdoor means of harmonising criminal law in the Community. Others including numerous members of the European Parliament, on the other hand, have pressed consistently for extending provisions to the realm of issues involved in the Lomé Conventions which provide for special trade and aid relations between the EC and African, Caribbean and Pacific states.

Problematic though extradition matters may be, the Community remains committed in principle at least to the idea that (in keeping with the objective in the Dublin Agreement) terrorists should be prosecuted in the state of their arrest if extradition is refused and irrespective of where the terrorist act was committed. However, there are no easy answers to the problem of agreeing on and implementing even limited measures among states that otherwise engage in a good deal of informal and formal cooperation on security and terrorism matters. Supranationalism in this respect poses as many questions as it answers. As each of the following chapters makes clear, reconciling this with national practice is far from straightforward.

Divergent practices and traditions among EC states will continue to inhibit common action. This does not imply, however, that such action is either unattainable or unthinkable. Instead, flexibility is necessary if the implications of other decisions relating to the Community—notably the completion of the internal market, the realisation of a People's Europe, and possibly EC citizenship—are to be appreciated properly. Already, reference has been made to the opportunities such a goal holds for criminals and terrorists. Contentious as legal action may be under Article 235 of the Treaty of Rome,[63] it is clear that the new Single European Act has lifted some of the taboos that surround Community action in fields that inevitably spill over and compromise member states' sovereignties in ways not foreseen by the drafters of the treaties establishing the European Communities. More pertinent still, perhaps, EC member governments remain ready to contemplate a range of coordinated responses to terrorism that can be elaborated both under the supranational aegis of the European Community, alongside it, in conjunction with it through European Political Cooperation, and in other fora where parallel action may be envisaged.

NOTES

1. See for example R. Gaucher, *The Terrorists: From Tsarist Russia to the OAS,* London: Secker & Warburg, 1968; E. Hyams, *Terrorists and Terrorism,* London: Dent, 1975; N. O'Sullivan (ed.) *Terrorism, Ideology and Revolution: The Origins of Modern Political Violence,* Brighton: Wheatsheaf, 1986; and P. Wilkinson, *Terrorism and the Liberal State* (2nd edn.) London: Macmillan, 1986.
2. J.J. Paust, 'A Definitional Focus', in Y. Alexander and S.M. Finger (eds) *Terrorism: Interdisciplinary Perspectives,* New York: John Jay Press, 1979: pp. 18-29, at p. 19.
3. J.A. Miller, 'Political Terrorism and Insurgency: An Interrogative Approach', in Alexander and Finger, *op. cit.,* pp. 65-91.
4. R.A. Friedlander, 'The Origins of International Terrorism', in Alexander and Finger, *op. cit.,* pp. 30-45 at p. 33.
5. D. Rapoport, 'The Politics of Atrocity', in Alexander and Finger, *op. cit.,* pp. 46-61.
6. G. Wardlaw, *Political Terrorism: Theory, Tactics and Counter-measures,* Cambridge: CUP, 1982, p. 4; D. Rapoport and Y. Alexander (eds) *The Morality of Terrorism: Religious and Secular Justifications,* Oxford: Pergamon, 1982.
7. Wardlaw, *op. cit.* See, too, J. Collins, 'Definitional Aspects', in Y.

Alexander and E. Ebinger (eds) *Political Terrorism and Energy*, New York: Praeger, 1981.

8. R. Clutterbuck, *Guerillas and Terrorists*, London: Faber, 1977; J. Bowyer Bell, *A Time of Terror*, New York: Basic Books, 1978; Wardlaw, *op. cit.*, and Wilkinson, *op. cit.*

9. P.H. Merkl (ed.) *Political Violence and Terrorism: Motifs and Motivations*, Berkeley: Univ. of California Press, 1986, p. 141.

10. J. Becker, *Hitler's Children*, London: Michael Joseph, 1977.

11. F. Ferrajoli, 'Critica della violenza come critica della politica', in L. Manconi (ed.) *La Violenze e la politica*, Rome: Savelli, 1979, pp. 36-39; and G. Bocca, *Il Terrorismo Italiano 1970-78*, Milan: Bompiani, 1978.

12. G. Pasquino and D. Della Porta, 'Interpretations of Italian Leftwing Terrorism', in P. H. Merkl (ed.) *op. cit.*, pp. 169-90, at p. 186.

13. Merkl, *ibid.*, p. 358.

14. P. H. Merkl, 'Rollerball or Neo-Nazi Violence', *ibid.*, p. 229.

15. K. Wasmund, 'The Political Socialisation of West German Terrorists', in Merkl, *op. cit.*, pp. 191-228, at p. 199.

16. Merkl, *op. cit.*, p. 347.

17. Thornton, 'Terrorism as a Weapon of Political Agitation', in H. Eckstein (ed.) *Internal War*, London: Macmillan, 1964, p. 73ff.

18. P. Wilkinson, 'Proposals for Government and International Responses to Terrorism', in P. Wilkinson (ed.) *British Perspectives on Terrorism*, London: Allen & Unwin, 1981.

19. D. Capitanchik, 'Terrorism and Islam', in O'Sullivan (ed.), *op. cit.*, pp. 115-131.

20. Wilkinson (1986) *op. cit.*

21. Friedlander, *loc. cit.*, p. 33.

22. Wilkinson (1981) *op. cit.*, p. 163.

23. R. Crelinsten *et al.*, *Terrorism and Criminal Justice*, Lexington: Lexington Books, 1978; R. Friedlander, *Terrorism: Documents of International and Local Control* (3 vols) New York: Oceana, 1979; Y. Alexander and D. Bell, *Legislative Responses to Terrorism*, Lexington: Lexington Books, 1985.

24. Wilkinson (1981) *op. cit.*, p. 169.

25. J. Loughlin, 'Regionalism and Ethnic Nationalism in France', and C. Diaz Lopez 'Centre-Periphery Structures in Spain: From Historical Conflict to Territorial-Consociational Accommodation', in Y. Meny and V. Wright (eds), *Centre-Periphery Relations in Western Europe*, Allen & Unwin, 1985.

26. E. Mickolus, 'Transnational Terrorism', in M. Stohl (ed.), *The Politics of Terrorism*, New York: Marcel Dekker, Inc., 1979, pp. 147-190, at p. 148.

27. Mickolus, *op. cit.*

28. D. Pluchinsky, 'Political Terrorism in Western Europe: Some Themes and Variations', in Y. Alexander and K.A. Myer (eds) *Terrorism in*

Europe, London: Croom Helm, 1982, pp. 40-78.

29. Crelinsten *et al., op. cit.,* pp. 39-43. See too, A.P. Rubin, 'International Terrorism and International Law', in Alexander and Finger, *op. cit.,* pp. 121-7.
30. C.C. Aston, 'The United Nations Convention against the Taking of Hostages: Realistic or Rhetoric?', in Wilkinson (ed.) (1981) *op. cit.,* pp. 139-60.
31. Wilkinson (1981) *op. cit.,* p. 164.
32. Aston, *loc. cit.,* and Crelinsten *et al., op cit.,* Ch. 6.
33. Wilkinson (1981) *op. cit.,* p. 177.
34. B. Jenkins, *International Terrorism: A New Mode of Conflict,* Los Angeles: Crescent, 1975, p. 1; Gaucher, *op. cit.*
35. Wilkinson (1986) *op. cit.,* p. 48.
36. A. Merari and N. Friedland, 'Social Psychological Aspects of Terrorism', in S. Oskamp (ed.) *International Conflict and National Public Policy Issues;* special issue of *Applied Social Psychology Annual,* 6 (1985) pp.185-206.
37. *Ibid.*
38. D. Fromkin, 'The strategy of terrorism', *Foreign Affairs,* 53 (1975) pp. 683-98, at p. 697.
39. Merari and Friedland, *loc. cit.,* p. 194.
40. Stohl, *op. cit.,* p. 3.
41. *Ibid.,* p. 4.
42. *Ibid.,* p. 10.
43. R.H. Kupperman, 'Treating the Symptoms of Terrorism: Some Principles of Good Hygiene', *Terrorism,* 1 (1977) pp. 35-52.
44. Wardlaw, *op. cit.,* pp. 76-86; and H.H. Cooper, 'Terrorism and the Media'; B. Johnpoll, 'Terrorism and the Media in the United States' all in Alexander and Finger, *op. cit.*
45. See N. Gal-Or, *International Cooperation to Suppress Terrorism,* London: Croom Helm, 1985.
46. *Ibid.,* p. 121ff.
47. See M.O. Hudson (ed.) *International Legislation,* (9 vols) Washington: Carnegie Endowment for International Peace, 1931-50, vol. 7, pp. 862-5. For a brief overview of international attempts at combatting terrorism, see R.A. Friedlander, 'Terrorism and International Law: What is Being Done?', *Rutgers Camden Law Journal,* 8 (1977) pp. 383-92.
48. See J. Lodge, 'The European Community and Terrorism: Establishing the Principle of Extradite or Try', in Lodge (ed.) *Terrorism: A Challenge to the State,* Oxford: Martin Robertson, 1981, p. 166ff. For details of various UN and international efforts to combat terrorism since the mid-1970s see Wilkinson (1986) *op. cit.,* Chs. 14 and 15.
49. Wilkinson (1986) *op. cit.,* p. 277.
50. *Ibid.,* p. 215.

51. *Ibid.,* p. 214ff.
52. *Ibid.,* p. 280ff.
53. See J. Lodge with D. Freestone, 'The European Community and Terrorism: Political and Legal Aspects', in Alexander and Myers, *op. cit.,* p. 77ff; for details of the specified offences that may not be regarded as political see Article 1 of the ECST, and Lodge (ed.) *op. cit.,* p. 170.
54. See D. Freestone, 'The EEC Treaty and Common Action on Terrorism', *Yearbook of European Law,* 4(1984) pp. 207-30.
55. Wilkinson (1986) *op. cit.,* p. 292.
56. Lodge (ed.), *op. cit.*
57. For details of the negotiations behind the ECST see Gal-Or, *op cit.,* p. 207ff.
58. See Lodge (ed.), *op. cit.*
59. Freestone, *loc. cit.*
60. See Crelinsten *et al.,* pp. 40-1.
61. See A.E. Evans, 'The Realities of Extradition and Prosecution', in Alexander and Finger, *op. cit.,* pp. 128-38.
62. Freestone, *loc. cit.*
63. For a rehearsal of the legal arguments see the report drawn up on behalf of the Legal Affairs Committee on the European Judicial Area (Extradition) known as the Tyrell Report after its rapporteur, *European Parliament Working Document, 1-318/82.*

2 British Policy on Terrorism: An Assessment

Paul Wilkinson

EXPERIENCE OF VIOLENCE BEFORE 1970

Compared to other European countries the British mainland has been remarkably free of domestic political violence for over 200 years. The last rebellion against the British Crown was the unsuccessful Jacobite rising of 1745. The Gordon riots of 1780, instigated by the Protestant associations attempting to force the repeal of the 1778 Catholic Relief Act and resulting in many deaths and destruction of property, was the last major outbreak of sectarian violence and rioting on the British mainland. It is true that extra-parliamentary protest and pressure often played a major part in securing social reforms, but this was generally remarkable for its non-violent character.[1] Only very rarely, as in the struggle for votes for women, did the conflict give rise to a deliberate campaign of violence. This is a remarkable record, especially when one bears in mind the deep social divisions, the traumatic effects of mass industrialisation and urbanisation, and the ready availability of theories and doctrines of revolutionary violence such as those of Marx, Bakunin and their followers. A main problem for historians of political violence between 1780 and 1970 is to explain Britain's capacity for non-violent political and social conflict and change. Even the massive British General Strike (1926), lasting nine days, managed to remain peaceful in most areas, and at no stage did it escalate into armed confrontation.

Britain's major experience of acts of terrorism in the period 1780 to 1970 stemmed from the campaigns of the Irish Republicans. Following Wolfe Tone's rebellion against British rule in 1798, a number of Irish Fenian groups carried out intermittent campaigns of violence against the British, both in Ireland and, occasionally, on the British mainland. Among the most notorious of these incidents were the Phoenix Park murders in Dublin, on 6 May 1882, when Lord Frederick Cavendish, the Chief Secretary of Ireland, and T.H. Burke, his under-secretary, were ambushed and stabbed to death as they walked in Phoenix Park, by members of the Irish Invincibles, a Republican secret society. (It is worth noting that this outrage caused a temporary revulsion against terrorism in Ireland, and was almost certainly a factor in strengthening support for Charles Stewart Parnell's constitutionalist Home Rule Party in Parliament.) The Fenians also attempted bombing campaigns in London, which in turn led to the formation of the Special Branch of the Metropolitan Police.[2] The Fenians were also active from an early stage in America, where they organised a number of abortive cross-border attacks into British Canada in 1866, 1870 and 1871. The Irish Republican movement's history of using the Irish-American community as a base for support, propaganda and fund-raising really goes back to the earliest days of the movement.

Although Irish Home Rule was eventually approved in principle by the Westminster Parliament in 1914, it was suspended for the duration of the First World War. However, before the war had ended the mood of the majority of Irish people changed dramatically in the wake of the republican insurrection in Dublin in April 1916, known as the Easter Rising.[3] A small group of nationalists from the Irish Republican Brotherhood, the Irish Volunteers and Sinn Fein, involving an estimated 2,000 strong 'citizen army' seized control of Dublin General Post Office and other key points and proclaimed the establishment of the Irish Republic. After a week of street fighting the Republican insurgents were overwhelmed and their leader, Patrick Pearse, and his colleagues surrendered. When it started, the insurrection was regarded as a dangerous folly by most of the Irish people. But the public mood changed dramatically when Pearse and thirteen of his co-leaders of the rising were executed by the British authorities. Support for peaceful constitutionalist efforts for Home Rule collapsed, and the extreme nationalists, under the leadership of Michael Collins and Eamon De Valera, fought and won a bitter war of independence against the British from 1919 to 1921.

Alas, this was not to be the end of the violence. The British government, led by Lloyd George, was willing to negotiate but was not prepared to risk trying to force the staunchly Protestant Unionist population of the North to be part of the newly independent Irish Free State. The British cabinet was, correctly, sure that the Unionists would resist any such move by force of arms. This led to the partition of Ireland under the Anglo-Irish Treaty (1921) which became, almost immediately, a source of continuing violence in Ireland. A section of the Irish Republican Army (IRA), known as the 'Irregulars', bitterly opposed the partition and fought a particularly bitter civil war against the army of the Irish Free State government which supported the peace treaty.[4] Although the IRA Irregulars lost this particular struggle they never abandoned their aim of uniting Ireland by force, and the IRA continued as an illegal underground organisation opposing both the British presence in Northern Ireland and the legal government in Dublin. In 1939 the IRA organised a series of bombings in England. The Irish Free State government responded by major efforts to suppress the organisation, including internment without trial. Between 1956 and 1962 the IRA began a fresh bombing campaign against the authorities in Northern Ireland, but this failed due to a complete lack of support from the Catholic population in the North.[5]

Meanwhile the Unionist government in Ulster had taken full advantage of its devolved powers, and the ignorance and neglect of Ulster affairs in the Westminster parliament, to impose a system which severely discriminated against the Catholic minority in terms of housing, jobs and voting. By the mid-1960s there was a new spirit of political activism generated by the Catholic civil rights movement. The IRA saw this as an opportunity to start a fresh campaign of violence. This broke out in 1969-70, with the Provisionals, a breakaway from the Official IRA, taking the lead in organising the violence, claiming that they were the only movement capable of defending the rights and homes of the Catholics in the North against what they saw as the aggressive violence of the militant Protestants led by the Rev. Ian Paisley and his followers.[6] This new Provisional IRA was much more militant than the old-style IRA, attracted more young activists, and was totally committed to terrorist tactics. It was the emergence of this movement which, above all else, created a major terrorist challenge to successive British and Irish governments after 1970. Northern Ireland terrorism, occasionally spilling over into mainland Britain, developed into the worst-protracted and most deadly terrorist conflict experienced in the post-war history of Western Europe.

It was undoubtedly very lucky for the British that they happened to possess an army with unrivalled experience of combatting terrorist violence in a whole variety of colonial insurgencies against British rule in the nineteenth and twentieth centuries. For example, assassination and bombing were tactics frequently used by extreme nationalists in India against the British *Raj,* for example in opposition to the 1905 partition of Bengal, and in the lead up to Indian independence.

There were some cases where terrorism was far more than simply an auxiliary weapon against British rule. For example, in Palestine 1945-48, the bombing and assassination campaigns of the Irgun Zvai Leumi, led by Menachem Begin, and the Stern Gang, played the crucial role in undermining the will of the colonial authorities and the British government and public to stay on until an agreed solution between Arabs and Jews for the future of the country could be found.[7]

The same could be said of the terrorist tactics of EOKA (Ethniki Organosis Kyprion Agoniston—National Organ isation of Cypriot Fighters) in Cyprus and of FLOSY (Front for the Liberation of Occupied South Yemen) in Aden.[8] Rela tively tiny numbers of well-organised and determined terrorists were able to take advantage of their intimate knowledge of local terrorism and the mainly willing support and assistance of large numbers of the native population. This made the task of the British soldiers and police, trying to collect intelligence and to apprehend suspects, virtually impossible. They were met with a wall of silence. Any member of the population who did give valuable information on terrorist plans or identities to the British immediately became a terrorist target.

These examples of terrorists succeeding in their strategic aims of forcing British withdrawal and establishing their own rule are, however, relatively rare. Modern terrorists are deceiving themselves if they believe that these conditions are replicated in, for example, present-day Israel or Northern Ireland. Israeli Jews and Northern Ireland Protestants do not have anywhere else to go, and have a massive determination to resist and defeat the terrorism of their opponents, if necessary by using counter-terror against them.

Although these colonial terrorist struggles had additional negative effects on British security, for example by inspiring others to believe terrorist leverage against Britain could work, one must not neglect their positive effects. The most important and lasting advantage was that the British Army acquired a hard-won expertise in fighting this type of war which no other army, except perhaps the French, could match. Just as the French developed and refined their theories and doctrines of *la guerre revolutionnaire*,[9] so the British perfected their own techniques of counter-insurgency.[10] Moreover they achieved some remarkable successes in this field, adding to their confidence, and enriching their methods of training and operational planning.

The most notable success was the Malayan Emergency, in which a major communist insurgency was decisively defeated and a viable independent Malayan government ultimately established. Many writers have pointed out that the British security forces had certain key advantages in Malaya: the insurgents did not have a common border with a friendly communist government upon which they could rely for military supplies, support and sanctuary; the basis of the terrorist movement was too heavily centred on the Chinese population; and the security forces were able to maintain a ratio of about ten to one against the insurgents. (It is instructive to compare this with the situation in the Vietnam War in the 1960s, where the Vietcong did have a friendly communist power over the border, where the insurgents were Vietnamese, and where the counter-insurgents operated with a ration of around four to one against their enemy). Nevertheless, Sir Robert Thompson and other counter-insurgency specialists[11] make a powerful case that the British emergency administration in Malaya only succeeded in defeating the insurgency because it successfully fought a two-front war; a political and socio-economic war to win the support and active cooperation of the people, and a counter-insurgency war to isolate the terrorists from the population, to destroy their lines of supply, communication and recruitment, and to destroy their bases and weapons. From Malaya and other counter-insurgency operations the British Army learned over and over again the crucial contribution of high-calibre intelligence gathering and analysis, the need for the closest possible coordination between the army and the civil authorities and police, and the vital necessity of operating within the rule of law to make clear to the population that even in an emergency situation the laws would be administered firmly and fairly and that the people's safety and welfare would be protected.

EXPERIENCE SINCE 1970

The British Army's experience in countering terrorism stood it in good stead when, in August 1969, the Labour government of the day decided that it had to put the army into Northern Ireland to maintain public order.[12] The police system, the Royal Ulster Constabulary and the 'B Specials', had cracked under the physical and mental stress of constant marches, protest demonstrations and mob violence on the streets.

There are very strong reasons why governments of liberal states should only employ troops for internal security purposes with the very greatest reluctance, and why they should seek to withdraw them at the earliest opportunity. First, in any conflict of this scale it may be assumed that the belligerent faction or factions enjoy at least some support of sympathy in sections of the general population. Hence an unnecessarily high military profile may merely serve to escalate the level of violence by polarising pro- and anti-government elements in the community. Second, internal security duties under the strict limits imposed in a constitutional liberal democratic system conflict fundamentally in many respects with the professional instincts, traditions and ethos of the military. The soldier's main task is seen as the identification and destruction of the enemy. In internal security duties it is often extremely difficult to know who or where the enemy is, for friends and enemies all look the same. Moreover according to the constabulary ethic, the prime objective is not to kill lawbreakers, but to apprehend them and secure their conviction before a court of law. There is a constant risk that a repressive over-reaction or a minor error of judgement by the military may trigger further civil violence. Internal security inevitably imposes considerable strain on the soldiers, who are made well aware of the hostility of certain sections of the community towards them. A further danger is that the civil power may become over-dependent upon the army's presence, and there may be a consequent lack of urgency in preparing the civil police for gradually resuming the internal security responsibility. On the other hand, governments may become lulled into a false sense of security by the skilful peacekeeping of professional troops, and rush into premature troop withdrawals only to find that the police are unable to hold the line. Last but not least there is the important strategic consideration that we have already noted above: prolonged internal security duties absorb considerable manpower and involve diverting highly trained military technicians from their vital external defence role.

A government in full knowledge of these factors that commits its armed forces to taking over the internal security role in a whole city or province does so because it has no option. The army is needed because the government faces the threat of a full-scale insurgency or civil war. Unfortunately the civil authorities are often unable to appreciate the full implications of this threat in military terms. They sometimes try to pretend that if the army could only function like a substitute police force all would be well and the security situation would somehow automatically rectify itself. The British Army in Northern Ireland has unfortunately all too often suffered at the hands of government ministers and officials labouring under such illusions.[13]

When troops are really needed in a liberal state to restore and maintain law and order, by definition the conditions of normal policing do not obtain. The very fabric of the state and the life, safety and property of its citizens are under attack by ruthless and fanatical opponents. When a state of internal war exists it is no earthly good trying to keep a low profile, or restraining the soldiers from pursuing and defeating the insurgents. What on earth is the good of attempting to defeat ruthless armed insurgents, fanatically determined to destroy the state, strictly according to Queensberry rules which are not even acknowledged by the enemy? There is only one sensible objective for an army engaged in internal war, and this is to root out and defeat the enemy, to destroy the insurgent movement as a military and political force so that the constitution and laws can be restored and upheld.

The British Army has achieved a truly impressive record in countering revolutionary war and major terrorist outbreaks around the world since 1945. British soldiers have shown enormous skill, courage and patience in carrying out these tasks, and their loyalty in carrying out instructions from the civil government has never been put in question. The army is steeped in the democratic ethos. It is doubtful whether any other army in the world could have performed the internal security role in Northern Ireland with such humanity, restraint and effectiveness. In 1972 and 1973 the army chiefs in Northern Ireland clearly recognised that they could not defeat the Provisionals simply by acting as 'substitute policemen' giving effect to the ordinary law. The Provisional IRA had in effect declared war on the government and the whole system of

law, and by terrorism and intimidation they had rendered
normal policing in certain areas (the so-called 'no-go' areas)
impossible. Moreover, by intimidating witnesses and juries
and terrorising whole districts, they had succeeded in causing a
breakdown of the normal procedures of the law. The army was
charged with restoring order, but political constraints ruled
out the use of martial law, i.e. the complete takeover of the
machinery of civil government for the period of an emergency.
Hence the British government adopted the only sensible
alternative: the use of special powers legislation for the
emergency to give the army and the civil authorities the
necessary measures to suppress the insurgents. This middle
course involves maintaining the independence of the civil
power, while at the same time establishing special army-
government cooperation at all levels.

By means of operations such as 'Motorman' the army was
swiftly able to end the 'no-go' areas; the 1973 Northern Ireland
(Emergency Provisions) Act enabled the army, by late 1974, to
get on top of the security situation in Ulster. The 1973 special
powers gave them *carte blanche* to enter any premises at any
time and to question anybody at any time for up to four hours.
By late 1974 the army intelligence system had built up an
impressive bank of detailed intelligence on over 40 per cent of
the population of the Province. These details were fed into the
centralised master intelligence computer based at Lisburn
Army Headquarters. A vast amount of this intelligence was
gathered by means of 'P-tests', whereby people would be asked
at random for personal information concerning every detail of
their families, friends, occupation and religious and political
affiliations and involvements. In addition random close
searches of houses were undertaken, 'head-checks' were
conducted to scrutinise all occupants of a house, and extensive
open and covert photographic surveillance was utilised. This
massive intelligence effort paid enormous dividends in 1974. In
that year 71,914 houses were searched, 1,260 guns and 26,120
lb. of explosives were found. The Provisionals' main
explosives experts were inside Long Kesh, and the Belfast
Brigade was in such weak shape that it comprised only fifteen

or so active bombers and marksmen, mostly boys aged between fourteen and seventeen. Internment had begun literally to throttle the IRA's organisation on the ground, because the army's intelligence had become so accurate that it had been able to identify the terrorists. The IRA's main force of bombers was, by November 1974, either interned or imprisoned. Overwhelming evidence that the army had beaten the Provisional IRA to its knees by December 1974 is provided by the figures of bombings and shootings for the month: bombings were down to fewer than one a day and shootings to an average of five per day (three per day involving the army and therefore indicating at least a strong likelihood of contact with the enemy). These figures for terrorist incidents were the lowest in Northern Ireland since 1970.

With benefit of hindsight it is now possible to see that the army had practically beaten the Provisional IRA by December 1974. Hence the Provos' Christmas truce, and their so-called 'cease-fire', proffered in January 1975, were declared from a position of desperate weakness: they had been decimated as a military force and they urgently needed time to lick their wounds, recruit and train new members, await the release of their key men from internment, and regroup. There was absolutely no evidence of a sincere desire for peace on the part of the IRA. Nor is it clear what possible basis could have existed for agreement or compromise between the terrorists and the government. It is difficult to escape the conclusion that the so-called IRA 'ceasefire' which ushered in a year in which total deaths through terrorism increased by 15 per cent, was bought at the cost of a fatal degree of appeasement by the British government.

When one looks at the escalation of terrorism in Northern Ireland in 1972, with 467 killed, it is easier to understand why the British government was fully prepared to support a determined crackdown on the terrorists by the army, combined with the use of internment, introduced in 1972. The government saw itself faced with the prospect of full-scale civil war in the Province, and was willing to use draconian methods to restore order. They were not looking for a military solution because they were intelligent enough to realise that there was no such 'solution' possible in Northern Ireland which would be compatible with democratic values and standards in the United Kingdom. The army and the temporary emergency provisions were designed to facilitate the brave political initiative of a power-sharing government in Ulster, which Edward Heath's government achieved through the Sunningdale Agreement. This bold experiment, the most radical and far-sighted political initiative ever taken by a British government to bring peace in the Province, needed a long period with a much-reduced level of violence if it was to have any chance. Tragically it was brought down not by terrorism but by a combination of the Ulster Workers' Council (UWC) general strike and a UK general election which came before the new Northern Ireland Executive could put down real roots.[14]

Internment, or detention without trial, was introduced in 1972 in response to the desperate pleas of the Northern Ireland Stormont government. It was argued that the normal judicial processes had proved incapable of providing essential protection for society. Lawyers, magistrates and witnesses were being intimidated. The police were hamstrung in their efforts to bring known terrorists to trial, and to have them convicted. Such action is always bound to cause an outcry among the terrorists' supporters and families. However, in 1972, the initial rounding up of large numbers of suspects was handled so clumsily that it became a major propaganda weapon for the terrorists both in the Catholic community in Northern Ireland and in the United States. The measure was inevitably condemned by civil libertarians as an infringement of civil liberties. But this opposition was given far greater cutting edge as a result of the fact that many of those netted by the security forces had little involvement in IRA terrorism.

By the end of 1975 Mr Merlyn Rees, then Secretary of State for Northern Ireland, had carried out his declared intention of releasing all internees.[15] But as fast as they were released they were returning to active service with the IRA units that had been so depleted by army and police success in 1974. The army estimates that up to 70 per cent of released internees became reinvolved.[16] The plain fact is that normal liberal democratic government and the rule of law have not been able to function in Ulster properly for the last sixteeen years because they have been under direct attack not only from the IRA but also from a multiplicity of 'Loyalist' assassination squads and private armies such as the Ulster Volunteer Force (UVF), the Ulster Freedom Fighters (UFF) and the Protestant Action Force.[17] There are long terrorist traditions in both Protestant and Catholic communities. Where evil men are determined to disrupt the law, and render normal judicial processes unworkable through intimidating and killing witnesses, the government has surely a duty to invoke special powers to protect the community, restore order, and re-establish the rule of law. In such situations detention without trial may be seen as the only way to bring about a substantial drop in the level of violence and to quickly demobilise the terrorist leadership structure. But it constitutes a denial of the fundamental right of habeas corpus.

In the climate of greater optimism engendered by Sunningdale, and with the phasing-out of internment, the emphasis of British security policy underwent a significant shift. The decision was made that the Royal Ulster Constabulary should be reformed, strengthened and expanded so that it could become a thoroughly professional and impartial police force accepted by the law-abiding of both Protestant and Catholic communities and capable, in due course, of taking the major burden of the battle against terrorism. This policy of 'police primacy' was well under way in 1976 and the dynamic leadership of Sir Kenneth Newman, who later moved from Ulster to be the Commissioner of the Metropolitan Police, played a considerable part in converting the RUC into the modern professional force it is today. Few outsiders can fully appreciate the stresses and risks faced daily by this courageous and highly disciplined body of men and women. Between 1969 and the end of December 1986 the force lost 235 officers through terrorist violence. By the early 1980s they were able to patrol in all the major urban areas. The so-called 'bandit country' of the rural border areas are the only districts where the British Army, with its greater firepower and mobility, of necessity takes the major role.

Clear evidence that the strategy of police primary and judicial control is slowly but surely winning the battle against terrorism can be seen in the falling casualty figures and the numbers of terrorist suspects charged and convicted. The total number of deaths through terrorism dropped dramatically from 467 in 1972 to 216 by 1974, rose again to 247 in 1975 and 297 in 1976. Since then they have been below 100 per year except for 1979 (113) and 1981 (101). Civilian deaths as a proportion of the total have also dropped sharply from 321 in 1972 to 44 in 1983. And between 1976 and April 1984, 8,281 persons were charged with terrorist offences.

In the light of the enormous personal stress and strain placed on every member of the RUC it would be surprising if errors of judgement resulting in over-reaction did not occasionally occur. Why should we expect the RUC to be superhuman as well as brave and loyal? Their reputation suffered a considerable setback in the attempted arrest of Martin Galvin, US Noraid organiser, in Belfast in August 1984, during which a Provisional Sinn Fein supporter at the rally, Sean Downes, was killed by a plastic bullet. Serious over-reaction in the circumstances of a fairly orderly political rally, under full glare of the television cameras, was an operational blunder. But it should be seen in the context of enormous provocation presented by the appearance of Galvin, a financier of IRA terrorism, a man officially banned from entering Northern Ireland by the authorities. Major responsibility for the confrontation and the death of Sean Downes must lie with the IRA's political front, Provisional Sinn Fein, which staged this propaganda demonstration to get just the publicity which, unfortunately the RUC gave them. Mistakes of this kind, inevitable in the terrible circumstances of the Province, should not be allowed to detract from the RUC's tremendous and devoted sacrifices in the battle to uphold the rule of law against the ruthless bombers and gunmen who have mown down so many of their brave colleagues and British soldiers.

The Northern Ireland conflict has also shown very clearly

the severe limitations of terrorism as a weapon. Terrorist atrocities have secured plenty of publicity for the terrorists and their various threats and demands, but these propaganda 'victories' should not delude anyone into thinking that terrorists of either extreme have 'won' their wars. On the contrary, terrorism has only tended to stiffen the determination and intransigence of the adversary community. Violence and sectarian attacks by one set of extremists inevitably provoke counter-terror and defensive paramilitarism from the other.

The Northern Ireland conflict is exceptional in Western Europe because it is a classic case of ethnic minority terrorism: the Provisional IRA, a tiny minority of the Catholic minority population in Northern Ireland, seeks to 'liberate' a territory in which the majority refuse to be liberated. Meanwhile, the Orange extremists, fearful of being made a disadvantaged minority in a Catholic Irish Republic, are ready to wage a bloody civil war if necessary, to prevent any attempt at unification.

In spite of the cries of doom by Unionist politicians, the long-term prospects for greater stability in Northern Ireland are better than they have ever been throughout the past seventeen years of conflict. Many decent law-abiding Protestant citizens of Northern Ireland have the good sense not to be carried away by Ian Paisley's emotional calls of 'betrayal'. Even if they do not like the terms of the accord, they are unlikely to want to plunge the Province into massive chaos by rebelling against the British government. They also realise that if the police and army had to divert their resources to quelling 'Loyalist' rebellion, the only true beneficiaries would be the real enemies of democratic government and stability in Northern Ireland, the IRA.

In the short term it is certain that the petulance and hysteria of some Ulster Unionist politicians will make the political climate within the Province more unpleasant than usual. But sullenness and refusals to enter dialogue and cooperate with Her Majesty's government are, alas, routine experience for ministers and officials in Northern Ireland. It is highly doubtful whether the Orange leaders and their followers are really prepared to take up arms against the British Crown and try to declare a unilateral independence.

Meanwhile, the governments in London and Dublin should keep their nerve and steadily pursue real improvements in bilateral cooperation through the inter-governmental conference. Both governments know that they face a ruthless and determined terrorist threat in the shape of the IRA, on both sides of the border. The IRA, despite recent arrests of its activists and other setbacks, is still an extremely dangerous organisation. On the British mainland the bombing of Harrods and the Grand Hotel, Brighton, and the conspiracy to bomb seaside towns in 1985, show that it is still capable of lethal and indiscriminate terrorism in Britain. In Northern Ireland there has been a worrying escalation in the destructiveness of its explosive bombing attacks, and it has intensified its policy of mortar attacks on police stations.

It is urgently necessary for Britain and Ireland to coordinate significant improvements in cross-border security. Such moves will also be of immeasurable help in slowly persuading the Unionist majority in the North that the advantages of the new Agreement outweigh what they see as its liabilities.

If the British government can keep its nerve in the face of current Unionists' vitriolic propaganda, they may at least be in a position to save Northern Ireland from chaos and endless terrorism in spite of itself. The Unionist politicians may not realise it, but if London and Dublin maintain the will to make the Anglo-Irish Agreement work, it gives them the means to decisively defeat the ghastly terrorism of the IRA, the cancer in the Irish body politic. The IRA knows that and this is why it is desperately stepping up violence to undermine the accord. It is only to be expected that the Orange and Green extremists should join forces to defeat this vehicle of potential stability. Blind and narrow nationalisms feed off each other. Yet more far-sighted and reasonable people in both communities in Northern Ireland can join forces to prevent this. The extremists of both sides constantly hurl wild accusations of 'betrayal'. Surely those who are guilty of betraying the real interests of the Northern Ireland people and their future generations, are those who fuel and fan the fires of sectarian bigotry, hatred and suspicion.

In the absence of any continental-style ideological terrorism of the extreme left in Britain, the main continuing terrorist threat on the mainland has been from the IRA's bombing attacks. These attacks started in 1973, intensified in 1974, the year of the Birmingham pub bombings, only to peter out again after the Balcombe Street siege. However, the bombing of Harrods, the massive explosion at the Grand Hotel, Brighton, during the Conservative Party Conference in October 1984, and the IRA plot to bomb English seaside towns in 1985, uncovered by the police, are evidence that the IRA still has the ability to organise deadly attacks on the mainland. There is a constant struggle by the British police and intelligence services to keep a step ahead of the increasingly sophisticated and devious methods of the IRA bombers.

In this battle there is little doubt that the Prevention of Terrorism Act's (PTA) provisions are likely to be seen as increasingly useful and necessary for the police. Moreover, this Act has now been amended to apply to international terrorist activity in Britain in addition to the IRA. This followed the recommendation of Lord Jellicoe's major review of the PTA.[18]

The Prevention of Terrorism Act was not a panic measure.[19] Its main provisions had already been prepared well before the carnage of the Birmingham pub bombings of 21 November 1974, in which twenty civilians were killed and 180 injured. And it was right and necessary that the government had such legislation ready, because the war in Ulster had already spilled over into the mainland over the previous eighteen months. Indeed before the Bill was introduced into Parliament nearly 700 people had been injured by IRA bombs in Britain. On a single day in March 1973 nearly 250 people had been injured and one killed in two bomb attacks at the Old Bailey and Great Scotland Yard. In 1974 there had been attacks at the National Defence College, Latimer, and on a coach on the M62 in February, at the Tower of London in July, at Guildford in October, and at Woolwich in November. But it was the

Birmingham pub bombings that finally convinced public opinion, MPs and the government that emergency measures were necessary to try to prevent the spread of this barbarism.

The Act introduced by Mr Roy Jenkins provided a valuable example of the kinds of special powers that can be used effectively to protect a society under severe terrorist attack, without simultaneously suspending the constitution or destroying civil liberty. One of its major provisions, the proscription of the IRA as a terrorist organisation, was, arguably, 'more spectacular than effective'[20]. Security experts have long argued that proscription simply tends to drive the target organisation completely underground and makes the tasks of intelligence-gathering and detection more difficult for the police. Nevertheless this move was politically well-judged, for it would have outraged public opinion if the IRA had been permitted to continue to meet, raise funds and recruit support openly in British cities. It was, after all, already a proscribed organisation in Ireland, both north and south of the border. Moreover the stiff penalties for belonging to, or professing to belong to the IRA, giving it financial or other support, or arranging or assisting in the arrangement of an IRA meeting, were a useful token of the government's determination to crack down on terrorist organisation. And one positive benefit of proscription is that it deprives the terrorists of the opportunity to march, demonstrate and provoke affrays with rival groups. This helps to free the police from the dreary and time-consuming work of crowd and riot control on the streets and enables them to concentrate on protecting the general public and catching criminals.

Of proven value to security forces is the power to exclude terrorists by denying them entry to Britain or by deportation. The Prevention of Terrorism Act 'enables the Secretary of State to make exclusion orders to prevent acts of terrorism, whenever committed, designed to influence public opinion or Government policy with respect to affairs in Northern Ireland'.[21] This enables the authorities to deny entry to (or to deport) any person suspected of terrorist offences, or suspected of entering Britain for the purpose of committing terrorism. As the necessary instrument of this Act, port controls by police and immigration officials have been considerably tightened. Port police have the power to stop, question and search any suspected person. These controls have already yielded much invaluable information to the security authorities.

Another very important power for the security forces is that of searching any person suspected of committing, preparing or instigating acts of terrorism. Apart from body searches of suspects, which may yield valuable evidence and intelligence, random searches of premises, and searches for specific equipment and materials used for terrorism, such as explosives and transmitters, may be specifically authorised by emergency legislation.

By far the most useful of the powers afforded by the Prevention of Terrorism Act, however, are those under section 7, clauses (1) and (2), dealing with arrest and detention. The police are thereby empowered to arrest without warrant a person whom they 'reasonably suspect' to be (i) a person guilty of a terrorist offence, or (ii) a person concerned in the commission, preparation or instigation of acts of terrorism, or (iii) a person subject to an exclusion order. Moreover, in particular cases the Secretary of State has the power to extend the period for which a suspect may be detained for questioning beyond the normal maximum of forty-eight hours. The additional period may not exceed five days, making the maximum period for which a person could be detained without being charged seven days. This power is an invaluable aid to the police, for it is interrogation that saves lives and provides the leads for catching other members of the terrorist organisation. And in the judgement of most intelligence experts forty-eight hours is not long enough for the process of interrogation to yield results. Seven days is generally just long enough to enable conventional police questioning methods to wear down the suspect's resistance. Frequently the longer period enables the police to use bargaining power. Exceptionally, with the cooperation of the Director of Public Prosecutions, they may be able to offer certain suspects immunity from prosecution in return for everything they know. This method can be particularly effective in cases where suspects are likely to have become enmeshed in terrorist activities more through blackmail and intimidation than political conviction. For example, the supergrass system in Northern Ireland has yielded invaluable information on terrorism for the RUC. This has resulted in scores of arrests of terrorists from the IRA and INLA (Irish National Liberation Army) and the Loyalist terrorist groups.

Second only to the terrorist threat from the IRA on the mainland is the problem of international terrorism, especially from the Middle East, spilling over into London and other major centres in Britain. London shares with Paris and other West European capitals the characteristic of ethnic diversity and political factionalism among a huge and increasing expatriate population. The whole range of Middle Eastern political movements is represented, many with a sizeable following and even with their own newspapers and organisations. For example, there are pro- and anti-Khomeini factions among the Iranians, Palestinians loyal to Arafat, anti-Arafat Palestinians, pro- and anti-Gadaffi Libyans, and agents and opponents of every other Middle Eastern state.

Three dramatic incidents in the 1980s illustrate the range of problems that the import of this type of violence can cause for Britain. In May 1980 a group of 'Arabistan' terrorists seized control of the Iranian Embassy at Princes' Gate, taking a large number of hostages.[22] The Metropolitan Police, drawing on its substantial experience with IRA terrorism, reacted with impressive efficiency. They first tried patient negotiation with the terrorists to persuade them to release the hostages peacefully. When the hostage-takers killed one of the hostages, the Police Commander rightly decided to call in the crack SAS hostage-rescue squad. The rescue operation was brilliantly planned and executed, the remaining nineteen hostages were released unharmed and five terrorists were killed. This operation, unique on the British mainland, proved the value of close police-army coordination and joint planning and exercising. It was also very useful in teaching the police more about the intricacies and complexities of such sieges,[23] especially where Middle East politics are involved, about the problems of handling the news media, and about the additional demands for police manpower and resources created by the siege itself and by the political demonstrations that built up as an accompaniment to the Embassy siege. Most important of all, in the longer term, was the fact that the total defeat of the terrorists helped to deter other groups from similar attempts to seize embassies. This lesson was not lost on other Western countries, and many of them proceeded to establish or radically improve their own capabilities for hostage rescue. Similarly firm responses in other incidents helped to curb the fever of embassy takeovers that had afflicted many capitals in 1980 and 1981.[24]

Although there is evidence that the Iranian Embassy hostage-rescue helped to deter similar embassy seizures in London, it is clear that this did not affect the readiness of terrorists to continue using less risky methods of terrorism, particularly assassinations and bombings, in London and other major cities. The activities of Libyan hit squads sent by Colonel Gadaffi to hunt down and murder exiled dissidents, continued. So did the violence of extreme Palestinian groups, such as Abu Nidal, a renegade Palestinian group.[25] It was this group which was responsible for the attempted assassination of the Israeli Ambassador in London, Mr Shlomo Argov. This outrage was the trigger for the Israeli invasion of Lebanon, or 'Operation Peace in Galilee' as it was called by the Israelis. The event was a reminder of the vulnerability of diplomats to terrorist attack, but it also showed the Metropolitan Police's efficiency in capturing both the Abu Nidal gunman and his colleagues so promptly.

A third important illustration of the international terrorist spillover into Britain was the incident in April 1984 when a Libyan gunman shooting from a window of the Libyan People's Bureau in St James's Square killed a woman police officer, WPC Yvonne Fletcher, and injured a number of anti-Gadaffi demonstrators who had staged a protest rally in the square. This outrage led to the British government severing diplomatic relations with the Gadaffi regime. But it raised a number of very important questions about weaknesses in Britain's defences against this type of international terrorism. Why had the Foreign Office failed to keep a close check on the personnel, diplomatic status and activities of the Libyan People's Bureau, especially following its takeover by a 'revolutionary committee' of Gadaffi extremists? Why did the Metropolitan Police and Home Office fail to act on various advance warnings of the possibility of confrontation at the embassy? Why was the demonstration allowed to take place so close to the embassy building?

In the longer term, the St. James's Square shooting revealed the great complications of dealing effectively with state-sponsored terrorism.[26] Her Majesty's government had to bear in mind throughout the siege the personal safety of our own diplomatic mission in Tripoli and the 8,000 or so British expatriates working in Libya. They were all potential hostages at Gadaffi's whim. Under these circumstances was it right for the British government to allow the Libyan People's Bureau personnel to return to Libya? Should the Libyan People's Bureau have been stormed and its staff arrested, in the light of the seriousness of Libya's breach of diplomatic and ordinary law? Was it sufficient for Britain to sever diplomatic links with Tripoli? Is it not desirable in such circumstances to cut all economic links also, and to thus impose some real economic costs on the state sponsors of terrorism? Should the democratic states either unilaterally or collectively take steps to revise or tighten the implementation of the Vienna Convention rules on the exchange of diplomats? None of these questions has yet been finally resolved.

The final category of terrorist threat is the attack on British targets abroad. This is the most difficult of all to guard against, and to deal with when it occurs, because it is likely to happen in areas where the host government is either weak or indifferent and where Britain has little or no military resources available to come to the aid of a British target. In such circumstances one must rely on good intelligence assessments and early warnings, cultivating cooperation with other friendly states or forces in the region, using military force for hostage rescue where necessary, and the general improvement of international cooperation—for example in aviation security measures—to help stop the terrorist getting through to his target.[27]

The British approach

A careful study of the British response to terrorism, both in Northern Ireland and internationally, shows that a well-defined and consistent approach has been adopted by successive governments since the mid-1970s. The underlying principles that inform the British policy, recently succinctly reiterated by the Home Secretary,[28] are: (i) a firm political will to uphold the rule of law and democratic government and to defeat terrorism; (ii) absolute refusal to surrender to terrorist extortion and demands; (iii) determination to act in accord with domestic and international law; (iv) treatment of convicted terrorists as common criminals with no special privileges, pardons, or amnesty; (v) the promotion of national and international measures to combat terrorists by minimising their rewards and maximising their costs and losses.

The major instruments developed by the British authorities to implement this policy are: the strengthening of the judiciary and the police, where necessary by emergency measures, and the provision of adequate resources and expertise for countering terrorism (e.g. the establishment and strengthening of the Police Anti-Terrorist Squad); improved intelligence gathering, analysis, and coordination; and active participation in bilateral and multilateral cooperation with our allies (e.g. the British-US Extradition Treaty and the TREVI (Terrorism, Radicalism, Extremism, and International Violence) system of European police and intelligence cooperation).

All these measures are the explicit characteristics of British response to terrorism. But there are also some very important indirect and implicit measures that should be added to complete the picture. British governments have no simplistic illusions that prophylactic economic, social and political reforms will somehow magically eliminate terrorism. But in Northern Ireland, and to some extent in the Middle East, they have realised the importance of addressing the deeply felt and legitimate grievances of whole ethnic groups or communities. The Anglo-Irish Agreement is first and foremost an exercise in bridge-building, a framework for potential power-sharing cooperation, and only secondarily a device for anti-terrorist cooperation with the Republic. Similarly the British Foreign Office has continued to favour moves, in concert with other European Community governments, to address the basic grievances of the Palestinian people in the Middle East. None of these policies has made any dramatic breakthroughs. How could they in view of the intractability of these conflicts? Nevertheless, there is undoubtedly an important element of constructive political reform and concern for human rights in British policy.

The British approach is widely respected and has been highly effective and consistent. It is one which the author is closely identified with and which he is ready to commend to other democratic countries. Nevertheless there have been many weaknesses and shortcomings in British *implementation* of this policy which must be honestly admitted and rectified.

One major problem which revealed itself in the early 1970s in Northern Ireland was a lack of adequate intelligence co-ordination between the army and the police.[29] The army set up its own intelligence system in 1969-70 because it has few other courses, and by 1974-75 it was extremely strong in this field. But as the Royal Ulster Constabulary (RUC) became more effective again, and 'police primacy' became adopted as official policy, the RUC's own intelligence gathering through informers and the work of the Divisional Mobile Support Units also made great strides. But unfortunately there was often some unhealthy friction between police and army in the mid-1970s, with neither side fully trusting the other or telling it what it was doing.

To curb these dangerous trends, in 1980 a new security coordinator, the experienced and gifted Sir Maurice Oldfield,[30] was appointed. His task was to assist the Secretary of State for Northern Ireland in improving the coordination and effectiveness of the fight against terrorism. Sir Maurice was extremely successful, mainly by making the security committees more effective by allowing the army and police to put their own cases, with himself, as a neutral, as chairman. Sir Maurice was forced to retire through ill-health within a year of taking office. Although there is reason to believe that his impact in Northern Ireland was beneficial and lasting, there has been continuing evidence of friction between MI5 and MI6 and further problems with morale and organisation in the secret services. This has worrying implications for British capabilities in countering terrorism. But there have also been problems of intelligence coordination and major security lapses on the mainland. By far the worst recent case was the events leading up to the IRA bombing of the Grand Hotel in Brighton during the Conservative Party Conference on 12 October 1984. Five people were killed in the blast, many were injured, some seriously, and the Prime Minister and many senior members of her government narrowly escaped death in the attack.

The Brighton bombing exposed major mistakes in security. There had apparently been a warning of an impending IRA terrorist attack sent by the intelligence services to all police forces. But the Sussex police, responsible for the practical security arrangements for the Conservative Party Conference, did not take the threat very seriously. In addition to an evident lack of adequate liaison between the Sussex police and the experts in countering terrorism, the Anti-Terrorist Squad and the Royal Ulster Constabulary, the physical security arrangements for the Grand Hotel were appalling. The hotel was not properly searched. The police did not use the best available techniques. Access to the hotel public rooms, unlike access to the Conference Hall, was not adequately controlled. Basic security precautions simply were not taken.

Urgent steps were taken to remedy these deficiencies in the wake of the Brighton bombing. An interdepartmental committee, named TIGER, was set up by the Home Secretary to evaluate intelligence from all available sources and to advise on appropriate security measures to all the police forces. In addition a special working group under the chairmanship of Sir Lawrence Byford was set up to study problems of security at party conferences and similar political events. These measures are welcome, but a question mark still hangs over the whole matter of coordination against terrorism. Is liaison between the forty-seven local police forces and the Home Office and intelligence services really good enough? Is there an adequate degree of specialist knowledge of counter-terrorism available within the provincial forces if and when they need it?

Another major weakness in Britain's response to terrorism has been the propensity of successive governments to allow British commercial interests to continue to conduct business as usual with the state sponsors of terrorism. This is extremely shortsighted because it underestimates the extent to which terrorist regimes such as Libya and Syria are vulnerable to concerted economic pressures by the West's leading industrialised states, and because it fails to see that the longer-term security and well-being of the economies and political systems of the Third World as well as the West depends to a large part on our ability to preserve general peace and security.

Despite occasional failures in intelligence of the kind mentioned above, the British government's record in combatting terrorism is impressive. Indeed it is one of the best in the democratic world. Britain has been one of the keenest supporters of moves to strengthen international cooperation against terrorism. For example, Britain ratified the Council of Europe's Convention on the Suppression of Terrorism in 1978 and backed the Bonn summit declaration on hijacking in the same year. Britain has also taken the initiative in seeking international, democratic measures against state sponsors of terrorism, for example, at the London summit of 1984, and the Tokyo summit of 1986 and throughout Britain's period in the European Community Presidency in 1986. Mrs Thatcher's leadership has been particularly remarkable for its courage and firmness in refusing to surrender to terrorist blackmail. The British model inevitably shows up the weaknesses and dangerously counter-productive aspects of the hostage deals pursued, for example, by successive French governments and the Reagan administration. In fighting international terrorism, as in other forms of defence, appeasement is the road to ruin. British experience shows that a policy of 'no surrender' is tough to implement, but at least it is honourable and helps to discourage further extortion attempts. But while there is such weakness and inconsistency in countering terrorism among other Western states, international terrorism will continue to be a major threat.

NOTES

1. For historians' interpretations of this process see, for example, E.L. Woodward, *The Age of Reform 1815-1870*, Oxford: OUP, 1939; R.C.K. Ensor, *England, 1870-1914*, Oxford, OUP, 1936; and C.L. Mowat, *Britain Between the Wars, 1918-1940*, London: Methuen 1955.
2. See the account in K.R.M. Short, *The Dynamite War*, Dublin: Gill and Macmillan, 1979.
3. This process of change among the Irish is discussed in an interesting analysis in William I. Thompson, *The Imagination of an Insurrection, Dublin, Easter 1916*, New York: OUP, 1967.
4. As described in Calton Younger, *Ireland's Civil War*, London: Muller, 1968.
5. J. Bowyer Bell, *The Secret Army*, Academy Press, pp. 310-55.
6. *Ibid.*, pp. 355-92.
7. Menachem Begin, *The Revolt*, New York: Henry Schuman, 1951.
8. G. Grivas, *Guerrilla Warfare and EOKA's Struggle*, London: Longman, 1964.
9. See P. Paret, 'The French Army and La Guerre Revolutionaire', *Journal of the Royal United Service Institution*, February 1959.
10. These techniques are analysed in F. Kitson, *Low-Intensity Operations*, London: Faber, 1971, and Sir R. Thompson, *Defeating Communist Insurgency*, London: Chatto and Windus, 1966.
11. Sir R. Thompson, *No Exit from Vietnam*, London: Chatto and Windus, 1969.
12. Mr James Callaghan gives an interesting account of this decision in his memoir, *A House Divided* London: Collins, (1972).
13. For a soldier's view of these frustrations see Robin Evelegh, *Peace-Keeping in a Democratic Society*, London: C. Hurst, 1978.
14. See Paul Arthur, *Government and Politics of Northern Ireland*, London: Longman, 1984.
15. For a comment on the internment measure, and its consequences, see Paul Wilkinson, *Terrorism and the Liberal State*, London: Macmillan, 1986, Ch. 10.
16. *Ibid.*

17. Martin Dillon and Dennis Lehane, *Political Murder in Northern Ireland,* Harmondsworth: Penguin, 1973.
18. *Review of the Operation of the Prevention of Terrorism (Temporary Provisions) Act, 1976* (Cmnd 8803) (1983).
19. Clive Walker, *The Prevention of Terrorism in British Law,* Manchester: Manchester University Press, 1986, p. 23.
20. *The Economist,* 30 Nov. 1974.
21. Explanatory Memorandum, Prevention of Terrorism (Temporary Provisions) Bill, 1974.
22. R.J. Andrew, 'The Siege at Princes' Gate', in Brian Jenkins (ed.) *Terrorism and Beyond,* Santa Monica: Rand, 1982, pp. 243-6.
23. John Dellow, 'Political Violence and the Response', in Richard Clutterbuck (ed.) *The Future of Political Violence,* London, Macmillan, 1987, pp. 173-6.
24. Richard Clutterbuck, 'Introduction', *Annual of Power and Conflict, 1980-81,* London: Institute for the Study of Conflict, 1981.
25. See Yossi Melman, *The Master Terrorist,* New York: Adama Books, 1986, for an interesting account.
26. See Paul Wilkinson, *op. cit.,* Ch. 16 for a fuller discussion of these problems.
27. *Ibid.,* pp. 240-58.
28. Speech by the Rt Hon Douglas Hurd to Police Management Association at Hendon, 30 Oct. 1985.
29. Richard Deacon, *A Biography of Sir Maurice Oldfield,* London: Futura, 1985, p. 38.
30. *Ibid.*

3   Terrorism in West Germany

Eva Kolinsky

SYSTEM STABILITY, OPPOSITION AND TERRORISM

Political terrorism in West Germany highlights a paradox of the German tradition and political culture. For opposition to advocate alternatives has been regarded with suspicion in a political environment anxious to defend stability as a precondition of democracy. Yet extra-parliamentary opposition has frequently sought the abolition and a transformative change of 'the system' as a prerequisite for effective political action. West German terrorism and the reactions to it have their common roots in a pre-democratic tradition of de-legitimising opposition and de-legitimising the political order.

In the 1950s, terrorism seemed a problem of the past. A strong institutional framework had been created to ensure political stability and to defend the fledgling democracy against too much diversity and too much opposition. The privileged position afforded to major political parties facilitated the political integration of initially disaffected groups. The use of violence was associated with the inhumanity of National Socialism by some, with communist regimes by others; it was not a tool of opposition. The political murders, street battles and terrorism which had proliferated during Germany's first Republic and accelerated its destruction, had virtually disappeared from the second. Since the 1960s, the integrative hold of the major parties on the electorate decreased as socio-economic and denominational cleavage lines lost some of their relevance. Political participation outside approved structures of representation increased, and modes of participation shifted from the conventional to the unconventional. Extra-parliamentary politics and opposition became newly important.[1] The student movement was the first in a series of new social movements which regarded themselves as correctives to state-affiliated party politics, and which articulated new issues outside established parliamentary or party channels. Since then, the citizens' initiative movement, the anti-nuclear movement, the women's movement, the squatters' movement and the peace movement have all laid claim to voicing issues which were salient in society but ignored by the political establishment.

It is necessary to consider West German terrorism in the context of this new volatility of political preferences and political participation. The 1960s saw a political mobilisation, but also a revival of anti-system fundamentalism among activists of the left and the right. Extra-parliamentary opposition movements have been inspired by expectations that the changes they demanded would also initiate a linkage between politics and people. Yet the policy adjustments which did occur remained within the party consensus and within the parameters of West German politics. The major parties proved flexible: the student movement sparked off educational reforms; an emphasis on co-determination and participation followed the citizens' initiative movement; the Social Democrats (SPD) incorporated core demands of the peace movement into its political platform; all parties are now addressing themselves to environmental issues; and legislation to pay foreign workers to return to their native countries has echoed demands from the right that all foreigners should be sent home.

A new equilibrium seems to be taking shape in West German politics: issues and movements surface at extra-parliamentary level, elicit adjustments, and decline only for different ones to emerge. This cycle of extra-parliamentary action and parliamentary articulation appears to have allocated to unconventional politics the prescribed function of limited innovation—an avant-garde perhaps, but not a leader. At this juncture, segments or factions which had anticipated a transformation of society or of the political system are radicalised into using coercive action, and ultimately terrorism. More specifically, on the left the student movement and the peace movement unleashed terrorism as they declined and as their aims began to lose distinctiveness. On the right, the temporary successes of the National Democratic Party (NPD) in the late 1960s, and its decay to a near-irrelevant fringe party in the 1970s and 1980s has led to a radicalisation which combined a deliberate recourse to Nazi language with aggressive actions against contemporary targets.

For both political camps, mass mobilisation appears to have conjured up expectations that a transformation of society was imminent. Regardless of political orientation, the use of terrorist actions in West Germany has two major purposes. It is intended to create a momentum which would somehow abolish 'the system'. It is also aimed at recruiting activists and convincing affiliated political forces that despite the adversity of the political environment—or worse still, its flexibility towards new issues designed to blur the distinction between opposition and mainstream parties—a determined few are capable of fundamentalist political action. Beyond the specifically West German determinants of terrorism, the apparent ability of self-styled liberation movements, guerilla fighters, and nationalists elsewhere in the world to make their demands known internationally and gain recognition as a political force in their respective regions through the use of terrorism, also served to persuade the German adherents of anti-system opposition that a recourse to terrorism could have similar pay-offs for them.

In faraway geo-political locations, terrorism may be about social liberation, political equality, regional independence. In West Germany, it testifies to the failure of creating a legitimate space for conflict in the political culture. The cross-party consensus and the tendency to brand opposition as potentially destabilising, have contributed to perceptions that change needs something more forceful than persuasion. By the same token, successive West German governments have reacted by intensifying state controls through tailor-made legislation, the perfection of surveillance networks and special police units. As in the founding days of the Federal Republic, political stability is valued as a precondition of democracy which appears threatened by terrorism. In the 1950s, the integrative capacity of the major parties and the commitment to non-violent politics at extra-parliamentary level had eliminated German terrorism; under the newly mobilised conditions of contemporary politics, and with violence no longer taboo, terrorism of the left and of the right has re-emerged as a facet of opposition in West Germany.

IN SEARCH OF THE LOST REVOLUTION: TERRORISM FROM THE LEFT

Attempts to explain why and how terrorism from the left could erupt at a time when West Germany seemed set to gain recognition as a 'model democracy' have been as plentiful as the answers they found. Some saw a straight line from the student movement, and indeed all left-wing politics, to terrorism; others suggested that the German events were largely copy-cat terrorism of events elsewhere or the backlash against restrictions imposed on liberties and freedom of dissent by the West German authorities. Biographical and psychological studies were also plentiful, and these set out to explain what made a bunch of middle-class and educated young people turn terrorist.[2] They detected tensions in the parental family, conflicts at school, mother fixations or the search for father-figures in a fatherless society tainted by its fascist past. Or was terrorism rooted in the inability of leftist factions to relate Marxist theory to the contemporary world?

The near-legendary fame of Baader, Meinhof, and Ensslin underlines the extent to which the study of terrorism in West Germany has centred on specific events in the 1970s, and on their presumed instigators. A government-commissioned analysis, charged with exploring the causes and assessing the prospects of West German terrorism, published painstaking accounts of thoughts, deeds and personality traits and concluded that having peaked in 1977, dealing with terrorism was merely a mopping-up exercise, i.e. arresting former terrorists who were still at large.[3]

What West Germany experienced in the 1970s was not just freak terrorism inspired by a mixture of charisma, circumstance and dismay at the 'over-reaction' of the political authorities, a Baader-Meinhof syndrome. It was a first sign of the new linkage between extra-parliamentary opposition and parliamentary politics, and of the dynamics within the extra-parliamentary camp between those intent on policy adjustments of the main parties and those pitched against the parameters of politics themselves.

Table 3.1: Terrorist Offences by the Left, 1969-1985*

Year	Offences	Year	Offences
1969	48	1978	52
1970	117	1979	41
1971	79	1980	77
1972	62	1981	129
1973	70	1982	184
1974	104	1983	215
1975	46	1984	148
1976	30	1985	331
1977	48		

Note: *excluding other offences such as assault, malicious damange, extortion or theatening violence.
Source: Terroristen im Kampf gegen Recht und Menschenwürde, ed. Bundesministerium Des Innern (BMI) Bonn 1985, p. 38, and annual BMI reports.

*Table 3.2: Offence with Left-Extremist Intentions 1982-1985.
(Specifically terrorist offences in brackets).*

Offence	1982	1983	1984	1985*
Explosions	68 (63)	55 (51)	47 (44)	63 (60)
Arson	310(120)	304(164)	172(101)	229(154)
Assault	22	41	65	88
Robberies	1	—	3	5
Breach of the peace				
Violence at demon-strations	119	90	117	112
Obstruction of trans-port	6	5	95	115
Malicious damage	1,071	1,045	770	990
Acts of violence:Total	1,597	1,540	1,269	1,602
Threats of violence	43	7	38	74
Other left-extremistoffences	249	157	216	167
Overall total	1,889	1,704	1,523	1,843

Note: *this also includes two terrorist murders.
Source: Betrift Verfassungsschutz, BMI, Bonn.

The data on criminal acts committed by terrorists such as
explosions, arson attacks, murders and robberies (see Table
3.1) show that far from having ceased, terrorism has soared to
a new peak in the 1980s. Comparative figures since 1982
indicate that terrorist offences have constituted 10 to 15 per
cent of offences perpetrated by left-extremists (see Table 3.2),
although matching offences with offenders has itself not been
without difficulty. In 1984, just thirty of the 148 offences
ascribed to terrorists were in fact traced to known terrorist

groupings or individuals; of the 331 terrorist offences reported for 1985, fifty-two were linked to groups or suspects.[4] Terrorist intentions are presumed for most bombings, and for a sizeable proportion of arson attacks, often relying on messages to the press or other identifying hints. The distribution of offences outlined in Table 3.2 points to a significant component of offences which involve violence of some kind. The sharp rise in traffic-related offences can be partly explained by more efficient detection and also by an upsurge of obstructions to prevent the transport of equipment for nuclear plants or military installations. Robberies in terrorism are substitutes for a social support system which guerilla fighters would have but which is lacking in West Germany. Their function is to replenish funds, to obtain guns or explosives, official documents for forging passports, driving licences and other means of identification.

Although a major thrust of terrorist attacks against banks and department stores, i.e. 'consumer society' and 'capitalism', against police and legal institutions, i.e. 'the system of repression', and against military installations of the West German and Allied forces, i.e. 'imperialism', has been evident throughout, new issues have surfaced. Since the late 1970s, terrorist actions have also been directed against construction firms involved with nuclear energy plants, with controversial projects such as the expansion of Frankfurt airport, and with programmes of urban modernisation. Computer centres and producers of electronic equipment became terrorist targets in the 1980s, as did a number of trade union headquarters which had withheld support from the striking British miners. Among the issues from the 1970s, military matters have soared to the forefront, while assaults on legal institutions and personnel receded somewhat.

The shift of issues points to a current link with extra-parliamentary opposition. The newly salient issues which inspired the new social movements have also defined some targets for terrorism. The splintering of the peace movement in 1983 into radicalised activisms ranging from obstruction of army exercises to killings and attempted killings points to the close link between contemporary terrorism in West Germany and the issue-based mobilisation of extra-parliamentary opposition since the 1970s. Over a decade earlier, the student movement had splintered into radicalised activisms when the 1968 events in France and demonstrations of 30,000 or 50,000 in West Germany were greeted as 'red swallows heralding the revolution in Western Europe.'[5]

The mass concern about the environment, about nuclear destruction or the dangers of war, which inspired the new social movement, were understood as the first stirrings of the transformative changes terrorism had in mind. The NATO twin-track decision of 1979 identified—in the eyes of one terrorist spokesman—the enemy, and also left him with the impression that the German population was on the brink of breaking with the established order: 'the logic of the system drove and drives towards war—and it will be conducted whenever victory seems possible. That in the process half of Western Europe and the territory of the FRG will be devastated, does not hold the pigs in the Pentagon back.'[6]

The differences between political movements and terrorism, however, are considerable. In the eyes of the law and most of contemporary society, terrorism is identical with unlawful behaviour and criminal acts. Contrary to ordinary crimes, terrorist actions purport to have political motives. While political activists usually see the physical destruction of objects or persons as their main purpose, terrorism aims at the psychological effects of destructive actions. These are designed to win support elsewhere in society—among the left, among the students, among the adherents of new social movements, among the West German population—and to unlease a transformative or revolutionary change of society which could not otherwise occur. Terrorist acts are intended as fanfares to set this change in motion.[7]

The step from appeal to action is a step in the terrorist direction:

Demonstrations and protests are preliminary stages of people gaining full consciousness of their situation. We have to awaken consciousness in more and more people, we have to mobilise them politically i.e. draw them into the anti-authoritarian camp which at present seems to consist only of a thousand or so students, and we have to do more than just protest. We have to move on to direct actions.[8]

When Dutschke called for action to supplant protests, the student movement was still wrapped in its utopian belief that the masses were about to awake. For the cacophony of communes, anarchists and so-called dope-rebels who followed, such awakening seemed possible only through shocking the masses, and through action untethered by conventions or consensus:

Shit on this society of half-seniles and taboos. Go wild and do lovely things. Have a joint. Whatever you see and you do not like, smash it to pieces! Have courage to fight! Have courage to win![9]

Laqueur's observation that terrorism is always nothing but action[10] does not altogether characterise the West German terrorists, who made considerable efforts to extend theories of revolutionary change by the doctorine of the 'primacy of practice': 'The analysis of class positions, which is needed, cannot be accomplished without revolutionary practice, revolutionary initiative.'[11]

What we are doing and what we want to show at the same time, is: that armed struggle can be carried out, that it is possible to pull actions off, where we can win, and not where the other side wins. And where it is, of course essential that they do not catch us, that is, so to speak, part of the success of the matter.[12]

As 'urban guerillas' West German terrorists placed themselves emphatically alongside freedom fighters in Third World countries, an avant-garde of revolutionary change: 'The urban guerila operates with the vast gap between apparatus and masses and is always on the side of the masses. The actions of the urban guerila are never directed against the people, they are always actions against the imperialist apparatus.'[13]

In reality, the nexus with the people proved difficult. In various attacks, innocent 'members of the people' were killed or injured. As neither the German population nor even the political left would give the expected support, many actions shifted towards an introspective elitism, with terrorism merely aimed at strengthening terrorism. Yet, since the mid-1970s, a collaboration with and alongside extra-parliamentary movements was also envisaged:

It is one of our perspectives, to get involved in a more comprehensive and more offensive way in the mass struggles, not in order to punish but in order to relate more or less formally to movements and use our actions to generate direct effects and advantages.[14]

In the 1980s, the presumed mass struggle occurred in the peace movement, and 27 per cent of terrorist offences were directed against personnel and installations of the US army in what was termed 'anti-imperialism'. Between 1984 and 1985, bombings rose by 47 per cent, arson attacks by 29 per cent with NATO installations, American personnel and equipment, manoeuvres and training programmes most frequently affected.[15] The fluidity of terrorist aims, and the location of 'mass' in the current issues of the day, indicates that in contemporary society, terrorism has become a facet of extra-parliamentary action.

There are other factors which make it difficult to draw neat boundaries between terrorism and parts of the extra-parliamentary left in West Germany. Although the Red Army Faction (RAF) has seemed to constitute an identifiable group or gang since the early 1970s, its organisational structure is by no means clear. The original six whom Heinrich Böll saw hunted by sixty million[16] were arrested by 1972, yet new recruits continued to adopt the name RAF and also a number of other names as the trade mark of their actions. Recruitment to the RAF, including coordination of terrorist attacks to free terrorists, has been conducted from within the prisons. The imprisonment of leading terrorists itself became a major issue in appealing for support outside, and in finding new recruits.

Specific allegations about the conditions of imprisonment gave rise to campaigns alleging inhumane treatment of terrorists, the most effective being the campaigns against 'isolation torture', against high security wings, and the 'red aid' or 'black aid' networks among the left.[17] Since 1973, nine coordinated hunger strikes have been organised by imprisoned terrorists. They claimed two victims, with up to ten being kept alive by force feeding. Of the seventy left-wing terrorists currently serving sentences, an estimated fifty-five joined in coordinated hunger strike actions.

The utilisation of imprisonment as an RAF issue has played a major part in the continued existence of terrorism after the early arrest of its initial perpetrators: prison authorities and courts came under suspicion of cruelty, aided by allegations that terrorists were physically or mentally tortured. Apart from presenting the imprisoned terrorists as victims of an inhumane punitive system, the campaigns also provided a focal point for the left, and could activate new support for terrorism. A hunger strike in 1984–85 was intended to secure prisoner-of-war status for terrorists, including being kept together in a large group and treated according to the Geneva Convention. Several thousand West Germans demonstrated in support of these terrorist demands, an indication that the mobilisation of support continues to be effective. During this hunger strike terrorist actions intensified, with thirty-nine arson or explosive attacks directly linked to it. The murder in February 1985 of a leading German industrialist by self-professed members of the RAF brought the hunger strike to an end, not without having shown that RAF terrorism continues to exist outside and inside West German prisons.

Intensive interviews with imprisoned terrorists of the RAF or other named groups have provided important clues as to how their illegal networks and recruitment operate. For the first generation of terrorists, the academic protest culture of Berlin and elsewhere was the formative environment. For the second generation, operating in the mid-1970s, the failure of factious communism and the orientation of the aid associations mentioned earlier played an important part. The present third generation were often active in the squatters' movement and in anti-nuclear protests or site-occupations in the late 1970s.

These networks can illuminate only a fraction of existing terrorism. If it is measured by the number of criminal acts perpetrated, the bulk of West German terrorism remains unknown. So called 'revolutionary cells' have occasionally claimed responsibility, but little has been discovered about their composition and activities. 80 per cent of recorded terrorist offences have been committed by groups and factions about whom nothing has yet transpired. It is assumed that activists appear to live ordinary lives and engage in 'leisure time' terrorism, i.e. perform terrorists acts from within society. Going underground as self-professed members of the RAF or some other named group or commando may only be done to avoid detection after terrorist actions had already been carried out, not to commence terrorism. For the 'leisure time' terrorists, close involvement in the new social movements and the various sites of protest in West German extra-parliamentary politics seems likely; it is here that the boundaries between left-wing activism prepared to endorse the use of violence, and terrorism determined to use it for its presumably political aims, become blurred. Some 500 activists are said to belong to the terrorist circle, 200 of these to the inner circle, and some twenty or so self-proclaimed RAF or revolutionary cell members.

An inclination among political activists of the left, however, to condone, advocate or personally exercise the use of violence for political ends has been observed in several empirical surveys of modes of participation. A propensity to regard the use of violence as an acceptable means of political participation has been recorded for just over 1 per cent of the German population; among the under 35s, it may be as high as 7 per cent; among young academics who are also dissatisfied with the political order and their own role in society, the proportion is closer to 25 per cent.[18] Coupled with the persistent belief among the West German left that the state is essentially repressive if not fascist in character, a belief which subsumes everything from parliamentary practice to the influence of the Americans in Western Europe, political activism is dramatised as resistance. This by itself appears to justify all actions, including for some the use of violence and terrorism.

The international dimension

Cooperation of RAF terrorists and Palestinian terrorists can be traced to 1970 and has been a major factor in the transition from extremism to terrorism. West Germans have received military training, weapons and explosives from the PLO and its splinter group the Popular Front for the Liberation of Palestine (PLFP). RAF terrorists were also trained and found refuge in the South Yemen, in Cuba, Algeria, and in the Soviet Union. Claessens argues that the para-military contacts with the PLO and especially the attack by the PLO on the Israeli team during the Munich Olympic Games in 1972 acted as a stimulus to terrorism in West Germany: not only did former academics learn how to handle weapons and explosives, how to conduct robberies and operate underground, they also deduced that the 'armed struggle' could be carried out by West Germans and within West Germany.[19] The cooperation of West Germans with PLO terrorists, with Carlos and others in the 1970s, has been extensively documented. It has not abated. The attack in Berlin on a night spot for American servicemen in April 1986 which killed two and injured over 200 people followed calls by the Libyan leader Gaddafi to hunt Americans wherever they are; since Palestinian terrorists have their headquarters in Libya and enjoy Gaddafi's protection, his call has activated terrorism. In Berlin, the RAF initially claimed responsibility with a Commando Holger Meins, named after a 1974 hunger-strike victim. Although an Arab has since been arrested, a consensus of terrorist intentions with West Germans cannot be ruled out. The event itself provoked an American air strike against Libyan military targets, and brought terrorism again on to the agenda of international politics.

In the 1970s Western European links were centred on

supporting imprisoned terrorists and presenting them as 'martyrs of a fascist police state'.[20] Founded in 1974 and 1976 respectively, the International Committee for the Defence of Political Prisoners in Western Europe (IVK) and the International Commission to Investigate the Cause of Death of Ulrike Meinhof (IUK) had collapsed by 1980 when members of other countries lost interest since the emphasis was too narrowly on German affairs. Red Aid groups in Switzerland, Austria, Denmark and the Netherlands have, however, remained active, in particular giving evidence in court cases on alleged maltreatment of imprisoned terrorists.

Since 1982, international cooperation in Western Europe has been geared towards a joint organisational base and coordinated action. In May, an RAF paper stated the principles of a European 'guerilla' campaign:

Now the question is settled whether one should and will in future engage in armed struggle in the Federal Republic and in Western Europe. It is obvious . . . struggles whose common aims make them into one struggle and generate from that political and practical links, will exist in the Western European centre in many guises.[21]

As an organisational tier of terrorism, the 'Anti-Imperialist Front in Western Europe' has so far failed to materialise. Yet West German terrorists have been able to find refuge in neighbouring countries, with a network of safe houses and support systems across most of Western Europe. During the hunger strike campaign in 1984-85, a series of attacks on German firms, embassies and institutions in the Netherlands, Belgium, Spain, Greece and Portugal, for instance, pointed to a high degree of international coordination. Police have established that bombings by the French *Action Directe* and the RAF used explosives from a robbery in which Dutch terrorists were also involved. The murder in January 1985 of the French general Audran in Paris was followed by a joint AD/RAF statement and a call for the 'unity of revolutionaries in Western Europe'.

BACK TO HITLER WITH A VENGEANCE: TERRORISM FROM THE RIGHT

Officially, West Germany has no place for political forces intent on restoring, reviving or rediscovering National Socialism and attitudes that went with it. The longitudinal studies of public opinion have shown that admiration for Hitler and National Socialism as a system of government have declined without altogether disappearing. The same is true for right-extremist attitudes among West Germans. Surveys conducted by military government in the American zone of occupation pointed to a core of 30 per cent right extremists. In 1981, a government-commissioned study estimated that 13 per cent, or 5 million, West Germans endorsed statements and held beliefs which could be classified as right-extremist.[22] Right-extremism was most common among the over-50s (20 per cent), among self-employed and farmers (between 6.5 and 14 per cent), among semi-skilled workers (14.5 per cent) and among the unemployed (13 per cent). All in all, 6 per cent of the electorate were found to endorse the use of violence for right-extremist purposes. It seems that a major part of extremist potential is among older people i.e. it can be regarded as a remnant of a former political commitment or socialisation process. While this is unlikely in itself to erupt in violence, it fosters a climate where right extremism and violence associated with it may be condoned or even encouraged. Among the under-21s, between 3 per cent and 5 per cent also look to National Socialism as a counter-ideology to the democratic political consensus.[23]

Terrorism from the right aims at a transformation of society back to a glorified National Socialist past by means of activism and violence designed to shock and generate a popular surge for change. The transition from extremist to terrorist actions occurred in the early 1970s when the *Aktion Widerstand* launched an aggressive campaign against detente and the recognition of the Eastern European neighbour states or the GDR in their post-war borders. It arose in direct confrontation with the NPD whose shirt-and-tie approach to politics was dismissed as ineffectual, and whose electoral decline had become apparent as it failed to retain the parliamentary representation won in the late 1960s. The disappearance of the neofascist NPD from all but pockets of local politics radicalised the extra-parliamentary sector on the right. The new militancy created a small yet growing neo-nazi camp; by 1984, the government listed thirty-four neo-nazi groups although it has been claimed a further 158 should have been included.[24] In addition, eighty-nine extremist groups existed which did not engage in violent activism, the so-called Old Right. In 1984, these had 22,100 members to the neo-nazi groups' 1,350; an estimated 230 of them were ready to use violence for their political ends.

Violent crimes with a right-extremist background had been high in 1971 with 12 per cent of all recorded offences on the right, and fell as *Ostpolitik* began to be accepted. Since 1974, right extremist offences have again been on the increase, with the violent component among these offences around 6 per cent. The proliferation of violent crime on the right (see Table 3.3) bears witness to this increased militancy. It is, however, a difficult task to distill the terrorist segment from the official reports. While terrorist offences are identified on the left, only certain criminal acts, such as the bombing at the Munich Beer Festival with the loss of seventeen lives in 1980, the bombing of a disco in Munich in 1984, some arson attacks and burglaries to obtain money and ammunition, are listed as acts of terrorism on the right. Of the offences included in Table 3.3 for 1983 and 1984, 11 were officially classified as terrorist in 1983; no such classification has been attempted for other years.

It is not so much the nature of a crime but assumptions about its perpetrators which determine whether it is listed as terrorist or not. In German criminal law, a group is identified as a terrorist association, its members as terrorists and their actions as terrorism if its organisational purpose consists of planning and executing terrorist acts. For the left, such purpose is assumed to exist, for the right, it is not and neo-nazi groups are not classified as terrorist associations. Thus only a few acts of violence on the right are presumed to be terrorist. Punishment also differs, since affiliation to a terrorist association is automatically counted as a serious crime, even if no act of violence has been committed by the accused himself. By contrast, affiliation to a radicalised group can be punished as a

Table 3.3: Terrorist Offences from the Right, 1978-1985

Offence	Year							
	1978	1979	1980	1981	1982	1983	1984	1985
Terrorist/violent offences								
Murder	—	—	2	17**	6	—	1	2
Explosive attacks	—	3	6*	4	5	1	1	—
Arson	—	1	15*	15	15	9	11	11
Robbery	—	—	2	4	4	2	—	2
Assault	13	26	27	24	11	30	44	33
Criminal damage	32	65	61	43	23	39	26	21
Terrorist/violent offences Total	45	95	113	107	64	81	83	69
Threats of violence	38	117	123	197	241	214	159	127
Other offences	864	1366	1530	1582	1742	1900	1472	1373
Right extremist offences Total	947	1578	1766	1856	2047	2195	1714	1569

Notes: *These bombings and arson attacks also killed 17 people and injured 204.
**Victims were mainly American soldiers and foreigners *(Gastarbeiter* and refugees.

Sources: For 1978-79 see *Betrifft Verfassungsschutz* 1979, Bonn 1980, pp. 46-48; for 1980 see *Betrifft Verfassungsschutz* 1980, Bonn 1981 pp. 43-44; for 1981 and 1982, see *Betrifft Verfassungsschutz* 1982, Bonn 1983 pp. 153-156; for 1984 see *Betrifft Verfassungsschutz* 1984, Bonn 1985 pp. 171-72; for 1985 see *Betrifft Verfassungsschutz* 1985, Bonn 1986 pp. 184-85.

minor offence with fines or probationary sentences. This official view of the right as a disjointed mass of groupuscules is not shared by observers from the left, who have tended to emphasise the coordination in an apparently loose organisational structure, and the personal and strategic cooperation between structures, and the personal and strategic cooperation between groups.

With neo-nazi groups not defined as terrorist associations, offences tend to be ascribed to deranged loners or to some small would-be

Führer such as Otte who testified in court that he kept discipline in his group by threatening traitors with the death penalty and warning them that he might in suitable cases denounce somebody to the police, not before depositing incriminating evidence in his apartment.[25]

The legalistic distinction between a terrorist left and a bunch of misguided hot-heads on the right blurs some striking similarities. To date, the right and the left have each executed one ex-terrorist. Despite the variance of presumed political aims, targets of terrorism are often identical. Terrorism from the right has been directed against American service personnel and installations to free Germany from a presumed foreign occupation; security personnel and institutions including courts and police who are seen as serving an allegedly illegal—the West German—state; foreign workers and immigrants into Germany who are denounced as swamping the genuine German race and causing unemployment; and finally, against Jews, their property and their places of worship. This is backed by a mixture of rabid anti-semitism and accusations that Jews fabricated 'the lies' about concentration camps and the Holocaust in order to slander Germany's good name. The right has also embraced environmentalism as meaning the preservation of the 'racial purity' of the German people and nation.

Similarities between terrorism from the left and the right have also been evident in links with the PLO: both sides received training, refuge from prosecution and probably funds and weapons from that source and both have cooperated with terrorist groupings in Western Europe. While the right emphasises a common anti-system militancy, the left has been at pains to deny any similarities, and has intensified demonstrations against events regarded as neo-nazi.

Table 3.4: The Social Composition in 1980 of West German Terrorism (Right and Left)

	Right Terrorists %	Left Terrorists %
Year of Birth		
1955 or after	51	3
1951-54	12	29
1946-50	4	34
1930-45	33	34
1930 and earlier	12	0
Sex		
Male	90	67
Female	10	33
Education		
Volksschule (Basic)	49	17
O-level; Technical	22	15
Grammar; A-level	17	19
University	10	42
n.a.	2	7

Source: Friedhelm Neidhardt, in *Gruppenprozesse*, pp. 447-50.

Table 3.5: The Occupational Status of Terrorists (Left and Right)

Occupation at time of offence	Left Terrorists (1) %	Right Terrorists (2) %	Right Terrorists (3) %
Self employed	13	8	no data
White collar/civil servants	33	9	12
Skilled workers, artisans	34	41	49
Unskilled workers: In education/training	13	34	17
Others/n.a.	13*	8**	22**
Percentage of unemployed	no data	22	25

Notes: *All 13% listed as giving No Answer; Niedhart interprets this as reflecting the low emphasis on the terrorist left on employment and the socio-economic integration that goes with it.

**For the right, these figures may include some unemployed; for 1984, all self-employed, pensioners and other non-working people were listed as 'Others'.

Sources: (1) Data for 1980, from Friedhelm Niedhart, 'Linker und rechter Terrorismus' in *Gewalt von rechts* ed. Bundesministerium des Inneren, Bonn 1982: 164; (2) Data for 1983, from Betrifft Verfassungsschutz 1983, Bonn 1984: 119; (3) Data from 1984 from Betrifft Verfassungsschutz 1984, Bonn 1985: 136.

Despite overlaps of the two types of terrorism, their social composition, recruitment and organisational networks are distinctly different. Table 3.4 compares the social background of terrorists who were serving sentences in 1980. While it is impossible to determine how old people were when they turned terrorist, the table highlights differences in the age distribution: the left has been dominated by the middle ranges, the right polarised between the youngest and oldest age cohorts. The few women involved in terrorism on the right have tended to play traditional female roles of bride, wife or mother, aiding rather than spearheading terrorism; on the left, women have taken leading roles and seen the shackles on their socio-economic emancipation in contemporary society as proof of its repressive nature. The data on the educational background reveal the privileged situation of terrorists from the left with significant recruitment of academics, in particular from arts and social sciences subject areas. The profile of terrorists on the right reflects the average distribution of educational qualifications in West Germany today. Among academics turned terrorist on the right, engineering, law, sciences and medicine are more common as specialisms than the humanities which are so prominent on the other side. The social composition of terrorism would indicate that regarding age and education, the left is more coherent and, it has been argued, potentially more autonomous: 'the presence of both sexes enables the fulfillment of erotic and sexual needs within the group' and facilitates a subversive existence.[26] The male-dominated groups on the right have no such built-in advantages and may be less adaptable to illegality.

Data on the occupational background of terrorists have been patchy. Some material on offenders on the right is contained in the annual reports for the Protection of the Constitution, notably in the volumes for 1983 and 1984 (see Table 3.5). Neidhart set out to compare the social composition and background of imprisoned terrorists of the left and the right. This is only partly successful since he relied on a very small sample (51) for his assessment of the right and arrives at doubtful numerical values. Table 3.5 aims at a comparison of the socio-economic background of terrorists and its impact across the political divide. There are important socio-economic differences between the two camps, above all the experience of unemployment. Bearing in mind the radicalising effect unemployment had in the German past, a link between unemployment and the escalation of political extremism to terrorism cannot be ruled out. Studies of electoral behaviour of the unemployed in the 1980s have shown that the majority has remained loyal to the established parties, while an above average segment tended to opt for presumed anti-system groups, often hovering between the two extremes.[27] Table 3.5 points to an over-representation of unemployed among offenders on the terrorist right; on the left, the distribution of occupations confirms the academic and relatively privileged position of activists. Other studies have shown that a large proportion of self-professed Greens, self-professed adherents of alternative culture, and those with negative views about the political system of the Federal Republic are in fact unemployed and often sustained by social security payments. A similar pattern can be assumed for terrorists from the left. Since occupations refer to a pre-terrorist phase in respondents' lives, actual unemployment at the time of turning terrorist may be higher; the 'no answer' category may also include some who were unemployed prior to terrorism.

The salience of employment and unemployment as a political issue differs on the left and on the right. On the left, employment is not necessarily coveted, while not-working is seen as providing the freedom to follow a preferred life-style and set of values. On the right, unemployment is more likely to be experienced as deprivation; unskilled, semi-skilled and apprentices who cannot readily be absorbed into the labour market are most frequently affected by unemployment. They figure prominently among activists on the right. The experience of unemployment appears to be more immediate and threatening on the right than on the left and can be regarded as a mobilising factor of terrorism.

Table 3.5 highlights a further difference between the two camps: although the left hopes to appeal to the working class, the right has a larger proportion of workers among its activists. Most are employed in small to medium-sized firms in small to medium-sized towns, i.e. they come from a recognised reservoir of rightist and extremist attitudes. The geographical 'size' of extremism could influence recruitment and cohesion. While the left, and terrorism affiliated with it, has strongholds in university towns and some larger cities, where communication can be direct and contacts frequent, the right in West Germany and its terrorist appendage are more scattered. Only large conurbations with a high proportion of foreigners such as Frankfurt, Berlin and Munich also have a number of groups which might engage in terrorism from the right. Socially and geographically, terrorism on the right reaches across West Germany, while that on the left has a specific and narrow core.

It has been suggested that the lower educational levels of the right have impaired the emergence of anything resembling a unifying ideology, although one could argue that ideology of the extreme right has always been eclectic. There are other reasons for the differences in cohesion. A mixture of trying to save one's bacon and getting into the limelight and media may explain why, in contrast to their colleagues on the left, right-wing terrorists have tended to name their accomplices, and divulge information about their organisations and activities during police interrogations. Interviews with neo-nazi activists and self-portraits have reinforced the pride in having restored the leadership principle of National Socialist vintage, and at having created, or at experiencing a sworn community who would live and die together for whatever their chosen cause might be. The step from extremist to terrorist is often explained as a search for unconditional acceptance and a shared sense of purpose which other groups, parties or activities are unable to satisfy. While imprisoned terrorists on the left inspired actions outside designed to free them, imprisonment on the right had no such effect, and individuals have reportedly been model prisoners. Yet, parallel to the aid associations on the left, support networks for imprisoned terrorists have been created. These could draw on donations from inside and outside Germany, from new and old adherents of National Socialism. They could also draw on the experiences with the support system for former members of the SS, HIAG (*Hilfs-organisation auf Gegenseitigkeit*, a mutual aid association) which has given financial and personal assistance to SS veterans and their families since the early 1950s, and has also preserved what from the SS perspective is the true German ideology through regular congresses and its journal, *Der Freiwillige*. The Aid Association for National Political Prisoners and their Relatives (HNG) was founded in 1979 to coordinate neo-nazi and possibly terrorist activities. It developed close contacts, including access to safe houses with COBRA, a French group affiliated to the right-terrorist *Faisceaux Nationalistes Européens*, (FNE). In conjunction with militants in Belgium, Austria, Switzerland and their French counterparts, West Germans are planning a European movement to coordinate actions and to provide cross-border hide-outs. These moves complement the support received for years from the American National Socialists who have pumped funds and in particular propaganda materials into West Germany and other European countries.

Terrorists of the right can build on established right-extremist connections in Europe and the United States, and they found new ones. In particular the close contacts with the PLO, including the training of right-wing terrorists in PLO camps, are a new development which points to a radicalisation beyond the circles of 'unteachables' who kept the fires of National Socialism burning in the past. The endorsement of violence and the use of arms in right-extremist ideology, however, have made these terrorists less dependent on expert training elsewhere than their brethren from the left. Paramilitary groups who conducted regular military-type exercises with weapons, ammunition and suitable drills, have proliferated since the early 1970s, and have come to characterise much of neo-nazism in West Germany. Although three paramilitary and terrorist groups have been banned in the last few years, others have sprung up to pursue the same aim of using violence to re-orient contemporary German society and politics in a National Socialist and allegedly German direction.

TERRORISM AND THE WEST GERMAN STATE

The German perspective on terrorism, with its fears about the stability of democracy and the survival of the political order, has made terrorism into a national problem rather than an international one. Although successive West German governments have given support to European and international condemnations of terrorism, overt commitment to curtail terrorism, in the Middle East for instance, has been scarce. Presumed economic and foreign policy interests have so far prevented West Germany from emerging as a trail-blazer in the fight against international terrorism. The international dimension becomes instead a national one, with increased emphasis on the monitoring and prosecuting of terrorism or extremism perpetrated by foreigners living in Germany.

In the case of West German terrorism, the state tradition works both ways. Terrorists have regarded the state as the incarnation of power, which they want to unseat if they operate from the left, or shift back to national concerns if they come from the right. The state, on the other hand, has responded by consolidating and expanding its control over social and political processes in order to curtail a challenge which was interpreted as a challenge to democracy and the state itself. Beneath a cross-party consensus about the need to close apparent loopholes in democratic stability, the degree of state control and the legitimacy of political dissent and anti-state sentiment in West German politics have remained controversial issues. In the 1970s, the SPD faced two contradictory sets of expectations: as the senior governing party, it had to address itself to terrorism with legislative and executive measures designed to improve detection, prosecution and prevent a recurrence. With fears stoked by the media that terrorism could hit anybody at any time, public opinion favoured strong punitive measures, a clear segregation of terrorists from the rest of society, and even the death penalty. The SPD also had to heed political sentiments within its own ranks and among its younger electorate that 'too much state' rather than the terrorist activities themselves constitute the real danger to democracy. Spearheaded by its socio-liberal wing, the FDP at the time also adopted the position that state measures should be moderate while the Christian Democratic Union (CDU) and its Bavarian sister party the Christian Social

Union (CSU) demanded a strengthening of the powers of the state, and secure democracy by legislation. For the opposition, terrorism arose from the detrimental influences of a socialist government and from an intellectual climate which undermined the strong position of the state.[28]

The all-party consensus that legislation was deficient did not mean agreement on the extent to which political democracy was in need of protection through tailor-made legislation. While the Christian Democrats aimed at legislation to hit terrorism specifically from the left and its suspected protest environment, the socio-liberal coalition aimed at formulating legislation which would serve as deterrent against terrorism without being applicable only to it. For the CDU/CSU, the anti-terror measures in the 1970s did not go far enough, for the SPD left in particular they went too far and brought the government to the brink of parliamentary defeat as some members of the *Bundestag* hesitated to endorse more restrictions.[29] Prompted by the need to act against terrorism, four major areas were reorganised. In some cases, the process has not yet been completed:

(1) Legal procedures and rights of defence, including the rights of information, mobility and contact of terrorist suspects and prisoners were more narrowly defined and curtailed.

(2) Legislation defined terrorist associations and the so-called state monopoly of the use of violence. The anti-terrorist laws of the 1970s were designed as a tool to apprehend suspects and sympathisers as terrorists and to coordinate the regionalised police forces. In January 1987, supplementary legislation came into force which extended the scope. It lists traffic-related offences, actions against production plants, public services and communication networks as terrorist in intention. Complicity has been broadened to include people who may have passed on information, even if they had no personal involvement with a subsequent crime. Minimum penalties for all terrorist-related offences have been raised, and the police have been empowered to utilise data stored in the central traffic control computer system in Flensburg.

This legislative change underpins the established tendency to tighten the net of state surveillance and reduce the decentralisation and regionalistion of West German policing of terrorism. Thus, the Federal Criminal Office (BKA) was expanded to house a specialist terror unit, and a specially trained and mobile unit, GSG 9 was created in 1972 within the border police (BGS). Stationed in Bonn it comprised 4,000 members in 1985. Increased funding and increases in the personnel of the border police since the early 1970s point to a shift in policing, and the new relevance of a federal force in West Germany. In 1972, the BGS commanded a budget of just under half a million marks; in 1985, just over 1.1 million. In 1972, 15,900 posts were allocated to this area; during the 1970s, allocations rose by over 1,000 annually; in 1981, the BGS reached its peak with 22,731 posts.[30] Since then, numbers have decreased slightly to just over 20,000, although some 3,000 trainees and apprentices are no longer counted within the personnel establishment, and a *de facto* decrease may not have occurred. In 1985, the *Bundestag* agreed an improvement in the promotion structure at the intermediate level; this underlines the continued importance attached to this branch of policing although its activities are not only pitched against terrorism but include drug offences, environmental destruction and border patrols.

(3) Terrorism has also generated an increased emphasis on internal security other than protecting key institutions and representatives of the state. Legislation to permit the surveillance of suspects and the accelerated installation of surveillance equipment and data banks have created an unprecedented information network. In 1981, the *Bundestag* authorised a broad-ranging census to create data banks not only to gain an accurate picture of changes in the social structure, in demographic trends, income levels and housing patterns of the population, but also to earmark possible suspects, and follow their movements or discover their protective environments. In the face of public protest against a state-sponsored intrusion into the private sphere, and after a ruling by the Federal Constitutional Court (BVG), the census

had to be modified and postponed. More importantly, the *Bundestag* was called upon to legislate on data protection since the BVG suggested that the rights of the individual were not sufficiently protected, and that the system of interlinking data banks and information networks would curtail civil liberties. Clarifications of the borderline between the right to privacy and the state's interest in security will have to be part of this new legislation.

By the time the present coalition government of CDU/CSU and FDP took office in October 1982, the anti-terror legislation had been completed, but the dust has not yet settled. In 1987, a new machine-readable Euro passport will be introduced which can activate surveillance records and personal files at border crossings and police checkpoints. It has been claimed that these electronic passports cannot be forged. They should facilitate the identification of wanted criminals and make the cross-border mobility of terrorists difficult.

In the area of internal security, the government is looking towards tightening legislation concerning demonstrations and protest action. The very extent of surveillance, and attempts to build up personal files on offenders (sympathisers as well as occasional demonstrators) has produced a backlash among the oppositional forces. Increasingly, demonstrators have worn helmets, masks and shields, partly as weapons and partly as disguise, to be unrecognisable on police photographs. New legislation is aimed at banning *Vermummung,* the wearing of garments which obscure identification. The government argues that its predecessor had allowed 'freedom without limits' and also 'restricted the right of the state to act against disturbances of the interior peace'.[31] Demonstrators who hide their identity are branded as terrorists in the making:

the most militant demonstrators, those who are prepared to use violence, have used disguises to escape identification and arrest. They also went underground and formed the core of terrorism. From this group, terrorists received their personal and ideological recruits and continue to do so. Robbing the demonstrator in disguise or the disguised violent offender of his anonymity means acting against the field of recruitment and the sympathisers of terrorism and violence.[32]

Accordingly, the government is altering the legal provisions concerning a breach of the peace to be effective against protesters. The proposal would render it a criminal offence to wear disguise or to carry what could be regarded as an offensive weapon during demonstrations. The FDP coalition partner has, however, refused to endorse these changes, and argued that the borderline between a potential act of violence and a *de facto* act of violence would become blurred if both were counted as serious offences. Critics of the proposed legislation have pointed out that the distinctions are unworkable, and would have the effect of bringing all protests and demonstrations into the grey zone of criminality. After the 1987 federal elections, the Christian Democrats again failed to persuade their junior partner in government to pass legislation against the wearing of disguises *(Vermummung)* at demonstration during the current legislative period. The Minister of the Interior, however, continues to press for legislative changes. In March 1987, a detailed report highlighted an increase in acts of violence during demonstrations. Zimmermann raised the issue of stricter legislation in the Bundestag debate on 19 March 1987 on the West German equivalent of the Queen's Speech, and warned of a 'distorted awareness of Right and Wrong' in society: 'The state, I think, cannot and must not tolerate any type of violence, who ever perpetrates it. A state which tolerates violence has given itself up. I therefore declare for this government, that we shall not permit, that violence and law breaking are made to look acceptable by using terms such as "civil resistance", "civil disobedience" or the apparently innocent "offence against the rules".'

(4) The fourth area in which terrorism in the 1970s sparked off legislation concerns ownership and usage of weapons. The second package of anti-terror laws in 1978 made it a serious crime to transport weapons of any description without a permit. While this amendment may have helped to catch terrorists, it also proved a considerable nuisance to other users of guns and weapons, whether farmers, members of shooting clubs, or hunters, who conflicted with the law if they did not

personally transport their weapons but asked their chauffeur, for instance, to do so. Against the protests of the German Judges Association who favoured the present laws, the government proposed a dual approach of a strict law for presumed terrorists, and another for ordinary citizens. While the judges protested that a specific group was to be singled out, and another shielded from punishment, the government maintained that their proposal remained well within the rule of law: reducing the minimum sentence from serious to petty crime 'will mainly concern people, who are in principle law-abiding and who would be treated harshly if they were charged with a serious offence.'[33] The decision whether or not the offenders in question are to be regarded as law-abiding depends on surveillance evidence or other data on the suspect.

This modification of the 1978 anti-terror legislation suggests that the government intends to strengthen the power of the state and its ability to discriminate between ordinary and potentially terrorist/criminal citizens by devising means to single out the latter for special treatment and harsher punishment. The moves against protesters and the legislation on weapons underpin the determination of the CDU/CSU and FDP to streamline legislation and 'to isolate the perpetrators and to finally apprehend them'.[34]

NOTES

1. For background see E. Kolinsky, *Parties, Opposition and Society in West Germany*, London: Croom Helm, 1984. W. Mommsen and G. Hirschfeld (eds), *Social Protest, Violence and Terror in 19th and 20th Century Europe*, London: Macmillan and Berg, 1982; J. Raschke, *Soziale Bewegungen. Ein historisch-systematischer Grundriss*, Frankfurt: Campus, 1985.

2. An overview of recent studies on terrorism is given in U. Backes and E. Jesse, *Totalitarismus, Extremismus, Terrorismus*, Opladen: Leske & Budrich, 1984, pp. 243-304. For an excellent evaluation see H.J. Horchem, 'Fünfzehn Jahre Terrorismus in der Bundesrepublik Deutschland', in *Aus Politik und Zeitgeschichte*, B5/1987, 31 January 1987, pp. 3-15.

3. The four-part (vols 1-4/2) series *Analysen zum Terrorismus*, edited by

the Interior Ministry, published by Westdeutscher Verlag, Opladen between 1981 and 1985.

4. For detailed accounts of events and groupings, see the annual reports of the Ministry of the Interior, *Betrifft Verfassungsschutz,* Bonn; also the interim reporting in *Innere Sicherheit.*

5. T. Fichter and S. Lönnendoncker, *Kleine Geschichte des SDS* Berlin: Rotbuch Verlag, 1977, p. 129.

6. Christof Wackernagel, 'Erklärung zur Sache' dated 12 June 1980, quoted in I. Fetscher and G. Rohrmoser, *Ideologien und Strategien. Analysen zum Terrorismus 1, op. cit.,* p. 94.

7. See D. Fromkin, 'Die Strategie des Terrorismus' in M. Funke (ed.), *Terrorismus,* Düsseldorf: Droste, 1977, pp. 83-99.

8. Rudi Dutschke, in *Kommune II: Versuch der Revolutionierung des bürgerlichen Individuums; kollektives Leben mit politischer Arbeit verbinden,* Luxembourg: Edition Ceuta (repr.), 1975, p. 17.

9. Wanda von Baeyer-Katte, Dieter Claessens, Hubert Feger and Friedhelm Neidhardt, 'Es ist Zeit zu zerstören'. Leaflet quoted in *Gruppenprozesse. Analysen zum Terrorismus 3, op. cit.,* p. 107.

10. W. Laqueur, *Terrorism,* London: Weidenfeld & Nicolson, 1977, p. 217.

11. Ulrike Meinhof, *Das Konzept der Stadtguerilla. Texte der RAF,* Utrecht: Verlag Rote Sonne, 1973, p. 350.

12. U. Meinhof, 'Natürlich kann geschossen werden', *Spiegel,* 25, (1970), 75.

13. See detailed discussion in Fetscher, *op. cit.,* pp. 98 ff.

14. *Revolutionärer Zorn,* 1 (May 1975), 4.

15. *Innere Sicherheit,* 1 (1986), 16.

16. Heinrich Böll, 'Will Ulrike Gnade oder freies Geleit', *Spiegel,* 3 (1972); Reply and refutation by Dieter Posser, *Spiegel,* 5 (1972).

17. Detailed account in A. Klaus, *Aktivitäten und Verhalten inhaftierter Terroristen,* Bonn: 1985.

18. See G. Schmidtchen, 'Jugend und Staat. Übergänge von der Bürger Aktivität zur Illegalität', in U. Matz and G. Schmidtchen (eds) *Gewalt und Legitimität. Analysen zum Terrorismus 4/1.* p. 187ff; also E. Kolinsky, *op. cit.,* Ch. 6.

19. See D. Claessens, in *Gruppenprozesse,* pp. 163-74.

20. *Terroristen im Kampf gegen Recht und Menschenwürde,* Bonn: BMI, 1985 p. 63.

21. 'Guerilla, Widerstand und antiimperialistische Front. Grundsatzpapier der RAF Mai 1982', *Innere Sicherheit,* 2 (1985) 9.

22. *Fünf Millionen Deutsche: Wir wollen wieder einen Führer haben. Sinus Studie über rechtsextremistische Einstellungen bei den Deutschen,* Reinbek: Rowohlt, 1981 pp. 17-81.

23. The lower figure is from E. Noelle-Neumann and E. Ring, *Das Extremismus-Potential,* Bonn: Institut für Demoskopie Allensbach, 1984 p. 44; the higher figure is from the *Sinus* study, *op. cit.,* p. 87.

24. 'Verharmlosung des Rechtsextremismus zurückgewiesen', *Innere Sicherheit,* 2 (1985) 11-14.
25. Quoted from the court report in *Gewalt von rechts,* Bonn: BMI, 1982, p. 190.
26. F. Neidhardt, 'Linker und rechter Terrorismus', in *Gewalt von rechts, ibid.,* pp. 161-162.
27. U. Feist *et al.* 'Die politischen Einstellungen der Arbeitslosen', *Aus Politik und Zeitgeschichte,* 45 (1984) 3-17; H. Krieger, 'Arbeitsmarktsituation und politische Stabilität', *Aus Politik und Zeitgeschichte,* 17 (1986) 3-18, esp. 11-12.
28. W. Althammer and B. Rombach, *Gegen den Terror. Texte. Dokumente,* Munich: Hanns Seidel Stiftung, 1977; H. Geissler, *Der Weg in die Gewalt,* Munich: Olzog, 1977; also a collection of quotations entitled *Die Verharmlosung des Terrorismus* was compiled by the CSU office in 1977. A critique of this type of terrorism debate is given in H. Glaser, *Jugend zwischen Aggression und Apathie. Diagnose der Terrorismus Diskussion,* Heidelberg: C.F. Müller, 1980.
29. For details see H. Vinke and G. Witt (eds), *Die Anti-Terror-Debatten im Parlament. Protokolle 1974-1978,* Reinbek: Rowohlt, 1978.
30. See 'Tätigkeitsberichte des BGS', *Innere Sicherheit,* 1 (1985), 19-35; 1 (1986), 28-30.
31. See the address by the Minister of the Interior, Zimmermann, at the congress of the *Junge Union,* 2 March 1985.
32. *Innere Sicherheit,* 2 (1985), 22; also *Innere Sicherheit,* 1 (1985), 14.
33. *Bundestags Drucksache* 10/1748; also *Innere Sicherheit,* 3 (1985).
34. Quoted from the address by the Minister of the Interior, Friedrich Zimmermann at the funeral of an industrialist terror victim, in *Innere Sicherheit,* 1 (1985).

4 Terrorism in Italy

Christopher Seton-Watson

BACKGROUND

Italy's first major act of terrorism occurred on 12 December 1969, when a bomb placed in a bank in Piazza Fontana in Milan killed sixteen persons and seriously injured eighty-eight. This was the work of terrorists of the extreme right, black terrorists, as they will be described in this chapter. In 1974 they were responsible for two more indiscriminate massacres (*stragi*): at an anti-fascist meeting in Brescia in May, which killed eight and injured ninety-four, and on the Italicus Rome-Munich express between Florence and Bologna in August, which killed twelve and injured 105. After 1974 black terrorism was for some years relatively quiescent: the headlines were occupied by red terrorists of the extreme left. Their most sensational exploits were the kidnapping, and subsequent murder, of Aldo Moro, president of the ruling Christian Democratic Party (DC) in March-May 1978; and three kidnappings during 1980-82: a leading judge, Giovanni D'Urso, in December 1980; a prominent member of the DC in Naples, Ciro Cirillo, in April 1981; and General James Lee Dozier, a senior American NATO officer stationed in Verona, in December 1981. Black terrorism meanwhile made a dramatic reappearance on 2 August 1980, when a bomb in Bologna station killed eight-five and injured 200.

The total number of persons killed or wounded in acts of terrorism between 1969 and 1982 has recently been calculated as 1,119.[1] In addition to the four indiscriminate *stragi,* and to physical assaults on individuals, whether homicide or wounding, the latter often in the form of kneecapping, terrorist attacks included attacks on property, such as factories, vehicles or DC premises; kidnapping for the purposes of publicity, political blackmail or the extortion of ransom; and raids on banks to acquire funds (*autofinanziamento*). The number of persons killed or injured in single acts of terrorism (i.e. excluding the victims of *stragi*) reached an annual peak of seventy-nine in 1979.[2] Only in 1982 did the level of terrorism at last subside. Italy therefore underwent a longer and more intense terrorist experience than any other West European country except Northern Ireland.

Both black and red terrorism flourished in the atmosphere of disorder and violence which accompanied the two cycles of mass protest between 1968 and 1979. The first cycle, in 1968-71, was based mainly in the factories and universities. The second, in 1977-79, which was peculiar to Italy, occurred mainly in the large conurbations. Black terrorism flourished on revulsion against excesses of left-wing protest and permissiveness, and on fears, however unfounded, that the ruling Centre-Left (DC-Socialist) coalition might allow Italy to lapse into anarchy or to drift into a communist takeover. The Piazza Fontana bombing was a reaction against the student militancy of 1967-68 and the victories of militant trade unionism in the 'hot autumn' of 1969.

Red terrorists found their support among those who felt frustrated by the limited achievements of legal protest movements and by the timid conservatism of the Communist Party (PCI), and drew the conclusion that only armed struggle could achieve their aims. Many of their leaders were former members of the PCI who had abandoned it for its lack of revolutionary zeal. Many more came from the protest movements, in which they had formed personal relationships and acquired their first political experience, in neighbourhood units, housing or squatters' collectives, student sit-ins or factory occupations, picketing, marches and demonstrations in favour of women's rights or prison reform. These common experiences often formed one of the chief bonds of terrorist groups. Terrorism flourished in the cities where protest had been most violent. A small minority of participants in these activities was ready to resort to the use of, first, stones, iron bars and knuckledusters, then petrol bombs and molotov cocktails, and finally the P38 revolver. Recruits for terrorism were also found in the *servizi di ordine* (armed stewards) which were a feature of some demonstrations. And it was often police repression of these activities which determined the choice of clandestine and armed struggle.[3]

Italian scholars and political commentators differ in their views of the extent to which terrorism was the product of the paralysis and immobilism of the Italian political system (*sistema bloccato*), which became apparent in the late 1960s, and from which there seemed no constitutional way of escape. There is no doubt that the system and its rulers were slow to respond to the legitimate demands of the protest movements. On the right the neo-fascist Italian Social Movement (MSI) had never won more than 10 per cent of the votes in national elections, and this manifest failure helped to nurture black terrorism. On the left the PCI had been growing steadily for twenty years, but still had little prospect of winning a parliamentary majority, either by itself or in alliance with other sections of the left, while the parliamentary ultra-left won only 1.5 per cent of the votes in the June 1976 election. For the New Left, and still more for red terrorists, the PCI's unremitting search for respectability, whether through a 'historic compromise' with the Catholics as proposed in 1973, or by entering the parliamentary majority in support of a DC government in 1977-79, was treachery. The failure of the conservative leadership of the trade unions to follow up their victories after 1969 was another cause of frustration. But though the *sistema bloccato* was probably a necessary condition for the flourishing of Italian terrorism, it was not a sufficient condition. It needed the existence of extremist groups within Italian society which were ready to exploit the opportunity which immobilism offered.[4]

BLACK TERRORISM

Between 1969 and 1975, 83 per cent of the 4,384 acts of terrorism, and 63 of the ninety-two assassinations, were perpetrated by black terrorists.[5] The two main organisations were *Ordine Nuovo* (ON: New Order) and *Avanguardia Nazionale* (AN: National Vanguard). ON was founded in 1956 by Pino Rauti, a young neo-fascist who broke away from the MSI because of its commitment to legality. ON was especially strong in the Veneto. AN was founded in 1960 by another neo-fascist, Stefano Delle Chiaie, as a splinter from ON. It nominally dissolved itself in 1965 but reappeared in 1970 as a counter to left-wing student militancy. Of the two, ON was the more ideological, AN the more actively terrorist, though they maintained close links and merged in 1975. ON's membership was estimated in 1970 as 1,500, AN's at 500. Both were paramilitary in character and indulged in methods of urban guerilla warfare which resembled those of the early fascist *squadristi* of the 1920s. They were responsible for innumerable clashes with left-wing students, and for attacks on PCI premises, or cafes and cinemas and other gathering places frequented by the left. In addition to ON and AN there was a multitude of other small groups, largely autonomous and usually short-lived, which indulged in similar activities.[6] In general the boundaries between militant neo-fascism and black terrorism were never well-defined.

In their earlier years ON and AN enjoyed the benevolence, and even protection, of elements within the intelligence service, SID (*Servizio Informazioni Difesa*), who saw in black terrorism a useful tool for containing a perceived threat from the left. Their calculation was that the so-called 'strategy of tension' would create mass fear, force the government into increasingly repressive measures, and so prepare a climate favourable to the restoration of 'order', either by a 'neo-gaullist' *coup d'état* or by the quasi-constitutional installation of an authoritarian regime. One of the minor figures on bail awaiting trial for involvement in the Piazza Fontana *strage,* Marco Pozzan, was smuggled out of Italy by a member of SID,

Captain Tonino La Bruna, in 1973, and SID gave a false passport and financial support in Spain to another of the accused, Guido Giannettini, a right-wing journalist who had for many years worked with the intelligence services. There were soon accusations, not only from the left, that the outrage had been planned and executed by employees of the state, that it had been a *strage di stato*. It is hardly a coincidence that to this day, despite judicial proceedings which dragged on for sixteen years, the perpetrators have still not been clearly identified and brought to justice.[7]

In 1974 this privileged position came to an end. After the Brescia *strage* the head of SID, General Vito Miceli, was replaced and subsequently arrested, but not convicted, for alleged involvement in subversive black activities.[8] ON was banned late in 1973, AN three years later, and many of their members tried, but most were acquitted. Some escaped abroad, notably Delle Chiaie, who found his way to Francoist Spain, and after Franco's death to South America. For the moment it seemed that black terrorism had been quenched. But in the climate created by the second explosion of social protest in 1977 it revived, with new labels and new aims. The two most formidable new groups were *Nuclei Armati Rivoluzionari* (NAR: Armed Revolutionary Groups) and *Terza Posizione* (TP: Third Position), both founded in 1979. Two founding members of ON, Franco Freda, a prolific journalist and one of the accused in the Piazza Fontana trial, and Paolo Signorelli, a professor of sociology, reappeared in TP, and Delle Chiaie gave it his patronage. NAR were closely linked with the neo-fascist student organisation, FUAN (University Front for National Action). NAR and TP were no longer concerned just with fighting the left, but declared their objective to be 'the disarticulation of the conveyor belts of state power'.[9]

The first sign of this new policy was the assassination in July 1976 of Victor Occorsio, an investigating magistrate who had shown unwelcome determination in tracking down the perpetrators of the Italicus *strage*. Armed clashes with the police became more frequent. It would seem that the new recruits had been impressed by the apparent success of the red terrorists, and felt that if they were to justify their existence, they must compete on the same ground. 'Armed spontaneity' became the new slogan. Between 1975 and 1980, 35 per cent of the 8,400 assaults on persons and property were carried out by black terrorists.[10] In 1979 the new strategy was described by Mario Tuti, while serving a term of life imprisonment for killing two policemen and under suspicion of responsibility for the Italicus *strage*, as 'pitiless terrorist offensives . . . striking where and when we wish'.[11] This was the spirit which lay behind the Bologna *strage* of August 1980.

After several months of apparently fruitless investigations into this outrage, it transpired that, once again, the intelligence services had been involved. The culprit was a senior general, Pietro Musumeci, who had obstructed the enquiries by laying false trails and providing cover for the guilty. Furthermore, evidence emerged of links between the intelligence services and the secret conspiratorial anti-communist masonic lodge, *Propaganda Due* (P2), founded by the ex-fascist Licio Gelli, and of P2's involvement in the Bologna *strage*. When the names of P2's 953 members were published in May 1981, it was found that all former and current chiefs of the intelligence services, including Miceli, and also La Bruna and Musumeci, had joined it. Gelli was promptly indicted for 'political and economic espionage', but had already escaped to Argentina, where he enjoyed powerful protection. In September 1982 an international warrant was issued for the arrest of Delle Chiaie and a close associate, Pierluigi Pagliai, together with a French and a German neo-fascist and one other Italian, all charged in connection with the Bologna *strage*. Delle Chiaie, who had apparently been able to make several clandestine visits to Italy since 1975, again disappeared. He resurfaced in Brazil in January 1983 to give an interview to a leading Italian journalist, Enzo Biagi, in which he proclaimed his innocence of both the Piazza Fontana and Bologna crimes. Meanwhile Gelli was arrested in Switzerland in October 1982, but escaped from his prison in August 1983 when on the point of being extradited to Italy, and returned to South America. In June

1986 the High Court of Cassation validated the indictment of four Bologna magistrates against Gelli, Delle Chiaie, Signorelli, Musumeci and one of his subordinates, Captain Belmonte, and thirteen others for complicity in the Bologna *strage*. In March 1987 Delle Chiaie was arrested in Venezuela and deported to Italy. At the time of writing a trial is pending.

RED TERRORISM

The most notorious of the red terrorist organisations were the *Brigate Rosse* (BR: Red Brigades) and the *Nuclei Armati Proletari* (NAP: Armed Proletarian Nuclei). The BR were initially based in North Italy, especially Milan and Turin, and mainly concerned with factories. The NAP were based in Naples and concerned mainly with prisons.The BR first announced their existence in October 1970. Their founders came from three sources: the Metropolitan Political Collective of Milan; a group of students from the University of Trento, whose leader was Renato Curcio; and some dissident members of the PCI from Reggio Emilia. At first they concentrated on the factories of Milan, especially Sit Siemens and Pirelli, exploiting industrial disputes, placing bombs under the cars of managers or the firms' lorries and committing other minor acts of industrial sabotage, and distributing leaflets intended to win over workers to the revolutionary cause. They also carried out assaults on members of the MSI. This was the period of what later came to be known as 'armed propaganda'.

Not much notice was taken in the press of these early manifestations of red terrorism, as they seemed not very different from those of the more extreme elements of the New Left. But in 1972 increasing police pressure forced the BR underground. Over the next two years they built up a new organisation of columns, sub-divided into brigades and cells, under the general direction of a small executive body (*direzione strategica*). Grouped round these columns, which numbered six at their peak (in Turin, Milan, Genoa, Veneto, Rome and Naples), were a large number of part-time 'irregulars', leading normal lives, who provided the logistical support for the full-time clandestine 'regulars'. Their social composition, which differed according to locality, included factory workers, public employees, members of the professions, middle-class students (often from Catholic backgrounds) and the rootless urban unemployed and precarious workers (*emarginati*). Many came from broken homes.

In April 1974 the BR carried out their most ambitious action yet: the kidnapping of Mario Sossi, a magistrate who had in 1972-73 prosecuted members of the XXII October group, a precursor of the BR. Sossi was chosen as a symbol of capitalist state repression and subjected to a 'people's trial'. The incident gave the BR the national publicity and recognition which they sought. Having achieved these purposes, they freed Sossi, despite the fact that their demand for the release of eight XXII October prisoners had not been met.

During 1975 and 1976 a steady increase in red terrorist activity brought vigorous police reaction, and very severe damage was inflicted upon both BR and NAP. Curcio had been arrested in September 1974, liberated in a sensational terrorist raid on his prison in February 1975 and arrested again in January 1976. By the spring of that year it was estimated that there were only fifteen BR 'regulars' still active, and a mass trial of the first generation of leaders, including Curcio, seemed to signal the end of red terrorism.

But, like the black terrorists, the BR's survivors found new leaders and recruits, and devised a new strategy, moving out of the factories in order to 'strike at the heart of the state'. Their new leader was Mario Moretti, the sole survivor of the original *direzione strategica*. The first sign of the new strategy was the assassination in June 1976 of the procurator general of Genoa, Francesco Coco. Next year the second cycle of mass disorder provided the base on which the most intense period of terrorism was to rest. It also brought into existence a new organisation, *Prima Linea* (PL: Front Line), which drew its members predominantly from the protest movements and remained mainly non-clandestine. By the spring of 1977 it had acquired about 100 'regulars' and 1,000 'irregular' sympathisers. One of its leaders was Marco Donat Cattin, son of a prominent DC senator. Over the next two years at least ten other minor formations made their presence known, often ephemeral and increasingly youthful, pursuing various tactics but all committed to the strategy of annihilation.[12] These were the years of 'diffused terrorism'.

In March 1978 the BR carried out their intention of striking at the heart of the state by kidnapping Moro in Rome in a well-planned operation during which his police escort of five was gunned down. The idea of abducting and 'trying' a DC leader appears to have been discussed as early as 1975. The operation was timed to coincide with a political development of critical concern to the BR, of which Moro was the architect: the formation of a government of 'national solidarity' supported in parliament by the PCI. The funds for launching the operation had been obtained through the kidnapping in January 1977 of a leading industrialist, Pietro Costa, for whom a ransom of about £700,000 was paid.[13] The 'commando' consisted of about ten persons, including two women, supported by up to 200 'irregulars'. Its leader was Moretti, who also seems to have conducted Moro's 'trial'.

The fifty-four days between Moro's abduction and execution were for most Italians a period of agony. The BR cleverly intensified the strain by issuing a series of communiqués on the progress and political significance of the 'trial', and by forcing or persuading Moro to write a succession of pleading letters, several of which they communicated to the press. The price publicly announced for Moro's liberation was the release of fifteen imprisoned comrades. The humanitarian urge to save his life was naturally strongest among his family, his close colleagues in the DC, and in the Vatican, with which he had intimate links. In the event the government, the parties and the whole of Italy split between the advocates of negotiation and those of intransigence, between *trattativa* and *fermezza*. The BR did not fail to exploit these differences. The PCI showed the most consistent intransigence, and the will of the DC not to concede was undoubtedly strengthened by its dependence upon PCI support in Parliament. The socialists, under the leadership of Bettino Craxi, were the main protagonists of negotiation. In fact the government, while publicly proclaiming its refusal to negotiate, turned a blind eye to the many unofficial attempts to establish contact with the BR. Proposals for an exchange of Moro with one or more convicted terrorists were widely mooted, and President Leone was ready to grant the necessary pardons. It appears that the DC leadership was moving towards some sort of deal on this basis when on 9 May the terrorists, unwilling to risk discovery any longer, executed their victim.

The Moro tragedy can now be seen as a turning point in the story of Italian terrorism. But at the time it seemed that the BR had achieved one of its main objectives, world-wide recognition as a major political protagonist capable of challenging the Italian state. In retrospect it is clear that the public image of the BR's power had been exaggerated out of all proportion to its real strength, which then consisted of about 300 'regulars' and between 2,000 and 3,000 sympathisers.[14] It is also now clear that the operation had failed in its ultimate object, the 'disarticulation' of the Italian state. The government kept its nerve, Parliament rallied to its support, and decrees prescribing severer anti-terrorist measures were approved in a matter of hours. On 14 May, only five days after Moro's corpse had been discovered, 4 million electors went normally to the polls in partial local elections: the turnout was 86 per cent. The BR had hoped to create panic, a collapse of confidence in the state, perhaps a military takeover: but nothing of the sort occurred. It is true that throughout the summer of 1978 the police and judiciary seemed to be moving with incomprehensible slowness, giving the impression of impotence and inefficiency. But in the autumn came a large number of arrests, and by the middle of 1979 there were 210 terrorists, including 143 BR, in custody awaiting trial. In the spring of 1980 the police forces inflicted further heavy losses on both BR and PL.

Nevertheless the years from 1978 to 1980 witnessed the most intense terrorist period, measured by the volume of incidents. The number of assaults on policemen, judges, prison guards, lawyers, industrialists and other symbols of capitalist oppression increased from 287 in 1977 to 716 in 1978 and 805 in 1979.[15] Two assassinations of particular significance were those of Emilio Alessandrini, an investigating magistrate concerned, ironically, with black rather than red terrorism, in January 1979, and of Vittorio Bachelet, vice-chairman of the *Consiglio Superiore della Magistratura* (Supreme Judicial Council) in February 1980. The first was the work of a PL column commanded by Marco Donat Cattin, the second by the BR.

On 12 December the BR kidnapped Giocanni D'Urso, a senior judge with responsibility within the Ministry of Justice for prisons. There followed what was in some respects a re-enactment of the Moro case, with the important difference that it ended with D'Urso's release. The BR's price was the closing of the top security prison of Asinara, situated on a remote island off the northern coast of Sardinia, and better conditions for their comrades in other prisons. D'Urso, like Moro, was subjected to a 'people's trial', and ten communiqués were issued. Once again Craxi and his party advocated negotiation. Even more insistent were the Radicals, the most ardent defenders of civil liberties, who abhorred repressive legislation almost as much as they abhorred terrorism. On 26 December Craxi announced that the government authorised the closure of Asinara. On 28 December terrorists in Trani prison, in Apulia, seized eighteen guards as hostages and warned of severe reprisals if the police intervened. Next day a special force of *carabinieri* landed in the prison from helicopters and released the hostages without loss of life. Three days later General Enrico Galvaligi, who had responsibility for prison security, was shot dead outside his home in Milan. On 6 January 1981 five Radical deputies, acting in agreement with Craxi and with the evident compliance of the Minister of Justice, visited Trani and another prison and held discussions with terrorist inmates, including Curcio. On 10 January the BR's tenth communiqué announced that D'Urso would be executed within forty-eight hours unless the Italian press published certain of their documents. Three leading dailies, including the organ of the Socialist Party, *Avanti!,* did so; on 15 January D'Urso was freed. The BR had won another propaganda victory.

The government and parties faced the same dilemma when Ciro Cirillo was kidnapped on 27 April 1981. Cirillo had a powerful patron in the secretary of his own party, Flaminio Piccoli, and within the DC the decision seems to have been taken that his life should be saved at almost any price. General Musumeci of the intelligence service took charge of the negotiation of a ransom and sought the mediation of a prominent member of the Neapolitan *camorra,* Raffaele Cutolo, who was serving a term in Ascoli Piceno prison. With the compliance, once again, of the Minister of Justice, Cutolo was enabled to make contact with BR leaders in another prison, as a result of which a ransom of between £1.5 million and £2.5 million appears to have been paid, split equally between the *camorra* and the BR. Who paid it is still a mystery.[16] Cirillo was freed on 24 July.

The organiser of both the D'Urso and Cirillo operations was Giovanni Senzani, a lawyer and criminologist who had worked with the prison service. He achieved prominence when Moretti was arrested in April 1981, but never became an effective leader. At this time the BR had four active columns, but they were working autonomously and without central direction. During the summer of 1981 two industrialists were kidnapped: Giuseppe Taliercio, manager of the Montedison chemical plant in the Veneto, who was murdered, and Renzo Sandrucci, an executive of the Alfa Romeo plant in Milan, who was released after the BR's demands for publicity had been met. But the most sensational exploit was the abduction of General Dozier on 17 December 1981. This was the work of the Veneto column, commanded by Antonio Savasta. Never before had Italian terrorists chosen a military or a foreign target, and their initial success caused astonishment. But their later conduct showed a remarkable degree of amateurishness, when compared with the professionalism of the Moro operation. The objects of the kidnapping were never clear, no demands were announced, and Dozier was not even interrogated, apparently because none of the abductors spoke English. On 28 January 1982 he was freed by a carabiniere anti-terrorist squad without loss of life. Savasta was captured during the operation, and Senzani had already been arrested earlier that month. These arrests, and the manifest failure of the Dozier operation, proved decisive blows to the BR.

IDEOLOGICAL PERSPECTIVES

Both black and red terrorists found theoretical justification for their actions in the writings of intellectuals. Most of the earlier practitioners of black terrorism had a fascist past, and later generations also drew their inspiration, not so much from Italian Fascism as from German Nazism and such movements as the Romanian Iron Guard. Julius Evola, a prolific philosopher of the radical right, became a cult figure in the 1960s in those circles from which black terrorism drew its recruits, and especially in ON. The leading populariser of Evola's writings was Freda. In such periodicals as *Ordine Nuovo, Quex* and *Costruiamo l'Azione,* he and others set out to explain the practical application of Evola's preaching to the contemporary Italian situation. They preached the mystique of Nieztschian heroism and the political guerilla warrior, and idealised violence. Their vision was of an authoritarian, hierarchic 'new order', governed by an 'aristocracy of the spirit', which would rescue Italy from its present decadence. They also looked beyond Italy to a new Europe based on traditional spiritual values and liberated from the materialist domination of both the USA and the USSR. One of AN's publications was entitled *Noi Europa.* ON proclaimed itself to be a national-revolutionary movement, with the aim, if not of destroying entirely the corrupt Italian political system, at least of transforming it on authoritarian lines.[17]

Red terrorists drew their inspiration from a confused amalgam of the writings of, amongst many others, Marx, Lenin, Mao and Marcuse, and the revolutionary literature of Third World national liberation movements. Events in Cuba,

Algeria, Vietnam and elsewhere convinced them that world revolution was on its way, but also that in the short term there was a real threat of a capitalist counter-revolution. In their view Italy, the weakest link in the international capitalist chain, was in a pre-revolutionary condition. The BR's numerous pronouncements were phrased in crude Marxist terminology and reflected the traditional 'maximalist' rhetoric of the Italian socialist and working-class movements, on which were superimposed the slogans and utopian myths of 1968. To a certain extent they also looked to the ideals of the armed resistance of 1943-45 and used the rhetoric of anti-fascism. They proclaimed themselves to be a 'combatant communist party' and the 'vanguard of the working class', in whose revolutionary potential they initially had unlimited faith. Their hopes of winning over a substantial part of the PCI soon had to be abandoned, but it was on Lenin's pre-1917 Bolshevik Party that the BR's increasingly militarised structure was modelled.[18]

The first writer to popularise a terrorist culture was Giangiacomo Feltrinelli, a millionaire publisher who founded his own private *Gruppi di Azione Partigiana* (GAP: Partisan Action Group), and died in March 1972 while attaching a bomb to an electricity pylon near Turin. He had had contact with Curcio, and after his death the BR inherited some of his ideas and some of the GAP's arms. Much more influential were the groups of intellectuals of the New Left, often known by the titles of their periodicals. The most influential were *Lotta Continua* (LC: Continuous Struggle), *Potere Operaio* (PO: Workers' Power), and *Autonomia Operaia* (AO: Workers' Autonomy). PO's great strength lay in the factories of industrialised Venetia. At its peak it was estimated to have 3,000 members and its national congress held in Rome in September 1971 was attended by delegates from fifty-eight sections and 108 cells. When it was dissolved in 1975, many of its militants passed to the BR. AO, which absorbed much of the PO, dominated *Movimento,* the loose umbrella organisation of the protest movements of 1977,[19] and placed its hopes of revolution less in the organised working class than in the *emarginati* of the big city slums. These groups defended and sympathised with red terrorists as 'errant comrades', but very few of their members openly advocated, and still fewer practised, terrorism. On occasions they condemned individual terrorist acts. The best known writer was Toni Negri, professor of political and legal theory at the University of Padua and also lecturer at the *Ecole Normale Supérieure* in Paris. He had numerous political discussions with Curcio and other terrorists. It was he who invented the concept of Italy as the 'imperialist state of the multinationals', which the BR adopted as their 'strategic directive' of April 1975. In reviews such as *Rosso* (Red), *Potere Operaio* and *Senza Tregua* (No Truce), Negri and his colleagues composed academic studies justifying political violence, reported sympathetically on revolutionary movements throughout the world, and popularised the concept of permanent civil war and the need to prepare for the seizure of power by military means.[20]

THE STATE RESPONSE

The Italian state authorities and political parties reacted more slowly to the terrorist threat than those in other West European countries, and took longer to recognise its nature and magnitude. But in one sphere, that of legislation, they moved quickly. After 1974 the trend of the previous five years towards an extension of civil liberties was reversed. The first comprehensive attempt to deal with problems of political violence and subversion was the *Legge Reale* of May 1975, named after the Minister of Justice of the day, Oronzo Reale. It was followed in 1977-80 by a succession of laws directed specifically against terrorism. Increased powers of search and of arrest, merely on suspicion (*fermo di polizia*), were granted to the police, and a wider use of arms authorised; the rules regulating the tapping of telephones were relaxed; the registration of lodgers by householders was made compulsory; the time limit of preventive detention without trial was extended to ten years; the granting of bail was restricted, mandatory sentences were increased and judicial discretion reduced.[21]

But parliamentary approval of tough anti-terrorist legislation did not mean that it produced rapid or decisive results. Opinions differ greatly as to the reasons for this. One school of thought explains it by the inefficiency and lack of preparation and training of the police and intelligence services. Another school of thought maintains that the reason was political. In the case of black terrorism the tolerance and collusion of the security services is well documented. But some commentators have asserted that the same tolerance was practised with regard to red terrorism, that some elements within the political system and state apparatus were willing to turn a blind eye in the calculation that red terrorism would discredit the constitutional left and so block the road to radical reform. Proof of such allegations is unlikely to be forthcoming, but speculation and controversy will doubtless continue.[22]

That there was much inefficiency is indisputable. Some of the blame may be attributed to Parliament's reluctance, at least until 1978, to vote the necessary funds. Another reason was the historical dualism and rivalry between the two principal police forces, the militarised *carabinieri* controlled by the Ministry of Defence (but in practice largely autonomous), and the public security force (*pubblica sicurezza*) administered by the Ministry of Interior.[23] In 1973 a special anti-terrorist unit was formed in Turin under the command of a *carabiniere* general, Carlo Alberto Dalla Chiesa. It was responsible for the virtual elimination of the first generation of BR leaders in 1975 and 1976. In May 1974 a Central Inspectorate for action against terrorism was formed in the Ministry of Interior under a senior police official, Emilio Santillo. It had marked success in breaking up NAP. But in 1976 both these units were dissolved in the course of a general reorganisation of the police and intelligence services. In January 1978 a new central office for anti-terrorist operations, UCIGOS (*Ufficio centrale per le investigazioni e le operazioni speciali*) was set up under the Ministry of Interior. These structural reforms were still in progress when Moro was abducted, which may partly explain the dilatory and confused course of the investigations.

When special top security prisons for terrorists were instituted in 1977, Dalla Chiesa was given overall responsibility for their security. After the murder of Moro he was appointed to a new post of anti-terrorist 'supremo', with plenary coordinating powers, and created a specialised and highly trained force of his own.[24] Its success, measured by the number of arrests, was impressive, and despite his disregard for civil liberties, he became 'perhaps the first popular policeman in Italian history'.[25] He seems to have been particularly successful in infiltrating terrorist units with police informers, and in initiating the procedure of inducing captive terrorists to turn state's witness, so earning themselves the title of *pentiti* (repenters). At the end of 1979 Dalla Chiesa was given the key *carabiniere* command of Northern Italy, with broad responsibility for continuing the battle against terrorism. His special force was disbanded, but the men whom he had trained for the job, *teste di cuoio* (leather-heads), showed their quality in 1980-82 in the quelling of the Trani prison revolt and the liberation of Dozier.

The reform of the intelligence services was much less successful. During 1976 and 1977 clear evidence of their collusion with black subversion emerged in successive trials and created irresistible pressures for reform. In October 1977 Parliament approved a law dissolving SID and replacing it by two services, SISDE for internal security and SISMI for foreign intelligence and counter-espionage, with an executive committee, CESIS, to coordinate their operations and facilitate cooperation between the two ministries concerned, Interior and Defence.[26] The problem of political control and accountability was tackled by giving the Prime Minister explicit responsibility for the services and setting up a scrutinising parliamentary committee. But it soon became apparent that not much more than the titles of the services had been altered, and that there had been little change in personnel or outlook.[27] The list of P2's members included the chiefs of both SISDE and SISMI, Generals Grassini and Santovito, and the secretary of CESIS, Walter Pelosi, as well as Miceli, his successor as head of SID, Admiral Mario Casardi, La Bruna and Santovito's deputy, Musumeci. This time a more efficient purge was carried out, and in recent years there have been repeated assurances from leading ministers that the intelligence services have now been truly reformed and placed under effective political control.[28]

PUBLIC OPINION

Public opinion and the media also, like the state authorities, were slow to take an unambiguous stand against terrorism. The black *stragi* were of course universally condemned. But at the time of the kidnapping of Sossi in 1974, the then still mysterious red brigadiers were widely regarded as proletarian Robin Hoods, and in the early years some of the sentences passed on red terrorists were remarkably lenient. Attitudes began to change with the assassination of Coco in 1976, and the Robin Hoods became inhuman monsters.[29] During 1976 and 1977 what little was left of press sympathy was destroyed by a series of assaults on journalists, notably the deputy editor of *La Stampa,* Carlo Casalengo, who died of his wounds. The BR and PL justified these actions by depicting their victims as agents and tools of the imperialist state. Yet some Italians still tried to remain neutral by following the precept, 'Neither with the state nor with the BR'. Many on the left found it difficult to deny a cultural affinity with the proclaimed ideology of red terrorism. As was remarked during the Moro tragedy by Rossana Rossanda, a leader of the ex-communist Manifesto group (which had no sympathy for terrorism), reading the BR's communiqués was like turning the pages of an old family photograph album. Nevertheless it was the Moro affair which finally brought about the decisive shift in public opinion. Significantly the PCI, which had opposed the *Legge Reale* in 1975, became an unswerving supporter of all subsequent anti-terrorist legislation. By 1979 condemnation of terrorism had become virtually unanimous.

Unanimity was harder to reach on the controversial issue of

how much publicity terrorists should be permitted. During the Moro crisis all the BR's communiqués, and many of Moro's letters from his 'prison', were published in the press. This gave the BR the world-wide notoriety they wanted. But gradually it came to be seen that publicity was their very life-blood, without which they would find it hard to survive. During the D'Urso crisis most of the press observed a blackout, though even then it was not complete.

For the media and for public opinion in general the greatest *cause célèbre* was that of Toni Negri, who was arrested, together with most of the leaders of *Autonomia Operaia*, on 7 April 1979. The magistrate who authorised the arrests, Pietro Calogero, asserted that AO and BR were merely the overground and underground sections of the same movement, and that Negri had been personally involved in the murder of Moro. This last charge was dropped a year later, and it was widely considered that Negri's sole misdemeanour had been to profess and propogate subversive political opinions (*reati di opinione*). In February 1983, after almost four years in prison, Negri was brought to trial on charges of planning armed insurrection and forming an armed band. In June he was adopted by the Radical Party as a parliamentary candidate and elected on its list. This led to his release and appearance in the chamber of deputies. But in September, after one of the stormiest debates in its history, which split the government and all of the parties, including the PCI, the chamber voted to deprive him of his immunity. To avoid arrest and reimprisonment, he disappeared to Paris. In June 1984 he was sentenced *in absentia* to thirty years' imprisonment. This verdict was confirmed on appeal in January 1986 and he and seven of his colleagues were acquitted of the charge of 'moral leadership' of the Red Brigades. But the sentence of 1984 still stands, and Negri remains in Paris.

INTERNATIONAL LINKS

The extent to which Italian terrorism has been indigenous or inspired from abroad has been the subject of much debate, and also much obscurity and disinformation. The international links of black terrorism are well known. Both Rauti and Delle Chiaie were frequent and welcome visitors to Greece after the military Junta seized power in 1967. After the Piazza Fontana *strage* Delle Chiaie, Freda, Ventura, Giannettini and many other minor figures found a haven and base in Spain, where they joined the so-called 'Black Orchestra'.[30] Delle Chiaie also visited South America, and in particular Chile, where he made contact with DINA, Pinochet's secret police, and appears later to have assisted it in dealing with political opponents of the regime.[31] After Franco's death he established his base in Buenos Aires, and is believed to have played a part in the coup of July 1980 which brought General Garcio Meza to power in Bolivia. One of Delle Chiaie's associates, Pierluigi Pagliai, suspected of involvement in the Brescia *strage* of 1974, worked for Meza's secret police. A very different kind of link with South America was provided by Gelli, who acquired wealth and influence under Peron and subsequent military regimes in Argentina. The restoration of democracy in Greece and Spain in 1974-76, and the collapse of military rule in Bolivia and Argentina in 1982, was certainly one of the reasons for the decline of Italian black terrorism. In October 1982, immediately after the restoration of civilian government in Bolivia, Italian *carabinieri* arrived to take delivery of Delle Chiaie and Pagliai. The latter was shot while resisting arrest, extradited in a coma and died within a few days of reaching Italy. Delle Chiaie got away to Argentina, and to this day has, like Gelli, so far eluded justice, somewhere in South America.

The international links of red terrorism are more obscure. Much of the scanty information available to the public has come from *pentiti*. Feltrinelli's international connections were multiple. He frequently visited Cuba and South America, and some writers have suggested that he has the ambition to become Italy's Castro. He also travelled to Czechoslovakia several times in 1971 apparently seeking advice and support in organising 'centres of resistance' to what he perceived to be an imminent right-wing coup. The BR certainly collaborated with kindred organisations such as the West German Red Army

Faction and the French *Action Directe*. It also seems likely that, despite Savasta's denial, the Dozier operation was part of a concerted international plan to disrupt NATO. If Madrid was the haven of black terrorists, many red terrorists found one in Paris, and in both cases extradition has proved a difficult and lengthy process.[32] Most of the red terrorists' arms were of Soviet or East European origin, but procured through the Middle East rather than directly. The BR had links with the PLO, and in later years some Italian red (and also black) terrorists attended training camps in the Lebanon, and possibly also in Libya and South Yemen. It is a reasonable assumption that the KGB and its East European satellites, as indeed all secret services,[33] took an interest in Italian red terrorism. But to deduce from this that they were tools of the KGB is fantasy. One is also bound to treat with scepticism the hints by Craxi and other leading Italian politicians, presumably based on intelligence sources, that there was, somewhere abroad, a 'grand old man' (*grande vecchio*) masterminding red terrorist operations. Certainly the BR had their contacts and collaborators abroad, but no convincing evidence has yet been furnished to the public that foreigners dictated their strategy or tactics [34]

The years from 1980 to 1982 saw a dramatic fall in the level of terrorist violence, and though this was not immediately apparent, the decline and death of both black and red terrorism. The number of terrorist acts fell from 294 in 1980 to 136 in 1981 and 92 in 1982.[35] There were many reasons for this. First, the political and economic climate had changed, and the protest movements had faded out. Many of their members were absorbed by the Radical Party, or by *Democrazia Proletaria,* the party of the extreme left which won six parliamentary seats in the June 1979 election. Industrial unrest had also declined, due largely to the economic depression, so depriving red terrorism of another of its bases. In December 1979 Fiat was able to dismiss fifty-one of its workers for violence in its factories and support for terrorism without serious protest. To a certain extent the same process of absorption occurred on the right, with some of the wild elements rejoining the MSI.

The second reason for the decline of terrorism was increased police efficiency, resulting from better pay, equipment and training, and consequently higher morale. The strong public sympathy for members of the police forces who were victims of terrorism was also an important factor. Better cooperation between the different police and intelligence services was also achieved. In 1981 the Ministry of Interior was given stronger powers to coordinate and direct police operations, and a central data bank was set up.[36]

The third, and perhaps most important, reason was the terrorists' growing isolation and loss of contact with political reality. Confronted with the increasing hostility of public opinion, many lost their faith. The BR's communiqués went on proclaiming the feasibility of armed insurrection, but even the working class, on which they had pinned their hopes, now rejected them. This had already been strikingly illustrated in October 1978 when Guido Rossa, a communist trade unionist, denounced a fellow worker for distributing BR leaflets in the factory, and gave evidence against him in court. The BR murdered Rossa in January 1979: 200,000 persons attended his funeral.

Both black and red terrorists were forced into a desperate struggle for survival, involving constant violent clashes with the police, and also—a new phenomenon—attacks on military barracks and transports, in order to obtain arms. One sign of desperation was the growing cooperation with organised crime, prominently revealed during the Cirillo affair. Though Senzani justified the policy ideologically by depicting the rank and file of the Neapolitan *camorra* as proletarians with revolutionary potential, it is clear that it brought discredit to the BR.[37] There were also signs of dissension and schisms among the terrorists themselves. From 1979 onwards the leadership of Moretti and Senzani had been openly challenged by the first BR generation, from inside their prisons. They were criticised for 'bureaucratic and militarist deviations' and for losing touch with the working class and popular protest. These disputes became public through leaks to the press. In 1980 the

Walter Alasia column of Milan was 'expelled' for indiscipline, and in 1981 Senzani created a virtually independent group of his own, the *Fronte Carceri* (Prison Front) in Naples.[38] Disillusionment also affected PL. In September 1979 Donat Cattin decided that a halt to active terrorism, a 'strategic retreat', was necessary, and in April 1980, to escape arrest, he disappeared to Paris.

This process of disintegration was accelerated in 1980-82 by legislative recognition of the practice initiated by Dalla Chiesa of inducing convicted terrorists to turn state's witness. Judges were now given discretion to reduce sentences, and even to authorise release, in appropriate cases.[39] By the end of 1982 the number of *pentiti* had risen to 389, of whom seventy-eight had actively collaborated with the police and judiciary. The most notorious, who became known as *superpentiti* (supergrasses), were Carlo Fiorini, a Milan teacher, associated with GAP, BR and PL, who incriminated Negri in December 1979 and provided much of the material for Calogero's indictment; Patrizio Peci, former commander of the BR Turin column, who talked to Dalla Chiesa in March 1980, revealing details of the Moro operation and Moretti's part in it; Roberto Sandalo, a leading member of the Turin PL, whose information in April 1980 led to PL's almost complete liquidation;[40] and Savasta and Emilia Liera, both captured when Dozier was freed, whose confessions led to 150 arrests during the summer of 1982. The most notorious black *pentiti* was Elio Ciolini, whose revelations in March 1982 about the Black Orchestra, the activities of Delle Chiaie and Pagliai in Bolivia, and the connection of P2 with the Bologna *strage,* led to the reopening of the investigations which SISME's obstruction had brought to a halt.

The motives of these *pentiti* were mixed. Some declared that they had undergone a moral or psychological crisis in prison and genuinely reached the conclusion that terrorism had been an error and a crime. Others doubtless were only interested in securing reduced sentences. Some of them, notably Ciolini, told lies, and many revelations amounted to little more than hearsay, which was subsequently rejected as evidence in court.

Several met death in prison at the hands of comrades whom they had betrayed or who believed, rightly or wrongly, that they had been police spies before arrest. In June 1981 Roberto Peci, brother of Patrizio, was kidnapped by the BR and executed. The growing use of these confessions aroused much public disquiet, for it was widely felt to be unjust that a murderer should be released because he had talked, while many who had committed lesser crimes remained in prison. But undoubtedly the *pentiti* made a major contribution to the defeat of terrorism.[41] In August 1985 the Prime Minister, Craxi, announced that 1,280 terrorists were in prison, 180 black and 1,100 red.[42]

Since 1982 Italy has not been totally free from black and red terrorism, but the relatively few incidents[43] appear to have been the work of very small groups, perhaps of only two or three persons, living a precarious existence in isolation from each other and lacking any coherent political strategy. Their decline, however, has coincided with the emergence, on an increasing scale, of two other phenomena, mafia and *camorra* terrorism, and terrorism, mainly Arab, imported from abroad. Space does not allow more than a few brief observations on these new developments. The mafia and *camorra* are criminal, not terrorist organisations. Unlike black and red terrorism, they have long been deeply embedded in Italian society, the first in Sicily, the second in Naples, and are fundamentally conservative in character and aims. Insofar as they have in recent years resorted to terrorism, this has been in response to the state's attempts to destroy their peculiar systems of power. Traditionally the state has been tolerant of them, but that tolerance was terminated when they took control of the drugs trade, acquired great wealth and extended their operations far outside their traditional areas. The threat they present lies not in any desire to destroy the Italian state, but rather to penetrate and even control it. In May 1982 Dalla Chiesa was appointed prefect of Palermo, in the hope that he would deal as successfully with the mafia as he had dealt with terrorism. On 8 September he was assassinated. This created a shock almost as great as Moro's murder, and has resulted in the most serious anti-mafia campaign for sixty years.

The most dramatic manifestation of imported terrorism was the attempt on the Pope's life in May 1981. If there is evidence that Italian terrorists were involved, it has never been made public. The same is true of the various acts of Arab terrorism, such as attacks on Israeli or allegedly pro-Israeli targets in Italian airports, and the very recent hi-jacking of the *Achille Lauro*. The aim of Arab terrorists is not to promote revolution in Italy, but rather to blackmail Italian governments into following a foreign policy more favourable to the Arab cause.

But though mafia and imported terrorism are fundamentally different from black or red indigenous terrorism, Italian governments have been faced with some of the same problems and dilemmas in dealing with them. A debate between the advocates of *trattavita* and *fermezza* took place at the highest level during the *Achille Lauro* incident. Another similarity is the appearance of *pentiti*. It was the information of the mafia's *superpentito,* Tommaso Buscetta, which made possible the mass mafia trial of 1986. Another *pentito* was the Pope's would-be assassin, Ali Agca, whose revelations of the 'Bulgarian connection' were dismissed as evidence in court for the same reasons as the revelations of many black and red *pentiti*. The problem of collusion, too, is particularly acute in the cases of the mafia and *camorra*. The Cirillo affair was not the only instance of the readiness of the state authorities to accept *camorra* assistance. More seriously, both mafia and *camorra* have enjoyed much more powerful and effective protection than black terrorists, though at a regional rather than national level.

Despite the anxiety caused by these new phenomena, there has been during the last five years a growing belief in Italy that the *anni di piombo* (the years of the bullet) are over, and that emergency measures can now be safely discarded. Already at the end of 1981 the *fermo di polizia* was allowed to lapse, and in July 1984 a substantial section of the anti-terrorist legislation was not renewed. In August 1982 a *Tribunale di Libertà* was instituted to safeguard the civil liberties which had suffered during the terrorist years. Italians are now assessing the significance of those years with greater calm and objectivity, and finding some cause for congratulation. Political terrorism has been defeated without resort to martial law, or even to the use of the army. No special courts were set up, nor was the jury system, though on occasions disrupted by terrorist intimidation, ever abandoned. The judiciary preserved and exercised its independence. The guardians of civil liberties (*garantisti*) were never silenced. In June 1978, only one month after Moro's murder, a referendum promoted by the radicals was held in which 23 per cent of the votes were cast in favour of the abrogation of the *Legge Reale*. There was always some limit to the suspension of civil liberties, and the Constitutional Court, while upholding anti-terrorist legislation, had always made it clear that it was extraordinary and limited in duration.[44]

More generally, the terrorist attack on the heart of the state can now be seen to have failed. The red terrorists had often timed their more ambitious operations to coincide with moments of political tension or crisis, but the electorate declined to be intimidated.[45] Terrorism had shown up many of the deficiencies of the Italian political system and state structure: irresolute and disunited governments, disloyal intelligence services, inadequate police forces, laxity in prison discipline and security, a cumbrous and slow-moving judicial system. But Italian democracy has survived, possibly even been strengthened, and the Italian people has once again shown its astonishing capacity for adaptation and its powers of resilience.

NOTES

1. Donatella della Porta and Maurizio Rossi, 'I terrorismi in Italia tra il 1969 e il 1982', in G. Pasquino (ed.) *Il sistema politico italiano*. Rome-Bari. Laterza 1985, p. 422.
2. *Ibid*.
3. Donatella della Porta, 'Political Violence in Italy during the 1970s', European University Institute paper, July 1985. I am indebted to Dr Carlo Levy, University of Kent, for lending me this unpublished paper.

4. This view is convincingly expounded by Gianfranco Pasquino in 'Sistema politico bloccato e insorgenza del terrorismo: ipotesi e prime verifiche', the fifth chapter of *La prova delle armi,* edited by himself, Bologna: Il Mulino, 1984.

5. Rosario Minna, 'Il terrorismo di destra', in Donatella della Porta (ed.) *Terrorismi in Italia,* Bologna: Il Mulino, 1984, p. 48.

6. Between 1974 and 1976, 32 acts of terrorism, including the Brescia and Italicus *stragi,* were the work of a still mysterious organisation calling itself *Ordine Nero* (Black order). It seems likely that its membership overlapped, if not coincided, with that of ON. See Minna, *op. cit.,* pp. 51-2.

7. According to the Ministry of Interior's figures, the number of black terrorists convicted between 1969 and 1982 was 432, that of red terrorists 1,414. It took four trials and almost ten years to reach a final verdict on those accused of involvement in the Piazza Fontana bombing. Two of the chief suspects, Freda and Giovanni Ventura, were first indicted in August 1972, released in September 1976 after serving the maximum term of pre-trial detention and sent under surveillance to the island of Giglio, from which Freda escaped in October 1978 and Ventura in January 1979. In February 1979, at the end of a two-year trial 33 persons at Catanzaro, Freda, Ventura and Giannettini were sentenced to life imprisonment, and two former members of SID, General Giandelio Maletti and La Bruna, to shorter terms. On appeal in March 1981 Giannettini was acquitted, Freda and Ventura, by then in Argentina, were acquitted of murder but had their 15 years' sentence for subversive association confirmed, and the sentences of Maletti and La Bruna were reduced. The Court of Cassation overruled this decision and ordered a new trial. In August 1985 all defendants were finally acquitted for lack of proof.

8. Miceli, like Delle Chiaie, had been involved in a farcical attempt at a *coup d'état,* led by Prince Valerio Borghese, in December 1970. After acquittal Miceli was elected to Parliament on the MSI list.

9. This strategy was first formulated by Delle Chiaie and Signorelli at the meeting at Albano Laziale in September 1975 at which the fusion of ON and AN took place. Franco Ferraresi, 'La destra eversiva', in Franco Ferraresi (ed.) *La destra radicale,* Milan: Feltrinelli, 1984, p. 73.

10. Minna, *op. cit.,* p. 63.

11. Tuti was acquitted of responsibility for the Italicus bomb in July 1983.

12. For a comprehensive list, see della Porta, 'Political Violence', *loc. cit.*

13. Giorgio Galli, *Storia del partito armato 1969-1982,* Milan: Rizzoli, 1986, pp. 115, 120.

14. *Ibid.,* p. 163. PL was also estimated to have a few hundred activists and about 2,000 sympathisers.

15. Della Porta and Rossi, *loc. cit.,* p. 421. Minna, *op. cit.,* p. 63, states that red terrorists were responsible for 65% of the 8,400 assaults on persons

and property between 1975 and 1980. For a full list of the incidents between March and December 1978 see Galli, *op. cit.*, pp. 166-7, 184-6.

16. Galli, *op. cit.*, p. 253.

17. For a detailed analysis of the literature of the radical right, including the writings of Evola and Freda, see Ferraresi, *op. cit.*, pp. 13-53. See also his summary of Delle Chiaie's manual of political action, *La lotta politica di Avanguardia nazionale,* in *Terrorismi in Italia, op. cit.,* pp. 262-7.

18. For a convenient summary of the BR's 'theoretical resolutions of September' 1971 and March 1973, and their first 'strategic resolution' of April 1975, see Galli, *op. cit.,* pp. 32-4, 54-5, 95-7.

19. *Movimento* was a very loosely structured organisation embracing all the disparate elements of the 1977 protest movements.

20. For the relationship between PO and BR, see Angelo Ventura, 'Il problema de le orgini del terrorismo di sinistra', in *Terrorismi in Italia, op. cit.,* pp. 128-38. LC split on the issue of support for terrorism in 1976 and many members of its radical wing passed to PL.

21. For details see Vittorio Grevi, 'Sistema penale e leggi dell' emergenza: la risposta legislativa al terrorismo', in *La prova delle armi, op. cit.,* pp. 20-45.

22. The chief exponent of this view is Galli, who argues that the police acted when they wanted to, or were ordered to, but on many occasions lacked the necessary political direction. Particular instances are, in his view, the inertia of the police in the early months of 1977, and the ease with which Moro's assassins abducted him and later parked the car containing his corpse in the centre of Rome, half-way between the DC and PCI headquarters. See Galli, *op. cit.,* pp. 92, 140-2, 147-8, 159-62, 175-8. The same view is held by Angelo Ventura, *loc. cit.,* pp. 118-19, who writes of 'the practice of immunity'; and by Paul Furlong, 'Political Terrorism in Italy: Responses, Reactions and Immobilism', in J. Lodge (ed.) *Terrorism: A Challenge to the State,* Oxford: Martin Robertson, 1981 p. 79, who suggests that the political value of terrorism outweighed the need for its control.

23. For a lucid analysis of the structures of Italian police forces, see Richard O. Collin, 'The Blunt Instrument: Italy and the Police', in John Roach and Jürgen Thomaneck (eds) *Police and Public Order in Europe,* London: Croom Helm, 1985 pp. 185-8.

24. Responsibility for prison security was taken over by General Galvaligi, who was assassinated by the BR in December 1980 (see above).

25. Collin, *loc cit.,* p. 185.

26. Servizio per le informazioni e la sicurezza democratica; Servizio per le informazioni e sicurezza militare; Comitato esecutivo per i servizi di informazioni e di sicurezza.

27. Galli, *op. cit.,* pp. 150-2.

28. In July 1985 Musumeci and a subordinate, Captain Giuseppe Belmonte,

were given prison sentences of 9 and 8 years for offences including conspiracy, diverting the judicial process and association with the mafia.

29. Carlo Marletti, 'Terrorismo e communicazioni di massa', in *La prova delle armi, op. cit.,* pp. 149-50.

30. Among the Black Orchestra's more prominent members, with whom Delle Chiaie and others collaborated, were Otto Skorzeny, the Austrian SS officer who rescued Mussolini in September 1943, and Yves Guérin-Serac, a member of the French OAS. For details see Stuart Christie, *Stefano Delle Chiaie: Portrait of a Black Terrorist,* London: Anarchy Magazine/Refract Publications, 1984 pp. 27-9, 71-4, 156-61.

31. Notably the attempt to assassinate Bernardo Leighton, vice-chairman of the Chilean Christian Democratic Party, in Rome in October 1975. Christie, *op. cit.,* pp. 85-6; Minna, *op. cit.,* pp. 55-6; Luciano Violante, 'Politica della sicurezza, relazioni internazionali e terrorismo', in *La prova delle armi, op. cit.,* p. 116.

32. Two prominent Italians whom the French authorities did finally agree to extradite were a colleague of Negri, Franco Piperno, in October 1979, and Marco Donat Cattin, in February 1981. Similar difficulties have arisen in London, where several black terrorists, apparently sheltered by members of the National Front, have escaped extradition owing to the inadequate evidence (by British standards) provided by the Italian authorities, (Christie, *op. cit.,* pp. 117, 120-1). The problem will presumably now be eased by the new British-Italian extradition treaty signed in March 1986.

33. Including, apparently, the Israeli, Violante, *ibid.,* pp. 110-12.

34. For a balanced study of the question, see Violante, *ibid.,* pp. 96-9. In his opinion there were international *rapporti* rather than *committenze.*

35. Della Porta and Rossi, *ibid.,* p. 421.

36. Grevi, *ibid.*

37. Galli, *ibid.,* pp. 250-2, 278-9.

38. For an analysis of this period of decline of red terrorism, about which accurate information is extremely scanty, see Gian Carlo Caselli and Donatella della Porta, 'La storia delle Brigate rosse: strutture, organizzazioni e strategie d'azione', in *Terrorismi in Italia,* pp. 201-16. The internal conflicts have been described, with over-simplification, as between *militaristi* and *movimentisti.*

39. Grevi, *ibid.,* pp. 45-8.

40. Sandalo's revelations provoked a major political crisis. He stated that Marco Donat Cattin, who escaped to France in April 1980, had been warned of his imminent arrest by his father, Carlo, who had in turn been warned by the prime minister, Francesco Cossiga. Having received the information from the investigating judges, parliament set its investigating machinery in action; but the PCI's attempt to have the prime minister impeached was defeated in an extraordinary joint session

of the two chambers in July.

41. Fiorini was released in February 1982 after 7 years in prison, Peci in April 1983 after 38 months, and Sandalo in November 1982 after 2½ years. Donat Cattin was given a suspended sentence of 8 years in December 1983 and conditionally released. Savasta and Libera, convicted of seventeen murders, had their sentences reduced by a court of appeal in January 1983 to 16 years.

42. The location of Dozier's 'prison' was revealed by a BR 'irregular', Ruggero Volinia, after his arrest on 27 January 1982: Dozier was freed the next day.

43. *The Times,* 12 August 1985.

44. The most serious was a fifth black *strage* on 23 December 1984, when a bomb exploded in a train, again between Florence and Bologna, killing 15 and severely injuring 116.

45. Grevi, *ibid.,* pp. 67-71.

5 Dictatorship, Democracy and Terrorism in Spain

Benny Pollack and Graham Hunter

Between 1968 and May 1986, according to Ministry of the Interior figures, 667 violent deaths resulted from terrorist activity in Spain. The perpetrators of these have ranged, in terms of ideological persuasion, from the extreme left to the extreme right. The overriding motivation behind the vast majority, however, has been an intense nationalism.

Such nationalist motivation has allowed for one particular organisation to achieve the indisputable, and unenviable, position of being clearly at the top of the terrorist league in Spain. Since 1968 *Euzkadi Ta Azkatasuna* (ETA)[1] has been responsible for three times as many deaths as the aggregate total of all other terrorist organisations in Spain. ETA has just recently added the 500th victim to its list of 'executions'.

Table 5.1: Deaths Attributable to Terrorist Acts in Spain, 1968-1 May 1986.

ETA	500
Extreme left	84
Extreme right	41
Unknown	42
Total	667

Source: Ministry of Interior figures. Extracted from *El Periodico De Catalunya,* 26 April 1986

In terms of its size, organisation and activities ETA, next to the Irish Republican Army, constitutes the second most important terrorist outfit operating in contemporary Western Europe. In Spain today ETA is the only extra-parliamentary, terrorist organisation with a degree of influence and potential for damaging the system.

CENTRIFUGAL NATIONALISM, AUTHORITARIAN CENTRALISM AND BASQUE OPPOSITION: THE EMERGENCE OF ETA, 1939-59.

In the preamble of a recently submitted report on *The Violence in the Basque Country* it is stated categorically that this violence 'does not originate from the exterior nor is it dependent upon international connections; it is a problem that is rooted in Basque history and its principal motivation is nationalism'.[2]

Centrifugal nationalist grievances and demands have been a persistent source of friction and conflict throughout Spanish history, dating back to the process of unification under Castilian hegemony. Whilst such general nationalist aspirations have spawned separatist movements in areas as far apart as Catalunya and the Canary Islands, it is only in Euzkadi (the Basque country) that separatism has acquired any real significance.[3] The explanation for this has to be sought in the pre-democratic (i.e. pre-1977) era which has marked recent Spanish history. Three specific, and interrelated, factors need to be taken into account here: (1) the particular nature of Basque nationalism; (2) the authoritarian-centralist response to the national question in Spain from 1939 to 1977; (3) the limitations and inefficacy of mainstream nationalist forces during the same period. The first would provide the potential for the emergence of a Basque separatist-terrorist organisation. The second certainly added the fuel, and the third possibly the spark.

Nationalism, and nationalist aspirations, cannot be treated as a generally uniform phenomenon in the context of the

Spanish state. The specificity of each particular case has to be taken into account. The examples of Basque and Catalan nationalism provide an illuminating comparison in this respect.[4] Basque nationalism, far more than Catalanism, would provide fertile ground for the generation of a militant separatist organisation. Whereas Catalanism has generally been restricted to cultural aspects of national identity, Basque nationalism has included a greater emphasis on ethnicity.[5] This accent on racial origin acted as a catalyst on Basque nationalism with demands for outright independence always being far more widespread than in Catalunya.[6] Aggravating this tendency toward separatism is the acute vulnerability of Basque culture and in particular the Basque language, *Euskera*. Totally distinct from the Romance languages, the origins of *Euskera* is a moot historical point. What is beyond doubt, however, is that this has accelerated the process of Castilianisation in the Basque country. The potential for a militant nationalist-separatist movement was thus exacerbated in the Basque country by a correspondingly higher level of 'cultural threat'.

Within the framework of the Spanish state, the most appropriate method of attenuating the likely transformation of this potential into socio-political reality was to concede far-reaching powers of national self-government and cultural affirmation to the Basques. Any such channels of integration were, however, effectively and brutally sealed off for forty years at the end of the civil war in 1939.

The suppression of regional aspirations and the maintenance of Castilian hegemony was to remain one of the major preoccupations of the Centralist-Authoritarian regime that was set up by the victors of the civil war. Autonomous political structures were dismantled, regionalist leaders exiled, imprisoned or executed, regional symbols and flags banned, and the public and educational use of languages other than Castilian outlawed. In brief, the response of the Francoist regime to nationalist aspirations was outright repression. The ultimate goal of this repression was not merely to undermine the nationalist movements in the short term, but also to restrict the inter-generational reproduction of distinctive cultural values and language.

The level of cultural threat as a direct consequence of the repression was furthered by the socio-economic transformation of Spain from the mid-1950s onward. The abandoning of the autarkic economic model and the development of a dynamic free-market economy was accompanied by a dramatic shift in the demographic pattern of Spain. As principal industrial areas, both Catalunya and the Basque country were hosts to a massive influx of an immigrant, Castilian-speaking, labour force. The vulnerability of Basque culture to repressive state policies within the context of sociological change would act as a catalyst on part of the traditional nationalist movement. It was the search for effective nationalist defence mechanisms that gave rise to an armed organisation that would outlive the dictatorship itself.

In his work on *Dictatorship and Political Dissent* Maraval has noted that 'nationalist demands . . . were never represented by an organised movement in the years of Francoism'.[7] Whereas independent working-class and student movements were able to be restructured during the years of the dictatorship, this was not the case with territorially based opposition movements. The mainstream nationalist parties tended to operate as oppositions in exile. The failure of the Basque Nationalist Party (PNV)[8] to present itself as a combative force led to a rift between younger PNV militants of the 'interior' and the 'exterior' leadership. By the mid-1950s, the youth wing of the PNV was becoming increasingly impatient with the inactivity of the party, and with what was considered the ossification of the leadership in exile. For many young militants the party failed to provide an effective nationalist defence mechanism to counter the centralist, anti-Euzkadi, policies of the authoritarian regime. It was after an unsuccessful attempt to convince the leadership to rejuvenate its internal activity by direct action that a breakaway group of the youth section formed the nucleus of ETA in 1959.

THE 'SPIRAL OF CONFLICT': THE PRAXIS OF ETA, 1959-75.

Initially, the main activity of the new organisation was the promotion of educational and cultural activities to reawaken the spirit of Basque nationalism. Throughout the 1960s, however, a process of radicalisation occurred and an intellectually weak variation of Marxism-Leninism was superimposed on the nationalist orientation of the youthful ETA. Inspired by Maoism and the heady influence of the success of the 26 July movement in Cuba (and perhaps more importantly by a misconception of the reasons for that success) ETA decided to embark upon its own military campaign of 'national liberation'.

The theoretical basis for such action was the so-called 'spiral of conflict'. This spiral was conceived as the hub of the revolutionary process—a process which would lead ultimately to armed insurrection and the Basque nationalist-socialist revolution. The spiral is schematically represented in ETA documents as A-R/C-A (Action-Repression/Consciousness-Action), with the spiral functioning thus: A^1-R/C-A^2-R/C-A^3 . . . etc. A^1 represents the initial action undertaken by the armed revolutionary foci (ETA). This primary action would provoke a repression reaction -R- on the part of the oppressor (the Spanish state). Such repression will in turn produce an increased awareness or consciousness -C- on the part of the 'oppressed' (the Basque people). The consequence of this will be further action, different from the first in that it will be undertaken by the oppressed themselves -A^2-. The logic of this schema is that the conflict between oppressor and oppressed will spiral. Each action will be qualitatively superior to the previous one—A^1, A^2, A^3 . . . and thus an advance in the revolutionary process.[9]

The spiral was set in motion shortly after ETA began its military campaign. The first actions of this campaign consisted mainly of acts of sabotage and bank robberies to raise funds. It was not until 1968 that ETA carried out its first 'execution'—that of a local chief inspector of the *Brigada*

Social renowned for his methods of interrogation. The most spectacular operation undertaken by ETA during the Franco years was the assassination of Prime Minister Admiral Carrero Blanco in December 1973.[10] The response of the Franco regime, as was its wont, was one of over-reaction and widespread repression. States of exception, show trials and suppression of all forms of opposition followed in the trail of ETA activity.[11] This repression, whilst not taking the 'spiral' to its theoretical conclusion, certainly provided ETA with widespread publicity and growing support.[12] Furthermore, whilst this repression had the immediate effect of disarticulating ETA and other opposition organisations, ultimately it led to a coalescing of the anti-Francoist movement. However, at no point during the dictatorship was this spiral a mere consequence of the actions of ETA: it was a manifestation of the growing popular demand for political change. Political change which, contrary to ETA's thesis, would be a consequence of consensus, not conflict, and a peaceful 'ruptura' rather than armed revolution.

FROM DICTATORSHIP TO DEMOCRACY: 'LA LUCHA CONTINUA'

The death of General Franco on 20 November 1975 set off a chain of events leading to an almost unprecedented peaceful transition to democracy after four decades of authoritarian rule. This achievement surely stands as a monumental example of reconciliation in a state with such long-standing and bitter divisions. Not all divisions were, however, so readily healed or easily forgotten. In the years following the death of Franco, the response of ETA to the changing political environment was one of the many unknown factors, Today, as Table 5.2 highlights, there is no doubt: for ETA 'the struggle continues'.

It is evident from Table 5.2 that ETA has not merely continued its campaign of violence under the present regime, but has in fact escalated it dramatically. In the first fifteen years of its existence, when Spain was still under the yoke of

Table 5.2: Violent Deaths Attributable to ETA Terrorist Activity, 1955-86*

The Francoist period From the founding of ETA in 1959 to the death of Franco in November 1975.	43
The transitional period From the death of Franco to the holding of first democratic elections on 15 June 1977.	23
The democratic period From elections of 1977 to present.	434

Note: *Periodised in relation to regime type.

Source: Ministry of Interior figures. Extracted from *El Periodico De Catalunya,* 26 April 1986.

authoritarianism, ETA carried out forty-three assassinations. During the fragile nineteen-month period of the transition to democracy, ETA intensified its activities. In the brief nine years of democratic rule, the death toll of ETA's campaign is ten times greater than it was during the dictatorship. It was the years immediately following the first democratic elections that witnessed the greatest increase in ETA terrorism, reaching a peak in 1980 of ninety-four deaths (see Table 5.3).

Tables 5.1-5.3 do not, of course, reflect anywhere near the true level of ETA terrorist activity. To recount the list of kidnappings, acts of sabotage, bank robberies, extortion (via so-called 'revolutionary taxes'), attacks on factories and tourist areas, reprisals against 'informers' and 'traitors' (quite often *ex-etarras* that is, former ETA members) would be all but impossible. The main targets of ETA's terrorist campaign, according to the organisation itself, has been the 'financial capitalist oligarchy' and the security forces. The latter have been particularly singled out by ETA assassination squads. Since 1968, 285 members of the security forces have been assassinated in terrorist attacks. Of those, the highest casualty rate has been amongst the *Guardia Civil*.[13] It was during the campaign of 1979-80 that this latter group was especially targeted.

That ETA chose to carry on its armed struggle under the present regime should not have come as any surprise. If it did, and it certainly did to many previous supporters of the organisation, this was often due to their having confused ETA's particular struggle with that of the broader anti-Francoist movement. As early as 1964, ETA had made explicit the difference between the two: 'The anti-Francoists struggled against Franco as if Spanish oppression of the Basque country did not exist. We struggle against Spanish oppression as if Franco did not exist'.[14] This overriding commitment to an anti-Castilian, rather than an anti-authoritarian, struggle bore ominous tidings for any future democratic regime. Such commitment does not, however, necessarily imply that the form of struggle should remain the same regardless of regime type. That it did, requires explanation. An explanation which

Table 5.3: Annual Rate of Violent Deaths Attributable to ETA Terrorist Activity, 1976-85.

1976 - 17	1981 - 30
1977 - 12	1982 - 40
1978 - 65	1983 - 40
1979 - 78	1984 - 33
1980 - 96	1985 - 30*

Note: *Up to October 1985.

Source: Figures extracted from *Desatado y Bien Desatado, El Periodico De Catalunya,* Barcelona, 1985, p. 314.

is to be found in the ideological and strategic developments of ETA from the mid-1970s.

THE IDEOLOGICAL AND STRATEGIC FRAGMENTATION OF ETA: 1974-81.

From the time of its first assembly in 1962, the history of ETA has been one of internal struggles, divisions and splintering. These splits have usually been provoked by differences of opinion over the definition of the primary socio-political contradiction within the Spanish state: whether the emphasis should be on national or class struggle. Aggravating these divergences were different conceptions of the most appropriate form of action to be undertaken. The most significant of these divisions occurred in 1974, when ETA split into two major formations: *ETA-Politico-Militar* (ETA-PM) and *ETA-Militar* (ETA-M). It was this division between 'Polis' and 'Milis' that would be of greatest importance in the democratic period.

The fundamental cause of this division was the 'confusion of ideology and nationalism' that had coexisted within the organisation since the early 1960s.[15] The ideologists (Marxists-Leninists) sought to develop the movement's activities at a mass level with pre-eminence given to political work amongst the working class. This 'workerist' tendency was vehemently opposed by the nationalists who also insisted on the primacy of the armed struggle. These differences came to a head over the so-called 'Pertur Thesis'.

Moreno Bergarache (Pertur), one of ETA's chief ideologists at the time, had sought to synthesise these two opposing positions and formulate a coherent strategy for the movement in the coming years. Pertur maintained that whilst there was a place for military action, a separate Basque Revolutionary Party was also needed to create a mass base. The most contentious point of his proposal was that the military wing of the movement should be subordinate to the decisions of the political wing. Furthermore, the ultimate objective was to phase out military operations in favour of strictly political activity.[16] Whilst this thesis was welcomed by many who considered a more flexible strategy appropriate in the changing political circumstances of the mid-1970s, it was rejected outright by the 'milis'. Thus, the dramatic political changes that occurred in Spain following the death of the dictator were accompanied by a sharpening of the contradictions within the ranks of ETA.

During the period of the transition, and the years preceding the attempted coup of 1981, this divergence between the two branches of ETA was accentuated. Although both continued with their respective military campaigns, the reasoning behind these followed two distinct conceptions of the socio-political circumstances within which they were operating.

In August 1976, ETA-PM VII assembly passed a resolution accepting Pertur's thesis in its entirety.[17] Correspondingly, a new political party, *Euzkal Iraultzarako Alderdia* (EIA), was set up to play the leading role in the Basque liberation movement. This would later evolve into the present *Euskadiko Ezkerra* (EE).[18] Although no specific timetable was drawn up for the abandonment of arms, by the end of 1980 EE had entered into talks with the central government to discuss the possibility of a ceasefire.

The following year, ETA-M also set up a political front, *Herriko Alderdi Socialista Iraultzaila* (HASI) later to become the hegemonic force within the present coalition of *Herri Batasuna* (HB).[19] For the 'milis', however, nothing had fundamentally changed. Unlike the 'polis', the military wing ETA-M was not subordinated to the decisions of the party. The primacy of armed struggle was thus re-emphasised. It was also during this period that ETA-M formulated its thesis of 'continuismo'. The evolution toward a 'bourgeois democracy', they argued, had not transformed the essential character of the Spanish state. The *poderes fácticos* (real powers) upon which the old regime was based, remained both intact and in control. The political changes were merely a superstructural facade. This thesis of 'continuismo' served to reinforce the 'milis' justification for continuing the armed struggle despite the newly-forged framework of a democratic polity. As was noted above, ETA claimed to be carrying on an anti-Castilian struggle under Francoism regardless of the authoritarian nature of the regime. In democratic Spain, ETA-M would justify its military campaign by claiming that there had been no real break from that regime. For the 'milis' the 'spiral of violence' would thus not only continue to function under the democratic system but it would also, they claimed, serve to reveal the true nature of the regime.

The basic difference between the 'milis' and the 'polis' is perhaps best summarised in the following passage from an interview with leaders of the latter in 1977:

> It is necessary to clarify our differences not in methods of action but in strategic objectives. (The 'milis') seek the overall destabilization of the system . . . We believe to uphold such a position would lead to a return to some form of the previous State. We believe that bourgeois democracy is a stage to be taken advantage of for obtaining our objectives.[20]

For ETA-PM the 'Spiral of Conflict' had ceased to function. The end result would be reaction rather than revolutionary mobilisation. The 'polis' military campaign would however continue, auto-justified as a means of 'deepening' the process of democratisation and of ensuring that the Basque question would remain a priority issue of the new regime.

Some three years after the above statement, the predictions of ETA-PM came near to being fulfilled. At 6.22 p.m. on 23 February 1981, (23-F) 200 *Guardias Civiles,* under the command of Lieutenant-Colonel Antonio Tejero, stormed the Congress of Deputies of the Spanish Cortes. Thus began the 'longest night' of Spain's young democracy. One of the main grievances of the would-be *golpistas* (conspirators) was the apparent failure of the liberal democratic regime to counter the rising tide of separatism and terrorism. The frustration of the attempted coup was not only a milestone in the recent history of Spain, but would also have important consequences for the future of the ETA terrorist organisation.

Despite ETA-PM's distinction between 'methods of action' and 'strategic objectives', their continued use of violence after 1977 also contributed to provoking this crisis. Also, however, there can be no doubt that the events of '23-F' accelerated the demilitarisation of this branch of ETA. By the end of the same year the 'polis' had formally renounced the armed struggle, although a fraction would continue a campaign of violence until 1984 under the name of ETA-PM VIII assembly. Many of these 'Octavos' would later join ranks with the 'milis'.

Since 1981, notwithstanding these splinter groups of ETA-PM and more obscure breakaway movements such as the *Commandos Autónomos Anticapitalistas,* Basque separatist-terrorism has come to be synonymous with the major remaining branch of ETA—the 'Milis'.[21] ETA-M remains the most intransigent and, despite the inclusion of many ex-'polis' having given a more ideological colouring in recent years, the most fervently nationalist in its demands. Although the events of 23 February 1981 revealed the limitations of ETA's 'Spiral of Conflict', the 'milis' continue as if nothing had changed. It is with this more militant element of Basque separatism that the Spanish authorities have had to deal since 1981.

COMBATTING ETA TERRORISM, 1981-86

The response of the Francoist regime to both Basque nationalism, and the emergence of ETA, was to utilise to the extreme the coercive apparatus of the state. The repressive anti-Euzkadi policies not only failed to undermine Basque nationalist aspirations but also served to nurture, and act as a catalyst upon, the very movement they were intended to crush. ETA terrorism is thus one of the many awesome legacies bestowed upon the present regime by its anti-democratic predecessor, and the attempt to combat and eradicate it within a recently forged democratic polity has proved a formidable task. The refusal by ETA-M to accept the political changes that have occurred since 1975 increases such difficulties. Apart from denying the democratic nature of the regime, ETA-M maintains that the Spanish Constitution was forced upon the Basque people. Furthermore, it refuses to accept the result of the referendum on the Basque Autonomy Statute. Whilst the majority, albeit slight, voted to accept the statute, ETA-M rejects its validity since it is dependent upon a constitutional framework which, in their opinion, had previously been rejected by the Basque population.[22] In the face of such intransigence, the Spanish authorities have formulated an anti-ETA terrorist strategy which consists of three central pillars: effective policing, international cooperation and a policy of 'social reinsertion'.[23]

1. Effective policing

The high levels of ETA violence in the years 1979 and 1980, coupled with the anti-separatist motivations professed by the leaders of the attempted coup in 1981, provoked a renewed sense of urgency on the part of the Spanish authorities. Apart from measures to counter insurrectionist tendencies within the military and security forces, a reinvigorated police campaign against the terrorists was set in motion. As Table 5.3 (p. 126) indicates, the annual rate of deaths attributable to ETA activity has declined considerably since this time. Whilst this is not solely due to the response of the public order forces, the success rate of uncovering and detaining numerous terrorist commando units had undoubtedly increased in recent years.

As the main area of ETA-M activity is in the Basque country itself, and the provinces of Viscaya and Guipuzcoa in particular, such operations have had great success.[24] Particularly heavy blows were dealt to ETA-M's military structure in 1984 and 1985. These years saw the complete destruction of key commando units such as those headed by Jesús Mariía Zabarte Arrogui and Zabarte Jaimaya in the Basque country, and also the 'Commando Navarra'. One of the chief reasons for this increasing success has been the coordination of police anti-terrorist activity under the control of the provincial civil governors of Viscaya and Guipuzcoa. Such success has not however been replicated in the Spanish

capital. During the early 1980s ETA-M activity was mooted in Madrid. Since late 1985, however, no doubt as a consequence of police success in the Basque country, ETA-M's 'Commando Madrid' has been increasingly active. So much so that the Spanish press in 1986 has made constant reference to the 'Battle for Madrid'.

Apart from this disruption to its military structure, ETA-M has also suffered financially from the increase in police efficacy. The frustration of numerous ETA-M kidnappings by the security forces in recent years has deprived the terrorist organisation of a considerable source of funding. This task of liberating ETA-M hostages has generally fallen to the 130-member strong elite corp of the *policía nacional*—the *Grupos Especiales de Operaciones* (Special Operations Group), formed in 1978 specifically to counter terrorist activity and other threats to state security. Whilst the successes on these fronts have been a considerable contribution to combatting ETA-M terrorism the question of police efficacy does not end there.

That ETA-terrorism is a major problem of public order in contemporary Spain there is no doubt. That effective policing has an important role to play in combatting it is generally not disputed. The appropriate form of policing within the constitutional framework is, however, another matter.

The extension of police powers to combat terrorist activity (and other forms of public disorder) has led to a growing concern on the part of many in long-established democracies. This concern has centred on the need to strike a balance between effective police powers and the safeguarding of basic constitutional and human rights. In the case of Spain such concern has an added significance, given that such rights have only been enjoyed for a relatively short period of time. It is in this context that the *Ley Antiterrorista* (anti-terrorist law) has been such a contentious and polemical issue.[25] Initiated by the previous UCD government, and criticised at the time by the Socialists in opposition, it has since been modified and reinforced, in December 1984, by the Socialists in government. The major concern expressed by many individuals and organisations has been that this law allows for the detention, incommunicado, of those suspected of terrorist activity, for up to ten days.[26] The government, and supporters of this law, claim that this is necessary for thorough police investigation. To critics of the law, on the other hand, it merely increases the likelihood of the abuse of basic rights.

Apart from such concerns, the efficacy of this law in combatting ETA terrorism is also questionable. As certain opponents have pointed out, 'at times, the same laws enacted to end violence, as, in this case the anti-terrorist law, do no more than poison the atmosphere'.[27] The application of this law in the Basque country (which accounts for the majority of cases) is illustrative in this respect. Of 1,181 detentions related to terrorist or political activity in 1985, 765 people were charged under the anti-terrorist legislation. Of these, only sixty-nine were sentenced to prison terms.[28] The fear of many is that the indiscriminate application of this law, rather than swelling the prisons with terrorists, will at best only serve to increase the hostility of significant numbers toward the police and security forces. At worst it may in fact increase support for the terrorist organisation.

Finally, effective policing alone is not enough to end, or to lead to a lasting reduction in, ETA-M terrorism. No matter how efficient, ultimately this would only be an exercise in 'damage control'.

2. International cooperation: 'The French connection'

At the end of 1984 the Spanish authorities commissioned a report on ETA's international connections. The report concluded that ETA had set up bases throughout Europe and was receiving support from other terrorist organisations, such as the IRA.[29] Since July 1985, the United States administration has made repeated accusations, without providing much in the way of substantial evidence, that the Sandinista regime in Nicaragua has been providing training and aid to the Basque Separatist organisation. In May 1986, a secret report of the Spanish State Information Service was 'leaked'. According to this report, since 1978 Libya has also been an important source of financial and material aid for ETA.[30] The importance of such links is, however, debatable. The findings of the International Commission in 1986 stress that such aid from other terrorist organisations or foreign countries has been minimal. ETA has acquired a high degree of self-sufficiency, raising funds from bank robberies, kidnappings and the imposition of 'revolutionary taxes' on Basque businesses. Weapons are either purchased on the international black market or obtained by theft in the Basque country.[31]

Both the report commissioned by the Spanish government in 1984 and that by the Basque autonomous government in 1986 are agreed that the most important international factor for the continued effective functioning of ETA has been the proximity of the French border, and the attitude of the authorities, until recently, in the neighbouring republic.

For obvious logistical reasons, France has been the traditional operational base for ETA. The fact the the Basque provinces are separated by the Pyrenees has allowed ETA to carry out terrorist activities with impunity and then retreat across the frontier to elude police action. Furthermore, the tolerance of successive French governments *vis-à-vis* the ETA exile community (many of the top leaders of the terrorist organisation having been granted the status of political refugee) has allowed for the consolidation of a relatively immune coordinating body within striking distance of its targets. Even when Spanish police activity was successful against commando units, the exiled leadership remained out of reach. Whilst such tolerance might have appeared justified when ETA was thought to be struggling against the previous anti-democratic regime, the continuation of such an attitude after 1977 was a continual source of consternation to Spanish democrats.[32] Repeated overtures by the Spanish authorities on the need for a bilateral accord on combatting ETA terrorism were, however, eventually successful in 1983. The accord reached between the socialist governments of the two countries (and continued under the present Chirac government) was an important step forward both in terms of international cooperation and also in the overall anti-terrorist strategy of the

Spanish government.

Since 1983, the French authorities have increasingly questioned the 'political' motivation of ETA activities, with ETA-M being denounced as an 'association of criminals'.[33] This change of attitude has been accompanied by a series of police and judicial actions against the organisation, with extraditions granted for the first time in September 1984. Given the legal difficulties of extraditing those who hold political refugee status, the French authorities have generally opted for a policy of deportation to third countries. The French and Spanish governments have reached agreements with Latin American and African states to act as vigilant hosts to expelled *etarras*. The justification for such deportations has been the failure to comply with residential requirements, and known members of ETA have been confined to areas well removed from the Spanish-Basque frontier. In this manner, many leaders of ETA-M have been deported to countries far from the field of operations.

In April 1984, the then French Minister of the Interior, Pierre Joxe, met with his Spanish counterpart to review the new-found cooperation between the two countries. At this meeting it was agreed to reinforce the joint anti-terrorist campaign by linking the measures of the French authorities to the Spanish government's policy of 'Social Reinsertion'. The French government would increase the restrictions on residence and work permits granted to Basque exiles, whilst the Spanish government for their part would facilitate the unhindered return of those exiles who had not participated directly in ETA terrorist activities.[34]

3. 'Social reinsertion'

The policy of 'Social Reinsertion', possibly the most imaginative and bold measure that has been undertaken to combat ETA terrorism, is one which in fact emanated from within the organisation itself.

The ceasefire called by the 'polis' in February 1981 was accompanied by an important initiative from the political branch of the movement, EE. The leaders of *Euskadiko*

Ezkerra, Mario Onaindia and Juan Maria Bandrés, put forward proposals to the then Minister of the Interior, Juan José Rosón, to negotiate the demilitarisation of ETA-PM. The substance of these negotiations was to discuss the question of militants of this organisation in prison or exile. The fruit of these talks, which continued throughout 1981, was the self-dissolution of ETA-PM on 30 September of that year. This was followed in the first months of 1982 by the launching of the government's policy of 'Social Reinsertion', which would permit the release from prison and return from exile of those members of the organisation willing to renounce the armed struggle. By the time of the third democratic elections, in October 1982, 250 members of ETA-PM had been 'reinserted' upon condition that they continue their campaign within the legitimate channels of Basque/Spanish democratic institutions.[35] The Socialist government which was swept to power in 1982 has continued with this policy of reinsertion and, especially since the agreements with the French government, has attempted to extend it to embrace the major existing branch of ETA—the 'milis'.

The present government's policy of reinsertion is, however, fundamentally different from that of its predecessor in key respects. Primarily it is an initiative of the Spanish authorities which does not have the official support of the terrorist organisation itself. It also lacks the endorsement of a political intermediary which has organic links with the terrorists, as was the case with EE in the negotiations of 1981-82. Whilst the PNV have played a pivotal role in the Basque country, *Herri Batasuna* (HB)—one of whose members was elected to the European Parliament in June 1987—have rejected the initiative. Furthermore, and partly as a consequence of the above factors, the Socialist administration considers 'Social Reinsertion' as a policy to be aimed at individual members of ETA-M rather than at the organisation *per se*. This concept of reinsertion is not therefore intended to lead to the dissolution of ETA-M, as was the case in 1981-82 with the 'polis'; rather it is viewed as a means of isolating the organisation.

The reintegration of individual militants is aimed at reducing

ETA-M to a rump, or 'hard core' element, and at denying them a wider support network. Correspondingly, the main emphasis has been on the reinsertion of members of the exile community in France. Ministry of the Interior figures put the number of ETA exiles living across the border at around 800. An estimate of those that have been directly involved in terrorist actions is less than 200. The vast majority do not have a history of 'front-line' activity and have generally been involved in back-up and support activities. It is to this latter group that the government's offer of reinsertion is specifically geared. The reintegration of a significant number of these exiles, it is argued, would isolate the 'hard core', leaving them without moral and material support, and more vulnerable to French police actions.[36] This policy of individual reinsertion has had a certain amount of success. About 120 *etarras* (not all 'milis') have accepted the road of reinsertion in the three and a half years of the Socialist government's first term of office.[37] Whilst this is only half the number of reinsertions that took place during the 1982 initiative, the supporters of individual reinsertion claim that this merely reflects the increased difficulties in dealing with the more militant members of ETA-M. Critics of such 'individual reinsertion' include PNV members who have played an important part in the return of many *etarras* to the Basque country. Joseba Azcárra, PNV member of the Spanish Parliament, renowned as 'The Senator of Reinsertion', has repeatedly argued that only by negotiating the question of exiles and prisoners at an organised level will a lasting solution of the problem be found. He has suggested that it is imperative 'to negotiate directly with ETA'.[38]

A NEGOTIATED SOLUTION?

The question of participating in negotiations with ETA has been a contentious one since the advent of democracy. The problems relating to, and the disagreements over, such discussions were dramatically highlighted by the events of 25 April 1986.

On this date, delegations of the PNV and HB held an initial meeting to discuss the violence in the Basque country and the measures necessary to eradicate it. At 7.15 a.m., three hours before the start of these talks, five *Guardia Civile* were killed by an ETA-M car bomb in Madrid. Despite this blatantly provocative move by the 'milis' the PNV insisted on the necessity of continuing with the meeting. *Herri Batasuna,* whilst refusing to condemn the terrorist act, also stressed that it should not impede the proposed talks. The socialists on the other hand, in their communiqués regarding the terrorist bombing, were adamant that the terrorist action served to show that 'In a democracy no type of political negotiation is possible with the terrorists'.[39]

As pointed out in the previous section, negotiations played a vital role in the early 1980s when the policy of reinsertion was initiated, and accelerated the demilitarisation of the 'polis'. Such success was as dependent on the particular strategic aims and the organisational structure of ETA-PM, as it was on the willingness of the authorities to seek a negotiated solution. Since 1976, the 'polis' had advocated an eventual abandonment of arms. Coupled with this, the primacy of the political wing of the movement was more conducive to a negotiated settlement. This is not the case with ETA-M, and the question of such a dialogue with the 'milis' is qualitatively different. Recent developments might, however, suggest that perhaps the 'threshold of dialogue' has not yet been reached.

The 'milis' have repeatedly claimed that they are predisposed to a negotiated pacification of the Basque country. The basis which they have traditionally put forward for such talks, and the conditions for abandoning the armed struggle, has been the KAS alternative (*Koordinadora Abertzale Socialista*).[40] The five basic points of this nationalist-socialist programme (although the 'socialist' element is restricted to one demand—point 4) are:

(1) A general amnesty for all ETA prisoners and the return

of those living in exile;

(2) Unconditional legalisation of all separatist political parties;

(3) Removal of all Spanish security forces from the Basque country;

(4) An improvement in the living and working conditions of the Basque working class;

(5) An authentic autonomy statute which is to include the incorporation of Navarra in the Basque country.[41]

Even if the central government were willing to negotiate on this basis, and it is unlikely that they are, ETA-M's adherence to its thesis of *continuismo* has ensured that such a settlement is impracticable. Whilst the failed coup attempt of February 1981 might have buried the 'Spiral of Conflict' theory, it did not serve to fundamentally alter the 'milis' position *vis-à-vis* the nature of the Spanish state. It has not been with the democratically elected government that ETA-M have repeatedly sought to negotiate but with the *poderes fácticos*. In April of 1986, virtually coinciding with the opening of the talks between the PNV and HB, in a rare interview of ETA-M leaders it was reiterated that 'it is the military and oligarchy that wield the real power in the Spanish State. It is they who have the responsibility of taking the definite decision of sitting with us at the negotiating table'.[42] On this basis, it is clear that ETA-M are in fact in agreement with the Spanish Socialists (although for entirely different reasons) that no 'political solution' is possible.

Since the close of 1984, however, there has been growing speculation, and a certain amount of evidence, that cracks are beginning to appear in the traditional negotiating posture of ETA-M. Divisions are said to exist within the organisation over the need to seek a compromise formula. These divisions are believed to be between a *línea dura* (hard line) which adheres militantly to the traditional negotiating conditions, and a *línea blanda* (soft line) which is willing to be more flexible.[43] This latter wing is thought to have the influential support of ETA-M's number one—Domingo Iturbe Abasolo (Txomin). It was reported that in a meeting with PNV members, in October 1985, Txomin had not insisted upon the presence of the *poderes fácticos* at the negotiating table, and indicated that it might be possible to open a dialogue with 'their representative'—the Spanish government.[44]

This move toward a more flexible position is not necessarily due to a change in perceptions of the nature of the Spanish state. More likely, it is a consequence of a realistic assessment of the increasingly isolated and vulnerable position of ETA-M. The disarticulation of key ETA-M commando units, the limited success of reinsertion, and the cooperation between the Spanish and French authorities have undoubtedly been key determinants in placing the 'milis' on the defensive. Apart from these elements of the government's anti-terrorist campaign, two other factors may also explain this flexibility. Primarily, there has been a marked decline in the level of support for, or tolerance of, ETA terrorism in the Basque country itself. During the years of the dictatorship, ETA's armed struggle was considered a just, if ineffective, method of replying to state violence in kind. In the uncertain years of the transition, ETA's military campaign was considered by many as a means of ensuring that Basque national demands would be treated as a fundamental priority of a future democratic regime. With the consolidation of democracy and the granting of Basque autonomy in 1979 (limited as this is in the judgement of many Basques) the justification for continuing a campaign of violence no longer existed. It was not until 1981, however, that popular condemnation of ETA (or at least the willingness to express such) increased dramatically. At the beginning of this year, a mere 24 per cent of the Basque population openly rejected ETA. By November of 1983 this figure had increased to 64 per cent. Twenty-five per cent of those polled in 1983 refused to give their opinion.[45]

The second additional factor that has possibly precipitated internal divisions in ETA-M, has been the growth in recent years of right-wing, anti-separatist terrorism of which the 'milis' have been the principal targets. Anti-separatist terrorism has a history almost as long as ETA itself and has continued up to the present day in the guise of the *Grupos Anti-Terroristas de Liberación,* (GAL).[46] The GAL first emerged in December 1983 and have since been responsible for more than twenty assassinations. Apart from the actual physical elimination of ETA militants, the fact that GAL operations have concentrated on the exile community has increased the determination of the French government to remove *etarras* (now both perpetrators and targets of violence) from French soil. Whilst the question of links between GAL and the Spanish state security forces is a highly contentious issue, there can be no doubt that its activities, indirectly at least, have aided the overall anti-ETA terrorist strategy of the government.[47]

It is too early to state categorically the extent of internal divisions within the ranks of ETA-M. It is imperative, however, that political decisions taken to combat ETA terrorism be based on an accurate assessment of the contemporary internal situation of the organisation. If such divisions do not exist to any significant degree, it may well be that the central government's position that no negotiation is possible is valid. If, on the other hand, the speculation regarding divergences within ETA-M is proved to have substance, the authorities must surely take advantage of the situation. If, as the government seems to accept, the total elimination of ETA-M is too optimistic a goal in the short or medium term, and if the limited goal of isolating a 'hard core' has been set, then negotiations with the *línea blanda* could be the key to achieving this.[48] The possibilities of dialogue should be taken to the ultimate threshold, and 'negotiations never ruled out as a political alternative'.[49]

CONCLUSION

The contemporary problem of ETA terrorism is rooted in the recent history of the Spanish state. More particularly, it is a legacy of forty years of authoritarian-centralist negation of Basque cultural and political aspirations. The continuation of ETA-M terrorism under the present democratic regime is, however, a consequence of the distorted and erroneous perceptions of socio-political reality held by the terrorists themselves. Perceptions which, unlike the vast majority of the Spanish/Basque population, fail to recognise the obvious *ruptura* that has taken place since 1975.

ETA terrorist activity contributed to producing the gravest crisis of the fledgling Spanish democracy in February 1981. The failure of the attempted coup was not only a landmark in the short history of the young democracy but it also marked the turning point in the fortunes of the terrorist movement. Since this date, as a consequence of internal developments within the organisation, a decline in social support and the relative efficacy of the Spanish authorities' anti-terrorist strategy, ETA-M has been increasingly isolated and marginalised.

Although its total eradication is unlikely, the prospects for a significant reduction in ETA-M terrorism are good. Bold political decisions over negotiating could help to deepen the process of isolating the hard-core terrorists. The initiative for such a negotiated solution will however have to emanate from within the terrorist organisation itself. Whether such an initiative will in fact be undertaken, by at least a section of ETA-M, only the future will elucidate.

NOTES

1. Basque Nation and Liberty.
2. *Informe de La Comision Internacional Sobre La Violencia En El Pais Vasco,* London, 5 March 1986. Reproduced in *Euzkadi,* 237, 10 April 1986, p. 39.
3. For example the Catalan separatist-terrorist group *Terra Lluire* (Free Land). Highly imitative of ETA its operations chiefly consist of amateurish small scale bombings.
4. For a concise and insightful outline of Basque and Catalan nationalism see K. Medhurst, *The Basques and Catalans,* London: Minority Rights Group, 1982.
5. *Ibid.,* p. 3.
6. *Ibid.*
7. J.M. Maraval, *Dictatorship and Political Dissent: Workers and Students in Franco's Spain,* London: Tavistock, p. 11.
8. Partido Nacional Vasco.

9. J.M. Garmendia, *Historian de Eta Vol. 2.*, San Sebastian: E. Itxaropena, 1980, p. 304.
10. For the official ETA version of this assassination see J. Agire, *Operación Ogro, Como y Porqué Ejecutamos a* Hendaye: Carrerro Blanco, 1974.
11. On this 'over-reaction' see G. Hills, 'ETA and Basque Nationalism', *Iberian Studies*, Vol. 1, No. 2, (1972) pp. 87-8.
12. This was particularly the case during the Burgos trial of 1970. This trial gave ETA both national and world-wide publicity.
13. Not all of these assassinations are attributable to ETA.
14. Quoted in Lo Rincón, *ETA: 1974-1984*, Barcelona: Plaza y Janes, 1985, p. 32.
15. P. Janke, *Spanish Separatism: ETA's Threat to Basque Democracy*, Conflict Studies No. 23, London: The Institute for the Study of Conflict, 1980, pp. 4-7.
16. For a detailed discussion of Pertur's ideas and the development of ETA-PM see A. Amigo, *Pertur, ETA 1971-76*, Itxaropena San Sebastian: 1978.
17. Although Pertur himself had been murdered a month earlier, presumably by opponents within the organisation.
18. The Basque Revolutionary Party and Basque Left respectively.
19. People's Socialist Revolutionary Party and United People respectively.
20. Interview with 'Tele express' in October 1977. Quoted in Rincón, *op. cit., p. 143.*
21. Autonomous Anti-Capitalist Commandos. A splinter group of ETA formed in 1975. Despite its title this group has frequently targeted left-wing parties and trade unionists.
22. In the referendum of December 1977 the Constitution was accepted by 87.87%, on a 67% turnout, at the level of the Spanish state. In the Basque country the PNV called for abstention and the Left Nationalists for a 'No' vote. Taken together these in fact amounted to a slight majority in Euzkadi.
23. See interview with present Minister of the Interior, José Barrionuevo in *Cambio 16*, 739, Madrid (27 Jan. 1986), p. 30.
24. Since 1968 there have been 625 violent deaths related to terrorism in the Basque country.
25. On the anti-terrorist law and its application in Spain see *España, La Cuestion de la Tortura: Documentos Intercambiados entre Amnistía Internacional y el Gobierno de España*, London: Amnesty International, 1985.
26. *Ibid.*, p. 10-11.
27. *Mundo Obrero*, Madrid (23 Jan. 1986), p. 9.
28. *Ibid.*, p. 9.
29. *El País*, Madrid (13 Jan. 1985).
30. *Cambio 16*, 756 (26 May 1986), p. 38-41.

31. *Euzkadi,* 237 (10 April 1986), p. 40.
32. *Ibid.*
33. *El Pais* (14 March 1986).
34. *Cambio 16,* 727 (4 November 1985), p. 24.
35. *Ibid.,* p. 24.
36. *Ibid.,* p. 26.
37. From Dec. 1982 to June 1986.
38. *Cambio 16,* (4 November 1985), p. 23.
39. For the reactions of the different parties to both this terrorist bombing and the talks between PNV and HB see *El Pais,* 26 April 1986.
40. Nationalist Socialist Coordinator.
41. These five demands reveal the overwhelmingly nationalist rather than socialist, motivation of ETA-M.
42. This interview was transmitted by Radio Popular de Milan. The text was reproduced in *Cambio 16,* 754, (12 May 1986), p. 75.
43. One interesting point to highlight is that these differences do not appear to follow the traditional ideologist/soft-line versus nationalist/hard-line divisions. Txomin, believed adherent to the *Línea Blanda,* is not reknowned for his commitment to Marxism-Leninism but rather to a militant nationalism. One of the staunchest defenders of the *línea dura* on the other hand is Eugenio Etxabaste Arizkuren (Antxon) who is also an ardent proponent of reinforcing the Marxist-Leninist commitment of ETA-M.
44. *Cambio 16,* (12 Dec. 1985), p. 38.
45. *El Pais,* 14 Jan. 1984. This should however be placed in proper perspective. In the autonomous elections of 1984, for example, HB obtained 16.5% of the votes cast, and thus remains the second most important party in the Basque country. Even when the abstention rate of 31.55% is taken into account one in ten of the Basque adult population still supports the political party closely associated with ETA-M. Whilst it would be mistaken to consider that this reflects the level of support for ETA-M's terrorist activities it is still too significant a figure to be ignored.
46. Anti-terrorist Liberation Groups.
47. This has been explicitly acknowledged by senior officials of the Ministry of the Interior, directly involved in the Government's anti-ETA terrorist campaign. See *Cambio 16,* 739 (27 Jan. 1986), p. 28.
48. Since writing this chapter the ETA-M leader, and presumed adherent to the *línea blanda,* Txomin, was detained by the French police and deported to Gabon on 13 July 1986. Txomin was killed in a car crash on 3 March 1987. It appears that the void left in the ETA-M command structure has been filled by one of the *línea dura,* Francisco Múgica Garmondia (his pseudonym is Artapolo). This will be an added obstacle to a negotiated solution as Artapolo has been a consistent critic of the policy of reinsertion.
49. *Euzkadi,* 237 (10 April 1983), p. 42.

6 Politically-Motivated Violent Activists in the Netherlands in the 1980s*

Alex P. Schmid

INTRODUCTION

There is at present no domestic terrorism in the Netherlands, and international terrorism has also largely by-passed Holland. Together with the Danes, the Dutch are in an exceptional position both within the EEC and within NATO. Nevertheless, the non-terrorism of the Netherlands deserves analysis as it might throw some light on the causes of terrorism elsewhere in Western Europe.

What is labelled 'terrorism' is a matter of definition. Many direct actions of political activists which take place in the Netherlands would qualify as 'terrorist' in a country like South Africa; some would also qualify as such in the neighbouring German Federal Republic. The Dutch authorities go to great lengths not to label politically-motivated violent activists 'terrorists' out of a (probably correct) apprehension that it could become a self-fulfilling prophecy. The media, by and large, follow the language used by the authorities in this area. Terrorism, therefore, is generally considered something foreign and the attitude of 'it cannot happen here' is widespread in the Netherlands. The South Moluccan incidents

* The data for this article was collected by Remko van den Dool whose assistance is gratefully acknowledged.

of the mid-1970s are widely regarded as regretful actions of desperate young people emulating foreign examples set by the Black Power Movement and the Palestinian Liberation Organisation. There had never been an organised underground terrorist *movement* among young South Moluccans, and their violent actions in 1970, 1975, 1977 and 1978 lacked the ingredients of a campaign that are necessary to create chronic fear of sudden victimisation (terror) among specific target groups. Some attempts to form cells and engage in political violence were made in the early 1970s by white activists under the name Red Youth, Red Help and Red Resistance Front but were discovered and defused before major damage was done to human beings.

At the same time the extra-parliamentary political landscape in the Netherlands became very rich and variegated. A Dutch handbook on action and work groups associations and other organisations active in the field of war and peace, politics and education, health care, emancipation, energy, environment, housing, working and traffic presently requires no less than five volumes to cover its subject-matter.[1] Most activists belong to perfectly legal lobby, pressure and action groups using conventional methods of political participation and contest. Their methods include information campaigns to persuade non-participants to engage politically for one or another (social) class or no-class issue; attempts to convince political opponents of the justice of the activists' cause; demonstrations in order to show to decision makers and opponents the size of their following; and litigation whereby juridical procedures are used to influence opponents, usually the government. A few groups within larger movements go further than these conventional extra-parliamentary activities: they take recourse either to methods of civil disobedience or to methods of contest.

The first type of these 'unconventional activities' is generally non-violent, even if at times illegal. In fact, the violation of laws is often part of the act in that laws considered 'unjust' are deliberately and without secrecy transgressed. Yet the punishment of the legal apparatus is accepted in order to draw attention to the rightfulness of a cause. Non-violent acts are at times even harmful in cases where non-cooperation creates victims by acts of omission. Nevertheless this type of unconventional activity is quite different from the second. Contest methods involve acts of commission which are deliberately damaging to an opponent. Its adherents—contrary to non-violent activists who recognise the basic legitimacy of the law of the state—refuse to accept the sanctions imposed by the law for illegal activities. Where contest techniques involve the intentional use of violence as part of the overall strategy, we are dealing with extreme groups. Such groups are generally situated on the fringe of larger social movements with similar goals but dissimilar methods of achieving these. While social movements might be radical with regard to their goals, the radicalism of means is a major mark of distinction between extremist radicals and other political radicals. This is not the only relevant distinction. Van der Loo uses altogether four for distinguishing mainstream from fringe groups. He considers whether or not a group

(1) makes an attempt to influence the government or ignores the government;
(2) principally refuses 'hard action' or accepts it as a method;
(3) adheres to principles of organisations accepted in our society, or rejects them;
(4) takes into account public opinion or ignores it, by and large.[2]

If in extrapolation of these four categories a terrorist movement in a democratic country is defined as one which rejects the authority of the government, accepts intimidating exemplary violent actions as a method, maintains a clandestine cell structure and largely ignores the disapproval of public opinion, then no such group or movement is at present active in the Netherlands. However, there are a number of groups that fulfil at least one of these four criteria and the possibility exists that at some point in time all four will be met.

The Dutch authorities use the term 'politically-motivated

violent activist' to describe the more extreme contestants among the political activists. When asked where they draw the line between a 'terrorist' and a 'politically-motivated violent activist' they point out that definitions of terrorism vary and that therefore no clear borderline can be drawn.

In the following pages an attempt will be made to portray the various violent activists now at work in the Netherlands on the fringe of larger movements. The basis for this account is a newspaper archive for the period 1980-86. Before discussing the groups and incidents, however, a few words on the Dutch political landscape are necessary.

BACKGROUND

Political life in the Netherlands has been characterised by an absence of major domestic political turmoil. There was some minor unrest in 1919 which was, however, completely in line with the rest of war-torn Europe. For the period 1948-77, the Netherlands consistently scores low on indicators of political protest as analysed by the authors of the *World Handbook of Political and Social Indicators* (see Table 6.1)

Part of the explanation for this domestic tranquility has to be sought in the 'pillarisation' which characterised Dutch society until the 1960s. This term refers to a neo-corporatist segmentation of society into four political cultures organised around Catholicism, Calvinism, liberalism and socialism respectively. The masses were guided by elites in churches, trade unions, business associations, media, education and other fields. Since the mid-1960s this political system has been diluted without, however, losing all its power to co-opt new challengers of the political life. It was only after 1979 that the limits of government support for new political demands became clearly visible, as the post-war economic boom came to a halt. After the Second World War, Dutch society had been rebuilding its economy and enjoying the fruits of increasing prosperity. In the war the communist party had played a significant role in the resistance against the German

Table 6.1: Political Protest in West Europe, 1948-77

	France	Denmark	United Kingdom	West Germany	Belgium	Nether-lands	Italy	Greece	Spain	Portugal
Protest demonstrations	378	38	691	300	76	19	230	158	358	246
Regime support demonstrations	94	3	34	84	9	3	44	28	42	43
Political strikes	154	4	142	22	51	1	173	21	173	35
Riots	207	7	372	143	60	9	444	127	265	187
Armed attacks	827	6	3931	157	42	28	544	670	313	117
Assassinations	4	0	50	4	1	0	6	2	7	1
Death from political violence	164	14	1463	61	81	13	259	9341	216	66

Source: Charles Lewis Taylor and David A. Jodice, *World Handbook of Political and Social Indicators*, 3rd edn. Vol. 2: *Political Protest and Government Changes*, New Haven: Yale University Press, 1983, pp. 24-51.

occupation and communists were, despite Stalinist traits, socially accepted and, until 1986, represented in Parliament, though with constantly declining support. On the political right there was a small 'Poujadist-like' farmers' party which showed some fascist traits. In 1982 the xenophobic Centre Party (CP) won one seat in Parliament, which they lost in 1986. On the right there were a few small fundamentalist Christian parties (GPV, SGP, RPF) and on the left a radical (PPR) and a pacifist (PSP) party who functioned as parliamentary voices of extra-parliamentary action groups. In 1986 these suffered a loss of seats in Parliament without, however, being completely wiped out as the communists were. The political centre was occupied by the main Catholic and Calvinist parties which fused into one in the 1970s, the 'Christian Democratic Appeal' (CDA). On the right, there were the Liberals (VVD) whose parliamentary strength never reached the size of the CDA. Left of centre are the Social Democrats (PvdA) who are at present almost as strong in Parliament as the Christian Democrats. In the period 1973-77 they headed a coalition government together with Christian Democrats but since then the CDA has, except for a short period in the early 1980s, governed with the Liberals. That too, is the prospect for the remainder of the 1980s. The Christian Democrats in the Netherlands are not comparable with those in, say, West Germany or Italy. They are more centrist and reformist and certainly less corrupt than Christian Democrats in some other West European countries. The position of the monarchy is secure, and without being particularly nationalistic the vast majority of the population shows appreciation for the queen. The Netherlands has been, since 1949, a faithful member of NATO, and popular support for NATO membership has rarely sunk below the 70 per cent level. The government's conditional decision to station forty-eight cruise missiles in the Netherlands, taken in 1979, and ratified in 1986, has been accompanied by an acrimonious public debate and lively extra-parliamentary actions, culminating in two mass demonstrations in 1981 and 1983. While the population was about equally divided between supporters and opponents of the introduction for a time, the

May 1986 general election showed that the issue was not considered of such paramount interest that it significantly reduced the votes of the Christian Democrats and the Liberals. In the period under consideration there was also a lively public debate about the future of civil nuclear energy. The parties on the left favoured the closure of the two existing nuclear power plants while the ruling coalition pleaded for the building of two more nuclear power plants. The Chernobyl incident, which took place shortly before the May 1986 election, caused them to have second thoughts, and for the time being the CDA-VVD coalition postponed a definitive stand on the issue. The economic performance of the Netherlands since the late 1970s has been below the average of the OECD countries, especially with regard to unemployment which soared to 17.2 per cent in 1984, without counting the unregistered unemployed. The export of natural gas, and a generally satisfactory export performance in other sectors, have, however, assured the continuation of a substantial level of economic performance. This, together with borrowings of the public sector, allowed the maintenance of a relatively generous and comprehensive social security system providing income to nearly 3.5 million people (1984) who were not gainfully employed.[3]

In 1986 the system was substantially changed, after a series of smaller cuts in the preceding years. However, it is not likely that the unemployed and dependent on social security will combine and turn to major violent action, despite the fact that many of them are in the 19-24 age cohort, an age group which also provides a sizeable proportion of terrorists in other countries.[4] The declining standard of living of hundreds of thousands of people and the lack of perspective for the future have not so far led to the rising of a 'new' proletariat of unemployed workers. Deprivation theory or Marxist theory cannot explain the 'puzzle' of the absence of a strong social movement of unemployed. Koebben and Godschalk have suggested six partial explanations to account for this absence:

1. the fact that many, though they are part of the unemployed, do not feel 'unemployed';

2. the heterogenity of the group of those entitled to social security benefits;
3. a still 'too' favourable position for part of the unemployed; and
4. at the other end, an already 'too' unfavourable situation. Then,
5. the existence of unemployed who strive not for collective but for individual action; and
6. the existence of unemployed who direct their collective actions not to the fight against unemployment but to other political goals.[5]

The last explanation is of particular interest here. A number of politically-motivated violent activists in the anti-nuclear energy and the squatter movements are without employment and use unemployment as an argument for legitimising their behaviour.[6] Xenophobic and racist parties and groups use immigrant workers as scapegoats, blaming them for stealing Dutch jobs.[7]

The use of violence by political activists in the Netherlands against government or sections of the society, is, as Table 6.1 indicated, comparatively infrequent. One reason for this seems to be that the government is not itself involved in illegal activities which would call for acts of legitimate popular resistance. Nor is the Dutch government responsive to grievances from sectors of the public. On the contrary, co-option of dissent is a hallmark of the Dutch political culture. As one Dutch political scientist put it: 'Before you pass the threshold of violence here, an action group has already obtained a government subsidy'.[8] The media, too, offer a freedom of expression and a degree of access to all sectors of the public which is not easily matched elsewhere in the world. It might be that this great freedom of verbal expression, which allows the statement of extreme positions, has so far limited the need for 'expressive' violence.

Governmental tolerance of political dissent and media access for dissenting voices appear to have played a part in preventing the survival of the kind of terrorism that emerged from the extreme fringe of the student movements of the late

1960s. The Dutch members of Red Youth (a name taken from a paper issued by dissidents of the pro-China Dutch Communist Party, NKP, which split off from the Communist Party of the Netherlands, CPN) who were inspired by Marighela's 'Minimanual of the Urban Guerrilla' did not get further than a few smoke and firebomb attacks in 1972 against a Holiday Inn and Philips establishments in Eindhoven and Rotterdam. After the arrest of two members Red Youth dissolved itself in 1973. Friends agitating for the release of the detained organised themselves as Red Help groups. Ten members of Red Help received training from the PLO in South Yemen for a period of three weeks in July 1976, for which they had to 'pay' by taking part in a terrorist attack in Israel. However, after the premature arrest of two members in Israel, the end of Red Help came in December 1976. Its successor, the Red Resistance Front (*Rode Verzetfront*: RVF) was established soon thereafter. Significantly enough it was organised as support for the German RAF (Red Army Faction) rather than for a Dutch cause.[9] While supporting foreign terrorists, the Red Resistance Front did not itself become a terrorist group.

Although there has not been a terrorist movement in the Netherlands so far, there are a number of social movements whose fringes are no strangers to political violence. In the following pages half a dozen of the more important ones are described briefly.

POLITICALLY-MOTIVATED VIOLENT ACTIVISTS IN 'NEW' SOCIAL MOVEMENTS

In the last two decades a number of basically single-issue social movements have emerged which generally see themselves as small prophetic minorities, trendsetters for the future, espousing various, mainly non-class issues. They have rallied around the themes of

1. Environment and energy
2. Squatting
3. Racism and anti-fascism

4. Third World solidarity
5. Anti-militarism

Although there is considerable overlap among the followers of these movements we shall discuss them separately here. Subsequently we shall also look at the few incidents of 'international terrorism' in the Netherlands in the 1980s.

1. Environment and energy

The environment movement came into existence in the mid-1960s with the Association for the Protection of the Waddensea and the action group *Oosterschelde*. Their actions in defence of waters and forests, against highway constructions, coastal and industrial developments and in support of urban conservation took the form of occupations and blockades. Many of the ideas generated by them met a favourable response from the political parties.[10] While confrontations with massive police forces took place, little violence was used by activists. One wing of the environmental movement, the anti-nuclear movement (*Anti-kernenergiebeweging*: AKB), which came into existence in the early 1970s, radicalised after a shocking experience of governmental display of force at the Kalkar nuclear power plant under construction across the German border.[11] Subsequent violent actions, however, never reached the same level as in France or Germany. One reason for this was that the government postponed a decision to build more plants in 1979, while soon thereafter initiating a 'Broad social debate' on the issue of nuclear energy, where opponents could voice their protest. A majority of the Dutch population was sceptical about the further use of nuclear energy, a scepticism which the government, however, chose to dismiss at least until the Chernobyl incident in May 1986. The violent actions emanating from extremist elements of the anti-nuclear energy movement included a case of arson, destroying trucks of a company in Beverwijk which was transporting nuclear waste.[12] There have been several instances of attempted sabotage against electric companies using nuclear-generated energy.

Such acts involved the short-circuiting or interruption of electric power lines. One such sabotage action in the night of 9-10 October 1981 near Oude Sluis was claimed by the Resistance Front Tim Turnip and Little Bulbs (*Verzetfront Willy Wortel en de lampjes*[13]). The group using this name later even produced a 'How-to-do-it' manual and a video-instruction movie to teach other activists how to interrupt electric high-voltage power lines. In another action members of a group calling themselves 'The revenge of Esq. mr. de Brauw'—a reference to the deceased chairman of the steering group of the 'Broad social debate' on nuclear energy whose conclusions the government had chosen to ignore—broke into the Ministry of Economic Affairs and 'liberated' a number of documents on the government's plans to construct two more power plants. At that point the impetus of the AKB was already declining and in order not to lose further ground the AKB tried to expand into another field, anti-militarism, the link being the use of plutonium generated in the Netherlands for the construction of French atomic weapons. As one of the driving forces behind the AKB, Hans de Jonge, put it:

Of course it was opportunistic from our part to turn our attention to anti-militarism. The peace movement had the publicity and the goodwill which we were lacking. Yet in addition the peace movement could certainly use a radicalization.[14]

In the meantime, the peace movement has been declining again and since the Chernobyl nuclear accident environmental questions have regained both publicity and goodwill. After a publicity campaign Greenpeace doubled the number of its supporters to 140,000, the Association for Environmental Defence (*Vereniging Milieudefensie*) increased its membership to 15,000, while other movements in this field such as the Association for the Protection of the Waddensea (31,500 members), World Nature Fund (*Wereld Natuur Fonds*: 116,000 supporters) and the Foundation Nature and Environment (*Natuur en Milieu*) slightly increased or at least held their present membership. On the fringe of such social movements there will always be some frustrated groups who feel that not enough is achieved soon enough. The temptation to resort to violent action is at present small, but could increase if the Dutch government decides on building two more nuclear power plants in the future. As the members of a group calling themselves the *Kema Keur Korps* put it in a declaration accompanying the occupation of a power grid switching station in North Holland in early 1986: 'This was still a nonviolent, friendly action. Yet the further the cabinet goes, the harder the actions will be'.[15]

One can also view the Animal Liberation Front (*Dierenbevrijdingsfront*) as part of the environment group. It argues that the Foundation for Anti-vivisection has already been active for eighty years without having achieved its goal. In 1983 one group 'Stop experiments with animals' (*Stop dierenprooven*) placed a powerful bomb in a laboratory of the Notox company in Den Bosch which could have hurt people if it had detonated.[16] During the Christmas period of 1983 the Animal Liberation Front threatened to inject strychnine into turkey, rabbit and chicken at supermarkets in seven Dutch towns.[17] The attention of the media is important to these activists. As one of them put it: 'The press stimulates us to conduct harder actions. When you do not obtain publicity with the liberation of three animals, you take twenty next time. When you get no publicity with the liberation of cats then you go on to bombings'.[18]

2. The squatters' movement

The squatters' movement emerged in the second half of the 1960s as a self-help organisation. The goals of the squatters widened as time went by. While cheap and good housing for young people was the original goal, it broadened to a demand for a new society, based on small-scale units, participatory democracy and increased attention for feminist values. Redress of grievances was no longer sought from the government (which in reaction to the grievances of the squatters had passed legislation enabling the confiscation of empty houses). In the eyes of many squatters the government was, from about 1978 onwards, seen as an instrument of the house owners, project developers and speculators. In their information bulletin *Bluf!*, the squatters of Amsterdam devote attention not only to squatting but also to anti-militarism, women's struggle, counter-culture, anti-fascism, drug addiction, Central America, repression by the legal and police apparatus, work and unemployment, racism in Southern Africa, anti-nuclear energy, communal living, the Berlin scene and the struggle for peace.[19] The political orientation of the squatters is generally to the left; anarchists and radical Christian and Social Democrats are also among them.[20] It is a conglomerate of individuals and protest- and pressure groups[21] without uniform and fully-developed ideology. In the first thirteen years of its existence, the squatters did not violently resist the execution of judicial orders to evacuate buildings occupied by them. In 1980, however, when a new queen was crowned, the ceremony was disturbed by street fighting and rioting in Amsterdam. With the slogan 'Geen woning—geen kroning' (No coronation without accommodation) 'Autonomists' announced a 'squatters' day' on 30 April 1980, in Amsterdam which ended in a violent confrontation with the mobile units (*Mobiele Eenheden*) of the police. The next two years were particularly violent as squatters threatened by evacuation orders turned their dwellings into barricaded forts and defended these with great ferocity. As one squatter put it in 1982:

In the yet rather short history of the squatters' movement it appeared that actual resistance, whereby police violence is not passively accepted but rather answered with violence, can be an effective means. In this context one has to refer primarily to the preventive effect which a violent conflict has for the future. In fact it is rather the threat of violent outbursts which protects an occupied flat from evacuation than the confrontation itself which . . . in a military sense is lost by definition. However, by seeking a confrontation each time, the government is forced to pay a high price each time that 'the law' has to take its course. Not only in a material sense, in the form of high costs in manhours, damage to material and persons, etc. but also morally, in terms of legitimacy. It is no sign of good government when tanks are required to keep the population under control. The threat of a loss of face, high costs, etc. connected to the evacuation of a flat, must remain credible. Therefore resistance is required each time.[22]

In the words of the squatters this represented 'the action course of maximum pressure or of maximum threat'.[23] However, in response, the police developed new penetration and arrest techniques which made more than symbolic resistance increasingly ineffective.[24] The violence of the squatters has been basically reactive and was not a result of the ideology of the squatters' movement; it was not seen as an instrument to change society. Its legitimacy was claimed on the basis of the offensive actions of the police force.[25]

However, not all has been defence. In July 1982 'Autonomists' in Amsterdam exploded a small bomb at the party office door of the Social Democratic Party, protesting against 'the lunatic policy of this party in the area of housing' and in connection with the 'Lucky Luyk' housing complex, which was marked for evacuation.[26] Autonomists' with the acronym MAF (standing alternatively for Militant or Military Autonomist Front) firebombed an underground station under construction in January 1983, protesting against the increase in fares which had been announced.[27] Another small bomb for which MAF claimed responsibility damaged the entrance of the city's housing office. In February 1983 MAF claimed responsibility for a bomb attack on the French consulate in Amsterdam, in protest against 'the continuing arms race in which the left and so-called independent French government participates'.[28] When Pope John Paul II came to the Netherlands in May 1985 the MAF was one of the three signatories of a pamphlet that promised HFL 15,000 for the 'liquidation' of the pope (the other two being the Northern Terror Front (*Noordelijk terreurfront,* a Groningen-based group of RAF sympathisers) and the *'autonomie operaie paese bassi'*). In February 1984 a 'Day of Unrest' was announced in Amsterdam on the occasion of which squatters, students, anti-fascists, ex-detainees, and others engaged in acts of destruction and street fighting with the police.[29] In the wake of forced evacuations of occupied buildings demonstrators have repeatedly taken to the streets and engaged in acts of destruction, like smashing windows, throwing firebombs at the palace of justice and into bank offices. Camouflaged with bivak caps and armed with iron rods, a number of squatters invaded the offices of four real estate agents, on one occasion destroying property, robbing files and money and beating up one person. Occasionally catapults were used with which marbles were shot at the police.[30] In August 1984 squatters also threw fire and paint bombs at tourist boats in order to protest against 'ignoring the interests of the people of Amsterdam on behalf of the tourist industry'. Tyres of touring buses were knifed and stink bombs thrown into hotel lounges.[31]

Such uses of violence alienated most of the people in Amsterdam. After a period of bloom between 1978 and 1982, the squatters' movement declined and the number of actions was decreasing. However, a hard core of activist squatters in the *Staatsliedenbuurt* in Amsterdam became increasingly violent. They managed to steal documents containing the private addresses of police officers in their neighbourhood and threatened their families by telephone calls. When one squatter died, apparently from an overdose of methadone in combination with a lung infection in a police cell after being arrested during an evacuation, street violence again erupted. In the wake of the death of the 23-year-old Hans Kok under circumstances which have not yet been fully clarified but which might involve acts of neglect of medical and police officers during the night after his arrest on 24 October 1985, a number of offices of the police and the city of Amsterdam became targets of arson and destruction.[32] The mayor of Amsterdam, Ed van Thijn, was labelled 'murderer' by squatters. On 7 November 1985, he escaped a bomb attack on his house. Two gasoline bombs with timing devices were found in the house next to where van Thijn slept. He escaped the threat at 3.30 a.m. after the bombs were discovered in time, following an anonymous tip.[33] Despite the fact that a thorough investigation of the circumstances of Kok's death was initiated by van Thijn, the charges of 'murder' were repeated. Even the Soviet Union became party to the conflict when its representative at the United Nations, Blishenko, cited the Kok affair as an example of human rights violations in the Netherlands. Following this support from an unexpected quarter, friends of Hans Kok and the collective squatting groups from Amsterdam demanded consultation with the Soviet ambassador in the Hague on the establishment of an international forum on human rights violations in the Netherlands.[34] In the meantime *Bluf!,* the newsletter of the squatters, found it appropriate to publish instructions on how to construct firebombs. With one 'martyr' as legitimation, they are likely to remain active in the future.

The housing shortage, the original grievance of the squatters, has become much less pressing through the policies of urban renewal and policy measures initiated in response to actions of the squatters. In a suburb of Amsterdam, hundreds of apartments can find no occupants.[35] The squatters are more and more becoming an anachronism, having lost almost all the sympathy of the population of Amsterdam, even among the 40 per cent of the town's citizens who have to live on a minimum income. As the mayor of the city of Amsterdam, Ed van Thijn, put it: 'With every stone that is thrown they become more isolated'.[36]

3. Extremists on the right and anti-fascists

Until 1971 right-wing extremists had sought a political home in the so-called Farmers' Party (*Boerenpartij*). In the early 1970s they managed to organise themselves on a more autonomous basis and began to contest elections on the platform of xenophobia. The growing number of immigrants from ex-Dutch colonies and Mediterranean nations surpassed the number of half a million Dutch who had emigrated permanently after the Second World War and since 1971 the *Nederlandse Volks-Unie* (Dutch People's Union: NVU) has attempted to capitalise on this. Its core is small; by the mid-1980s it had about 150 members.[37] In 1980 the party split and some three dozen members set up the Centrum Party (CP) which, in 1982, managed to obtain 70,000 votes and thereby one seat in Parliament, losing this again in 1986. On the level of local government, however, its influence still exists, as it does outside Parliament. While until the mid-1970s older men with Nazi sympathies constituted the core of the racist right, a number of more youthful members have since been recruited and organised in groups like the Viking Youth (*Viking Jeugd*), which is said to have about 150 members, divided into cells.[38] (Fearing prosecution the Viking Youth has since dissolved itself officially in the meantime.) Right-wing violence has so far mainly been verbal, consisting of pamphlets inciting to violence, threatening phone calls and letters to members of ethnic minorities and antagonists on the left. Physical violence by skinheads and others has sometimes been attributed to right-wing organisations but concrete proof is difficult to come by. Some examples illustrate the kinds of action of the extreme right. On 12 May 1983 the Tilburg party office of the Pacifist Socialist Party (PSP) was damaged by a bomb after an earlier attempt had failed. Responsibility was claimed by the National Youth Front (*Nationaal Jeugd Front*), a youth organisation of the NVU. In Eindhoven, the PSP offices were also targetted by two bombs. The perpetrator was a 16-year-old member of the Viking Youth who also admitted responsibility for numerous phone calls and threatening letters to politicians, and for bomb announcements by phone.[39] There has been a small number of incidents where people nearly got killed. In January 1983, three young men were arrested in Heerlen on the charge of having thrown a molotov cocktail in the house of a Moroccan family.[40] In October 1983, in Zwolle, a Turkish family became the target of a gunman.[41] On 20 August 1983, a black from the Antilles, Kerwin Duynmeijer, was killed by a 16-year-old white boy in Amsterdam. This was widely interpreted as a racist killing given the fact that the perpetrator had the Viking Youth sign tattooed on his skin and was said to have links with known right-wing party members.[42]

After this incident, which generated considerable commotion, anti-fascist groups became more active. Their goal is to combat the racist and neo-fascist groups on the right. One target of their violent attacks has been the house of the chairman of the extreme-right (Belgian-based) organisation *Voorpost,* B.Y. Wiersma in Bergen op Zoom. A molotov cocktail (which failed to explode) was thrown at his house. In May 1984 a bus carrying members of the Centrum Party was shot at, but no one was hurt.[43] An ideologist of the Centrum

Party, Dr W.J. Bruyn, the author of a text on 'The Netherlands for the Dutch' was chained to a block of concrete in Amsterdam by a group of eight anti-fascists.[44] The most serious incident so far has been the attack on the Cosmopolite hotel in Kedichem on 29 March 1986. About 200 people protested against the gathering of the Centrum Democrats (which had split from the Centrum Party but sought reunification). Two groups claimed responsibility, the Radical anti-Fascists (*radicale anti-fascisten*) and the Activists of 29 March (*actievoerders van 29 maart*). Smoke and firebombs were thrown into the hotel and the eighty people escaped just at the last moment, warned by the only two policemen present. The secretary, J. Janmaat, the member of parliament of the CP, lost a leg after jumping out of a window. The owner of the hotel later died in an accident when clearing up the debris of his hotel. The Activists of 29 March (which with 180 members constituted the bulk of the attackers) claimed that they had 'literally smoked out the fascists of the CP'. They said 'that the hotel Cosmopolite went up in flames was not intended'. 'If anti-fascists are hurt as well, we regret that', they added. The Radical Anti-fascists, on the other hand, wrote 'that the events in Kedichem are susceptible to repetition'. As rationale they said that 'Fascists should never be able to organise themselves. He who allows them to do so is a collaborator'.[45]

4. Third World solidarity: the anti-apartheid activists

The term 'self-appointed champion of a cause' (*zaakwaarnemer*) has been coined by Koebben to refer to 'a person who champions the interests—as he sees them—of a certain group in society, without himself belonging to that group and without being elected or hired by this group—or by its representatives'.[46] In the Netherlands there are a great number of such self-appointed spokesmen not only for domestic causes but also for foreign ones. Among the most active are a number of groups who identify with Third World liberation struggles. Most of these groups are non-violent. However, especially when repression against the championed group abroad increases, some activists are incited to take up more violent methods of protest. Such has been the case with the anti-apartheid movement in the Netherlands. When on 15 June 1986 5,000 people demonstrated against the apartheid regime on the occasion of the tenth anniversary of the Soweto uprising, some 100 activists who were not satisfied with calls for an economic boycott shouted 'action, action'.[47] The kind of action which they had in mind had become increasingly clear in the month before. Groups operating under names like Pyromaniacs against Apartheid, the Steve Biko Kommando, the ANC-Benjamin Moloise-commando, Revolutionary Anti-Racist Action (*Revolutionaire Anti-Racistische Aktie*: RARA), Night Damage have caused millions of Dutch guilders worth of damage in acts of destruction, arson and bombings. The single worst incident was the firebombing, on 17 September 1984, of a Makro supermarket in Duivendrecht, causing more than 20 million Dutch guilders worth of damage. Responsibility for the arsonist attack against a company doing business with South Africa was claimed by the Autonomists and RARA respectively. In a declaration of RARA in which the violent activists promised 'unconditional solidarity with the black revolutionary struggle in South Africa', Western imperialists were blamed for collaborating with the apartheid regime. Since nothing much could be expected from parliamentary action in terms of economic sanctions against South Africa, the accompanying press communiqué stated, capitalism had to be fought in Western Europe as well 'by attacking here—in the imperialist West—all the economic, political, military institutions which make oppression here and elsewhere possible'. The action paper *Bluf!* had published a list of companies doing business in South Africa which had included Makro, thereby offering a target to potential violent activists.[48] One of the activists for South Africa said 'that the confrontation takes place within Dutch society as well'.[49] Earlier actions of anti-apartheid activists included the damaging of a library belonging to the Dutch-South African Association (NZAV) on 19 January 1984; an arsonist attack on the villa of the oil dealer John Deuss in Berg en Dal on 7 January 1985; attacks in March and April 1984 against travel agencies in Mijdrecht and Bentveld, which were accused of encouraging tourism to South Africa. Other targets of damage and destruction by violent activists included the firm of a wine dealer who was importing wine from South Africa, a bank, and two garages selling cars whose producers Volkswagen and Mercedes Benz were said to have business links with South Africa, and Shell, the oil multinational. As one violent activist put it: 'Following the six executions in South Africa, recently, this was a good moment to get at Shell'.[50] In May 1986 a number of Shell pump stations were damaged and one was destroyed by groups calling themselves Night Damage and More Night Damage. In their justification, violent activists said Shell had 900 pumps in South Africa and that army trucks from which people were shot daily in South Africa were running on Shell gasoline. In an interview with the press three violent activists said:

We have no need of legitimation of our activities by half plus one. What a nonsense this is. . . . They said it is undemocratic. What matters for us primarily is the struggle against apartheid. . . . It is unavoidable that the breakdown of apartheid has consequences for our society as well. . . . If Dutch economic groups do not wish to sever links with apartheid, it cannot be prevented that the confrontation is also taking place in Dutch society. With this in mind we approach the confrontation. . . . We are not prepared to accept that more parliament-oriented anti-apartheid organisations decide for us how we should conduct action. The arrogance with which they claim to be the only ones with some strategic insight is contradicted by the countless instances that it is just a combination of information distribution, demonstrations and direct actions which brings about results. . . . We have conducted the actions expressly as part of a broader campaign which takes several forms. . . . It is the result that matters and the means we choose depend on the circumstances. Sabotage is one of the means effective in increasing pressure on Shell.[51]

Increased repression in South Africa is likely to increase the violence of anti-apartheid activists here. In one of their declarations they said: It is our task, as anti-racists to support the black population by means of actions here. Each victim shall be revenged by means of an action against a company supporting apartheid'.[52] How far they will go remains to be seen. One activist held that 'Violence against fascists is permissible'.[53] One action group, the Anonymous, threatened to poison canned fruit products from South Africa, in phone calls to three supermarket chains.[54]

So far the only shooting incident in connection with the struggle in South Africa took place at Hilversum on 31 December 1985, when four bullets were fired on the VARA building. Since VARA radio was collecting money for a radio station for ANC's Radio Freedom it is likely that the perpetrators have to be sought in circles sympathetic to the white minority regime in South Africa.[55]

5. Anti-militarism

The Dutch peace movement of the 1980s has been one of the most impressive in Western Europe. It has, in congruence with its goals, been overwhelmingly peaceful in its attempts to prevent the stationing of more nuclear weapons in the Netherlands. On 29 October 1983, more than half a million people demonstrated in The Hague against the impending stationing of cruise missiles. On that occasion an opinion poll was conducted which showed that 72 per cent of the participants said they were prepared to conduct actions going further than demonstrating if the government proceeded with the stationing of the rockets. During the slightly smaller 21 November 1981 demonstration in Amsterdam, 58 per cent of the more than 300,000 participants expressed their agreement with this. A process of radicalisation was apparently taking place. Women, in particular, were especially motivated: 76 per cent expressed themselves in favour of further action and 56 per cent rejected NATO membership, while the respective percentages for men in 1983 were 68 and 46.3.[56] So far, the peace movement has been peaceful, apart from some material damage. At the prospective base in Woensdrecht where forty-eight cruise missiles will be stationed, 1,034 demonstrations took place between 28 June 1983 and 1 November 1985, during which the fence was damaged 723 times, causing material damage running into millions of Dutch guilders. [57] The most serious incident at Woensdrecht so far was triggered off by anonymous opponents of the peace movement. In June 1986 one building, housing two female demonstrators, was the target of two dozen small-calibre rounds.

Actions by opponents of the introduction of new nuclear weapons have taken various forms. In Amsterdam, for instance, the offices of the Liberal party (VVD) were occupied in protest against the stance taken by this party on the question of cruise missiles.[58] Some of the people behind such actions have become radicalised in their campaigns against cruise missiles in particular and militarism in general. Take this statement:

> That you can prevent a war if you can stop the cruise missiles and the arms race is what Mient Jan [Faber, the secretary of the Interchurch Peace Committee, KV] thinks. Our point of departure is completely different. You cannot prevent war at all, because the war is already taking place. Our illegal situation is comparable to the one of the resistance in the Second World War. Only the form of appearance of this war is slightly different. Yet we are already occupied.[59]

Several groups have reportedly decided that they will continue their anti-militarist struggle underground, operating in closed groups under great secrecy, preparing for harder actions than have hitherto taken place.[60] The prototype for such a group is *Onkruit* (untranslatable, literally *onkruid* is weed, and *kruit* is gunpowder) and in the remainder of this section we shall take a closer look at *Onkruit,* the best-known anti-militarist group. Today, *Onkruit* is actually more like a trademark for certain types of action than the name of one specific action group.

Onkruit was founded in 1974 as a working group of the Association of Conscientious Objectors to Military Service (*Vereniging Dienstweigeraars*: VD). Anarchist in orientation, it opposed the state, capitalism and militarism by legal and illegal means. By the end of the 1970s *Onkruit* had about 100 members in fifteen towns. In the early 1980s national coordination was given up but new support came forth in 1982 when the male anti-militarists were joined by Women Against Militarism (*Vrouwen Tegen Militarisme*). Today there are autonomous groups consisting of squatters, members of the anti-nuclear energy movement and, now a minority, conscientious objectors, in various towns performing actions under the *Onkruit* label in protest against nuclear weapons, the arms race, NATO and the Dutch armed forces.[61] Their goals include solidarity and material support for revolutionary left-wing movements in the Third World, feminism, anti-fascism and opposition to hierarchical structures in general.[62] *Onkruit Amsterdam* seems to possess a leading function in preparing hard, direct actions. It has published brochures with a great number of names and addresses in the areas of the military, nuclear energy and the police, which are, in their view, suitable targets for direct action. Other movements, perhaps due to overlap in personnel, have copied *Onkruit* acts of sabotage and theft.[63] Theft has two functions for *Onkruit,* a material and a propaganda one. The material one is a service to revolutions in the Third World, such as the 1983-84 thefts of medical civil defence equipment from depots in Dubbeldam, Ommen, Numansdorp (twice), Tiel and Hoogwoud which was sent to Nicaragua and Eritrea as 'alternative development aid'.[64] Other thefts from military bunkers aim at the revelation of war preparations by NATO. 'Liberated' incriminating documents are published in book form or shown in public exhibitions with the goal of convincing larger sections of the population that militarism is a clear and present danger in Dutch society.[65] Because of the academic background of a number of *Onkruit* members, these classified documents, while tendentially selected and presented, are well edited. They are not unsympathetically received by certain sectors of the public. That, of course, is the intended effect. The Domestic Security Service (*Binnenlandse Veiligheidsdienst*: BVD) identified the following goals of *Onkruit*:

In longer terms the aim of these actions is to convince an as large as possible part of the public that 'Onkruit' is right and to inspire as many supporters as possible to go out and conduct for themselves—autonomous—actions. Many actions taken together can of course—even if they are not coordinated—cause much more damage than the pin-pricks of Onkruit itself. In order to reach these goals defence secrets are also made public: this provides information on the location of bunkers and on the role of army and civil defence in the preparation of [nuclear] war. In addition, one aims to create the impression on the basis of scenario books, cable traffic, mapsigns, etc. that the army and government are making preparations for taking action against [their own people] in case of unrest in war and peacetime.[66]

In addition to thefts, occupations and publications, *Onkruit* is also said to be planning acts of sabotage against military installations.[67] Working in small impenetrable 'affinity groups' and preparing their attacks meticulously with reconnaissance, *Onkruit* actions are among the most sophisticated at present taking place in the Netherlands. Whether or not *Onkruit* members will develop into terrorist groups remains to be seen. On the one hand there has been progress to what has been termed 'little violence', that is, the mailing of threatening letters and the making of phone calls at night to members of security forces, whose private addresses have been made public following a theft of documents.[68] This could be the prelude to hard actions. On the other hand, however, *Onkruit* has so far been careful to take into account what relevant sectors of the public think of their actions.[69] The purpose of their actions is more to provide discussion than to obtain material results in their war against militarism. Since they are not blinded by an ideology that justifies violence against people, it is likely that *Onkruit* will not pass the fuzzy line from politically-motivated violent activists to terrorists.

INTERNATIONAL TERRORISM IN THE NETHERLANDS IN THE 1980s

While there have been forty-eight incidents of transnational terrorism in which the Netherlands became involved between September 1969 and October 1979,[70] the 1980s have been less taxing for the Dutch. There have been only half a dozen incidents of international terrorism in the Netherlands in the 1980s, of which most were unsuccessful:

1. In 1981 the Indian embassy in The Hague was the target of a firebomb attack by a group fighting for the liberation of

Kashmir. The attack failed to cause damage.

2. In 1982 a heavy bomb placed in front of the Kuwait consulate failed to explode. It was apparently meant as a protest against the cessation of financial support for an Arab extremist movement.

3. On 21 July 1982 the Turkish consul Kemalettin Demirer was the target of an armed attack by four gunmen. Neither the consul general nor his driver were hurt, while the Dutch police escort shot and wounded one perpetrator, who was sentenced to six years imprisonment. Armenian terrorists, who had by that time already killed two dozen Turkish diplomats in more than one dozen countries were responsible.

4. The most serious incident took place in a suburb of The Hague in March 1985. In a building where the Surinam Liberation Council was housed, three young Surinamese musicians were executed and two wounded in a gun attack. The motive has not become clear; it might have been a case of mistaken identity. As perpetrators of this murder, a special killer team—'the flying brigades'—of the Surinamese military strongman Col. Bouterse has been suspected but no evidence has surfaced which would have given substance to this hypothesis. There is a large exile and emigré community of people from Surinam in the Netherlands, which is itself divided. Some groups have been involved in preparations of a *coup d'état*. In this connection a Surinamese *emigré* physician tried to blackmail the Heineken beer brewery into paying $20 million for the financing of a liberation army. He had threatened to poison Heineken beer with digitoxine, a medication for heart disease. The kidnapping of the beer magnate Freddy Heineken on 30 November 1983, however, was a purely criminal affair not linked to the above incident.

5. A firebomb which detonated in front of the Aeroflot building in Amsterdam on 30 December 1982, has to be mentioned, as well as a bomb found in front of the Soviet trade legation in Amsterdam on 23 June 1985.[71]

6. On 30 September 1985, a bomb was discovered in time in front of the El Al office in Amsterdam.

The targets of international terrorism in the Netherlands

have been connected with the Arab-Israeli conflict, with ethnic separatism in India and Turkey, with a former Dutch colony and one superpower. It is remarkable that despite the fact that there are about 10,000 Americans in the Netherlands as well as numerous NATO installations, there have been no attacks on these.

The near absence of national and international terrorism in the Netherlands is difficult to explain. Domestic terrorism, of course, is also (nearly) absent in a number of other small European countries such as Norway, Finland, Switzerland and Sweden. There is probably some correlation between national and international terrorism. One explanation might be that in the absence of local domestic terrorists, international terrorists have insufficient links for successful operations in a country like the Netherlands. However there are, for instance, 300,000 immigrants with a Muslim background in the Netherlands who could conceivably form a fertile substratum for Arab terrorism. Another line of explanation suggests that international terrorism has 'spared' the Netherlands because this country has been selected as safe haven where terrorists can retreat and make plans for new attacks abroad. This accusation is difficult to verify or falsify. It suggests an agreement among a multitude of foreign terrorist movements to that effect which is highly unlikely given their ideological diversity and weak or absent operational cooperation. It also suggests that international terrorists can restrain Dutch national terrorists from acting in their own country.[72] The accusation that the Netherlands harbours 'terrorists' has probably arisen from a number of cases of non-extradition of Irish and German suspects. The Dutch criminal code does not make conspiracy to commit acts of violence a crime unless the safety of the Dutch royal family or members of the Dutch government and Parliament is at stake. Foreign suspects of terrorist conspiracy do not fall under this narrow definition and cannot be extradited on conspiracy charges which exist under foreign criminal law only.

The explanation why the Netherlands has been spared from international terrorism is therefore unlikely to be found in a safe haven conspiracy theory. International terrorists like Abu Nidal have planned at least one attack in the Netherlands—against the moderate Palestinian spokesman Sartawi—but ultimately selected a less heavily protected scene for their murder. Good intelligence has played a role in preventing the Netherlands from becoming a major scene of international terrorism—and so has good luck.

CONCLUSION

This survey of politically-motivated violent action in the Netherlands is incomplete. There have been several minor and most often unsolved incidents of shooting, bombing and arson. To give some examples:

—29 February 1980: a bomb placed by members of the Red Resistance Front (RVF) explodes in front of the house of a judge in Heelsum;

—4 May 1981: a train between Enschede and Zwolle is fired at; none of the 11 rounds hurts passengers;[73]

—13 July 1981: arsonist attack on the house of the secretary of the Turkish workers' movement in Almelo, presumably by Grey Wolves;[74]

—31 May 1981: the house of the mayor of Meerssen in Limburg is destroyed by arson;[75]

—9 September 1984: a group called *Koetho Reh* explodes a bomb at the Van Heusz monument in Amsterdam in protest against the cooperation agreement between Amsterdam and Jakarta. One boy is injured.

—April/May 1985: in letters signed Red Army Faction (RAF) members of the Eindhoven soccer club PSV were threatened with violence unless a substantial sum of money was paid;

—4 January 1985: heavy explosion with professional explosives at the electricity plant Medemblik in North Holland;

—29 January 1985: a molotov cocktail is thrown into a building of the Ministry of Defence in Groningen, for which the Northern Terror Front (*Noordelijk Terreur Front*) claims responsibility;[76]

—7 August 1985: a molotov cocktail is thrown through a window into the building of the Dutch Parliament, a second, unexploded one is discovered outside the building;[77]
—4 April 1986: during an Indonesian festivity attended by more than 1,000 people, the Pasar Gambir, in the Ijsselhal in Zwolle, a molotov cocktail is thrown onto the roof of the hall.

Bombings in particular appear to be underreported in the press, the main basis of this survey. For the period January 1980-May 1986 we found on the basis of an analysis of two dailies, a total of thirty-one bomb attacks and eleven cases of bombs discovered before damage resulted. However, one study covering the period 1979-81 found, on the basis of the reporting of 143 police corps and districts (88 per cent of the total) more than 600 registered bomb threats per year. In 1981, for instance, the author of this study recorded 655 reportings, of which 90.68 per cent proved to be false, 5.19 per cent concerned fake bombs and 4.12 per cent real bombs. The last-mentioned percentage is the equivalent of twenty-nine bombs for one year alone. Even if corrections are made for bombs found from the World War Two period, it indicates a serious underreporting.[78] The fact that a substantial number of bomb threats were registered in The Hague and Hilversum—the seats of the government and of the electronic media—is already an indication that they refer to political violence.

On closer inspection then, contemporary Holland is not without political violence. However, it should be kept in mind that the survey given in the preceding pages covers a period of more than six years in a period of economic recession with more than 20 per cent youth unemployment. If we compare the Dutch average of about 200 criminal killings per year with political killings, which are practically absent, Dutch society must still be considered exceptionally peaceful. There has been no terrorist movement attempting to cause direct human victims whose murder would serve the purpose of creating a climate of terror or a setting for political extortion. The Dutch politically-motivated violent activists have directed their violence mostly at things rather than human beings. This is, as Herman Franke pointed out, one of the outstanding features of Dutch criminal behaviour.[79] By and large political and non-political aggression is channelled into property destruction. The latter, consisting mainly of vandalism, has increased by more than 1,800 per cent since 1950, causing more than 500 million Dutch guilders worth of damage per year.[80] Another reason why Dutch politically-motivated violent activists have not turned to anti-personnel violence on a substantial scale might be that they lack the discipline necessary for a terrorist movement. They certainly lack a self-righteous ideology which justifies killing. However, some activists are forming cells, others disregard public opinion, yet others have given up hope of seeking redress from government. If these elements should come together in one group, it is no longer unlikely that the Netherlands too will be haunted by the fantasy war of a miniscule group without significant popular backing for one good cause or another. Much will depend on the reaction of the Dutch authorities. It is to this question we turn next.

THE RESPONSE OF THE DUTCH GOVERNMENT

The Palestinian assault on the Olympic Games in Munich in 1972 was an eye-opener for many a government, including the Dutch one. Airport and embassy protection, the introduction of specialised arrest teams and the development of crisis scenarios became common. In a policy guideline of 22 February 1973, anti-terrorist measures were firmly placed into a criminal context.[81] However, in dealing with the South Moluccan incidents, the political dimension was not lost sight of, and a mixed Dutch-South Moluccan commission was established to sort out the grievances existing among the immigrant minority. The commission *Koebben-Mantouw* served as a forum for communication and as a political lightning conductor and thereby helped to clear the air. Especially felicitous was the idea of allowing young South Moluccan activists to visit their distant homeland Ambon to see for themselves how little political support there was for their struggle. These orientation travels brought about a sobering sense of realism and made them aware that they felt, after all, more at home in the Netherlands than in the fictitious South Moluccan Republic (RMS).

The experience with South Moluccan political activism helped the Dutch government to realise that it had a responsibility for the well-being of this and other ethnic minorities (the Surinamese, the Antillians but also the Turks and Moroccans). Consequently, a minority policy has been set up since the late 1970s which aims at the integration of immigrants, while at the same time respecting their cultural identity. This policy can be considered to have been stimulated or at least accelerated by the Moluccan incidents. The potential for ethnic political violence in the Netherlands has thereby probably been contained.

The idea of co-opting potential dissent is very strongly developed in the Netherlands. A member of the Central Intelligence Information Service (*Centrale Recherche Informatiedienst*: CRI)—which, together with the Domestic Security Service (*Binnenlandse Veiligheidsdienst*: BVD), keeps an eye on the political violence scene—expressed it in these terms:

> If you react too strongly as a government with your monopoly of violence, you run the risk that a hard core of an activist group finds a motive to detach itself and to develop into a cell of terrorists. It pays to keep on trying with all your energy to forestall a number of frustrated people becoming isolated. For this reason it is a good idea that we leave ample room in our society for extraparliamentary actions. This is not a plea for passively watching how our public order is eroded. . . . Tolerance has its limits and to turn a blind eye to the course of events is also dangerous. The Netherlands cannot be allowed to become a launching pad for terrorism. That is why we carefully monitor the moves of sympathisers who are in contact with terrorist groups. Together with the BVD we regularly develop situation assessments and threat analyses.[82]

Since 1981 the role of the CRI's Special Affairs Centre is to assess domestic and foreign intelligence on terrorism, while the BVD has its own agent network for domestic investigations. As targets of potential terrorist threats the military also has its own security units which are respectively termed *Marid* (for the naval forces), *Luid* (for the air force) and *Lamid* (for the ground forces). Given the fact that the ground forces alone have about 400 military areas to guard, the protection of these objects is incomplete. Repeated thefts of weapons from military arsenals mainly by criminal groups have been the result.

The Hague, as the seat of foreign embassies, has a special office for Protection and Guarding which coordinates police and *marechaussée* surveillance of objects like the Turkish, American, British or Israeli embassies.[83] Amsterdam Airport has also recently received a permanent protection unit. There is, however, no national anti-terrorist unit comparable to GSG-9 or SAS in the Netherlands. On the political side, attempts are apparently under way to develop a new structure for crisis management with integrated staff for the support of policy, and crisis centres.[84]

Internationally, in 1975 the Netherlands took the initiative for TREVI. They also signed ECST in the early 1980s. The fact that the Dutch government has generally been restrictive in its extradition policy of persons suspected abroad of terrorism, should not be interpreted as tolerance of political violence but as concern for the due process of law. In Parliament, there has been no cleavage of significance in matters of terrorism.

The Netherlands is one of the most open societies in the world. There is an extraordinary tolerance of political dissent whether it comes from foreign or from Dutch citizens. There is a danger that this tolerance may be abused. On the other hand, a contrary policy of political repression contains dangers just as great if not greater. One of the former members of the Dutch Red Youth of the early 1970s—the closest the Netherlands got to a terrorist movement of its own—expressed it in these words:

If you situate my case in Germany, I would have been dead, or imprisoned for life or I would still be a fugitive. It is very strange to realise this. In the Netherlands you get so much freedom that the motivation to take action dissolves. A rather strange effect if you notice it in your own behaviour. The liberal climate in the Netherlands has called a halt to terrorism; in Germany reactionary forces have kept terrorism artificially alive for ten years.[85]

NOTES

1. *Nederlands Bibliotheek en Lektuur Centrum. Nederland in Aktie.* The Hague: NBLC, 1984-86.
2. H. van der Loo, 'Moderne bewegingen: een culturele onderstroom', in O. Schreuder (ed.), *Moderne bewegingen. Oude thema's in een nieuw klimaat,* Zeist: Kerckebosch BV, 1985, p. 168.
3. A.J.F. Koebben and J.J. Godschalk. *Een tweedeling van de samenleving.* The Hague: OSA, 1985, p. 11.
4. *Ibid.,* p. 12.
5. *Ibid.,* p. 27.
6. *Ibid.,* p. 57.
7. *Ibid.,* p. 63
8. Bart Tromp, quoted in Eric Boogerman, 'Hoe tolerant is Nederland?' *NRC Handelsblad, Zaterdags Bijvoegsel,* (27 Feb. 1982).
9. Luuk Zonneveld, *Politiek Geweld in Nederland,* Leiden: COMT, 1986, p. 2-3.
10. Hans van der Loo, Erik Snel and Bart van Steenbergen, *Een wenkend perspectief? Nieuwe sociale bewegingen en culturele veranderingen,* Amersfoort: De Horsting, 1985, p. 24.
11. W. van Noort. 'Nieuwe sociale bewegingen: ideologische, strategische, organisatorische en personele verbindingen', in O. Schreuder, *op. cit.,* p. 144.
12. *Ibid.,* p. 157.
13. *Volkskrant,* 22 July 1985.
14. Cited in Flip ten Cate, Cor Groeneweg and Jurjen Pen, *Barst de bom? Het veranderde gezicht van de radicale vredesbeweging,* Amsterdam: Uitgeverij Jan Mets, 1985, pp. 49-50.
15. *Volkskrant,* 16 Jan. 1986.
16. *Volkskrant,* 6 Oct. 1983.
17. *Volkskrant,* 27, 28 and 31 Dec. 1983.
18. *NRC Handelsblad* (hereinafter *NRC*), 24 May 1984.
19. W. van Noort, *loc. cit.,* pp. 143-4.
20. Ton Dijst, *De bloem der natie in Amsterdam. Kraken, subcultuur en het probleem van orde,* Leiden: COMT, 1986. p. 14.
21. W. van Noort, *op. cit.,* p. 142.
22. Cited in Dijst, *op. cit.,* p. 109.
23. *Ibid.,* p. 108.
24. *Ibid.,* p. 116.
25. Agnes van der Voort. 'Legitimiteit en geweld bij het verschijnsel kraken. Een analyse van het konflikt tussen overheid en kraakbeweging'. Nijmegen, doctoral thesis, 1983, pp. 143-4.
26. *Trouw,* 31 July 1982.
27. *NRC,* 17 Jan. 1983.
28. *NRC,* 11 Feb. 1983.
29. *Parool,* 10 Feb. 1984.
30. *NRC,* 13 Oct. 1982, 4 April 1981 and 7 March 1981; *Trouw,* 4 June 1983.

31. *Parool,* 21 August 1984 and 17 Sept. 1984; *NRC,* 18 Sept. 1984.
32. *NRC,* 26 Oct. 1985.
33. *Parool,* 7 Nov. 1985.
34. *Volkskrant,* 18 March 1986.
35. *Volkskrant,* 26 Oct. 1985.
36. *Volkskrant,* 28 Oct. 1985.
37. *Volkskrant,* 11 Oct. 1985.
38. *De Nije,* 5 April 1984, as quoted in Knipselkrant 1984, p. 656.
39. *CIDI dokumentatie,* 13 Jan. 1983.
40. *NRC,* 5 Jan. 1983.
41. *Volkskrant,* 1 March 1984.
42. *Bluf!,* 1 Sept. 1983.
43. *Parool,* 15 May 1984.
44. *NRC,* 15 May 1984.
45. *Volkskrant,* 1 April 1986.
46. A.J.F. Koebben, *De zaakwaarnemer,* Deventer: Van Loghum Slateru;, 1982, p. 5.
47. *Volkskrant,* 16 June 1986.
48. *Telegraaf,* 18 Sept. 1985.
49. *Volkskrant,* 17 May 1986.
50. Cited in ten Cate *et al., op. cit.,* p. 101.
51. *Volkskrant,* 17 May 1986.
52. *Volkskrant,* 21 Oct. 1985.
53. *Volkskrant,* 21 Jan. 1984.
54. *Volkskrant,* 1 March 1986.
55. *Volkskrant,* 2 Jan. 1986.
56. *Volkskrant,* 2 Nov. 1983.
57. *Gelderlander.* 1 Nov. 1985; *Telegraaf,* 25 Sept. 1985.
58. *NRC,* 5 June 1984.
59. Cited in ten Cate *et al., op. cit.,* p. 101.
60. *Ibid.,* pp. 55 and 100.
61. *Ibid.,* pp. 19-20; van Noort, *op. cit.,* p. 151.
62. *Vrij Nederland,* 19 Oct. 1985.
63. F. ten Cate *et al., op. cit.,* pp. 20-1.
64. *Ibid.,* p. 103.
65. Martin Gerritsen, Bert Koolhaas and Karel van Langevelde, *De vallende macht. Anti-militarisme na 1984,* Amsterdam: Vereniging Dienst-weigeraars, 1985, p. 39.
66. The BVD analysis was made public by the Anti-Militarist Research Collective (*Anti-Militaristisch Onderzoeks Kollektief*: AMOK) and is repr. as an Appendix in F. ten Cate *et al., op, cit.,* p. 111.
67. *Ibid.* pp. 116-17.
68. *Ibid.,* p. 116.
69. Gerritsen *et al., op. cit.,* pp. 38-40.
70. Edward F. Mickolus, *Transnational Terrorism. A Chronology of Events 1968-1979,* London: Aldwych Press, 1980, p. 92.
71. *NRC,* 30 Dec. and 23 June 1985.

72. C. Visser, in lecture delivered on 6 May 1976 at the Netherlands Institute for International Affairs.
73. *NRC,* 5 May 1981.
74. *NRC,* 13 July 1981.
75. *NRC,* 1 June 1981.
76. *Volkskrant,* 30 Jan. 1985.
77. *NRC,* 7 Aug. 1985.
78. B.D. Willems, *Politie-optreden n.a.v. bommeldingen,* Bilthoven: Cursusscriptie Inspecteur der Rijksrecherche, 1983, p. 38.
79. Herman Franke, 'Het beheerste Nederland', *Haagse Post,* 29 March 1986, p. 29.
80. G. Heofnagels, quoted in *Volkskrant,* 26 Oct. 1985.
81. Brief from the Minister-President to the speaker of the lower house, 22 Feb. 1973; repr. in Joke Cuperus and Rineke Klijnsma, *Onderhandelen of bestormen? Het beleid van de overheid inzake terroristische akties,* Groningen: Polemologisch Institut, 1980, Appendix I.
82. *Elseviers Magazine,* 16 Feb. 1985.
83. *Vrij Nederland,* 1 Feb. 1986.
84. *NRC,* 9 Jan 1985.
85. Lucien van Hoesel, quoted in *Groene Amsterdammer,* 13 Feb. 1985.

7 The Evolution of Belgian Terrorism

David Laufer

When five kilos of dynamite exploded outside the Brussels office of Litton Business Systems on 2 October 1984, more than just windows were shattered. Although an act of terrorism within Belgium was not extraordinary in itself, the Litton attack marked the beginning of a phenomenon well known to other European states, but markedly absent from Belgian life: indigenous terrorism. Indeed, the official Belgian response to the campaign of the *Cellules Communistes Combattantes* (CCC) initially was hampered by the conviction that the attacks were 'imported', and thus did not reflect any serious flaws inherent in Belgian political structures or social life. Over the next fourteen months, however, twenty-seven bomb attacks against defence, political and business targets convinced the government that the CCC had its roots in Belgian soil, and was bent on tearing the political, social and economic fabric of the country apart.

More remarkable than the mere advent of a Belgian brand of terrorism, is why domestic terrorism did not develop earlier. European terrorist organisations fall into two broad categories: separatist groups such as the Irish nationalist terrorist groups the Provisional IRA and INLA, the Basque ETA, the Corsican FLNC: and the ideologically-motivated groups such as the Red Army Faction (RAF) and its forebear Baader-Meinhof in West Germany, the Red Brigades (BR) in Italy and Action Directe (AD) in France, to name only the most infamous. Certainly the conditions existed in Belgium to foster a separatist terrorist organisation. Deep-seated antagonism between the country's two linguistic/ethnic groups of Dutch-speaking Flemings and Francophone Walloons has existed for years and has often erupted into violence. In spite of significant devolution to regional and community councils, extremists from both sides continue to call for secession, albeit with little resonance among the electorate. The linguistic/ethnic debate, however, has remained primarily within the political sector because of factors peculiar to Belgian history and the Belgian psyche. As I will argue later, these factors mitigated the tendency to separatist terrorist violence, whereas the linguistic conflict as a whole stifled the earlier development of an ideologically-based terrorist group.

Objective conditions which would have allowed a domestic, ideologically-motivated group of terrorists to flourish also existed in Belgium. These are the same conditions that made Belgium a haven and a source of arms for terrorists from other countries. Historically, Belgium has had to maintain a very free and open society. Established in 1830 as a buffer state, Belgium's status of armed, permanent neutrality was guaranteed by the Great Powers. This fact of life necessitated good political and economic relations with the UK, France and Prussia. Liberal doctrine held that economic freedom was founded in political liberty, a concept which was enshrined in the Constitution of 1830, viewed by some historians as the archetypal expression of nineteenth-century liberalism.[1] Belgian society continues to articulate such openness, as does the economy, which derives half of the GNP from foreign trade. Permeable borders and relaxed customs regulations are the result, and work to the benefit of international terrorists. Justice Minister Jean Gol has remarked that 'terrorists know they can enter a democratic country like a nightclub and leave it like a cinema'.[2]

Belgium has perennially served as an easy source of arms for terrorists. The arms industry first developed in Belgium around Liège, in the fifteenth-century. The city is still the home of *Fabrique Nationale d'Armes de Guerre,* one of the largest arms manufacturers and most aggressive arms sellers in the world.[3] As a big export earner, arms sales are subject to very few export and transit controls. Belgium ranks as one of the most lax of all West European states in exercising control over this area of trade.[4] Recently, however, measures have been adopted to improve gun control.

In addition to ease of mobility and access to arms, Belgium has also offered a plethora of suitable targets to terrorist groups. As the seat of the EEC since 1957 and of NATO since 1966, Belgium provides many symbols which a domestic group could attack if so inclined. The question, then, is not why the CCC developed, but why so late. In analysing the issue of the origins of the CCC, however, one is initially struck by the anomaly of its development within Belgian political and social contexts, almost as if it developed *ex nihilo*. Political violence was simply not invoked by extremist parties, and those fringe groups which did espouse violence were primarily Flemish and right-wing, such as the *Vlaamese Militanten Orde* (VMO). The CCC is an extremely left-wing and evidently Francophone group, two factors which differentiate it from the previous, marginal record of Belgian political violence. To more fully understand the phenomenon, it is necessary to place it against the background of Belgian history.

CONFLICT RESOLUTION IN BELGIAN POLITICS

For a nation born in revolution and inclined toward internal disputes, Belgium has succeeded remarkably in defusing the tensions that divide the society. Over the years, various political parties and interest groups have 'developed an aptitude for negotiation, which contributes to solutions which never satisfy everybody, but which are generally accepted'.[5] Compromise and coalition dictated by political expedience are as firmly rooted in Belgian history as is conflict. Indeed, it was common opposition to the inferior status accorded Belgium in the United Kingdom of the Netherlands (established in 1815), which united the Catholic, conservative clergy and bourgeoisie of Flanders with the more liberal, free-thinking entrepreneurial class of Wallonia.[6] This 'Union of Oppositions', formed in 1828, took advantage of a popular revolt in Brussels in 1830, and with the blessing of the Great Powers, forged an independent Belgium.

Political parties in the new state originally developed along religious lines, mirroring the Catholic/anti-clerical dichotomy of society in a Catholic and a Liberal Party. Class divisions became institutionalised in the party system in the 1930s with the development of the Socialist Party (*née* Workers Party) to the left of the Liberals. Linguistic differentiation did not begin until the mid-1960s, but eventually all parties split into Flemish and Francophone blocs. Proportional representation, instituted in 1900, ensured that virtually all parties could achieve some representation, and coalition governments have been the norm ever since. As a 'consociational' democracy,[7] Belgium's pluralist system is truly multi-dimensional in character, and power is not concentrated in the hands of any one governmental branch, party or interest group. Such a system encourages not only a sharing and a fair distribution of power, but also a formal limit to power. Most importantly, however, this system permits the access to power to any legitimate, viable group willing to compromise in order to achieve it. The widespread acceptance of this practice by parties from right to left has been a key factor in stultifying radical political ideas and preventing political violence.

For parties to continue to tell they need a stake in the system, the system has to be effective in addressing demands, redressing grievances and avoiding, preventing or resolving conflicts. Through consultation, conciliation and arbitration, the Belgians have become adept at legislating problems out of existence, or at least in removing the elements of political conflict.[8] The government has slowly attempted to resolve social differences in much the same order in which they arose historically: the Catholic/anti-clerical split was addressed in the 1958 *Pacte Scolaire* which essentially delineated areas of responsibility for the state and the Church in matters of education. Next, a determination not to let socio-economic disagreements spawn political conflict led to the extension of social welfare legislation, with many of the financial and management responsibilities of the Belgian welfare state devolved to the unions themselves.[9] There has thus developed a strong emphasis in Belgium on cooperation among the 'social partners': trade unions, employers' federations and the government.[10] The Belgian labour force is among the most skilled and well-educated in Europe, and is highly unionised (67 per cent membership). Membership is about evenly divided between Christian and socialist unions which 'have long ago scratched words like "class struggle" from their vocabulary'.[11] Class divisions in Belgium, therefore, are much less clear-cut than in other European countries, and no simplistic relationship exists between social class and the party system. Belgian workers are much less likely to vote on class grounds than their counterparts in other countries, since the presence of religious and linguistic divisions cut across the politics of class.[12]

LINGUISTIC CONFLICT AND 'NEW LEFT' POLITICS

Even in Wallonia, where socialism has always been the dominant political force and where the unions are strong and militant, traditionally the extreme left has remained weak and non-violent. There is not even a history of an autonomous, organised anarchistic squatters' or subversive movement, such as *Onkruit* which developed in the Netherlands. Thus the absence of a well-defined working-class consciousness and the lack of a violent tradition, made for very infertile soil for the growth of an extreme left-wing terrorist movement. Whereas the origins of the ideological terrorist groups in Italy, France and West Germany can be traced to workers' struggles and student activism in the 1960s, the Belgian CCC appears to have few roots in the events of that period. The reason for this is twofold: workers' struggles and student activism did not occur in Belgium on a scale comparable to that of its continental neighbours; and what did happen in Belgium in these areas was suffused with the overtones of the linguistic/ethnic conflict, which had the effect of stunting the development of violent, ideologically revolutionary groups.

Although the bitter and violent strikes and demonstrations in Wallonia and Brussels in 1960 and 1961 were ostensibly in direct response to the *loi unique,* which increased taxation and decreased public expenditure, they were also the result of a simmering resentment about Walloon economic decline and insecurity about the position of the Francophone community. Significantly, the Catholic trade unions and the Flemings generally did not participate in the strikes (except in Antwerp).[13] Historically, the Walloon region was superior economically, and the Francophone community, although a minority, held cultural predominance. By the early 1960s, both positions were in jeopardy. Flemish productivity and industrial production began to outpace those of Wallonia during the period. Moreover, Flanders attracted a growing portion of new investment, much of which was concentrated in newer, technological industries. In contrast, Walloon investment remained concentrated in the more traditional steel and metalworking industries.[12] The Walloon nationalist movement began to develop about the same time (early 1960s), articulated by groups such as *Wallonie Libre, Renovation Wallonie* and *Movement Populaire Wallon,* which stemmed from the violent workers' strikes.[15] The linguistic equality laws which the Flemings succeeded in passing in Parliament in 1963 added force to the Francophone backlash: in 1964 the *Front Democratique des Francophones* was founded, followed in 1967 by the more working class-oriented *Rassemblement Wallon* (RW). RW had the strongest separatist tendencies among parties of the Walloon nationalist movement, which was overtly left-of-centre. It was not, however, paramilitary,[16] and even the most extreme groups, such as Jose Happart's *Action fouronnaise,* would have nothing to do with refugee terrorists from other countries.

By the late 1960s, just as the workers' struggles had found expression in and were incorporated within a nationalist movement, so Belgian student unrest was channelled into avenues of linguistic/ethnic protest rather than into the ideological activism more typical of the New Left. Student demands for increased democratisation, endemic to industrialised countries during this era, encouraged ethnic demands in Belgium. Coupled with the New Left 'post-bourgeois' values which emphasised quality of life, the need for belonging and for intellectual and aesthetic self-fulfilment, this agitation accelerated the communalisation of Belgian politics.[17] New Left demands for decentralisation, regionalisation, autonomy and grass-roots democracy all became reflected in regionalist politics. The New Left and the nationalist movements actually had little in common except opposition to the established social order, but the nationalists drew support from the same social base as the New Left and, in doing so, eventually eclipsed it.[18]

A microcosm of this experience is illustrated by the 1968 crisis at the University of Louvain. Of the time when students were fighting and rioting in the streets over a plan to expand the French section of the university into a Flemish area between Louvain and Brussels, a Belgian former Trotskyist militant has said, 'We lived May 1968 by proxy, by listening on our radios to what was happening in Paris'.[19] Clearly, linguistic/ethnic concerns subsumed the ideological activism of student politics in Belgium. After 1968, there was a greater trend towards political fragmentation along linguistic, not class lines: the major parties split into Walloon and Flemish parties (e.g. the *Parti Socialiste Belge* formed the *Parti Socialiste* and the *Vlaamse Socialisten*). From 1968 to 1971, support for the various regionalist parties as a percentage of the total national vote jumped to 24.1 per cent from 15.7 per cent (it has dropped steadily since). Nationalist parties made these gains by stealing wind from the sails of left and right alike, but it was the essential moderation of their demands (none advocated the outright break-up of the country) which led to the willingness of the major parties to try to accommodate them.

Their efforts led to the Constitutional revisions of 1967-71 and to the *Pacte Communautaire* of 1977-78. These established the framework and defined the details for the devolution of powers to newly-created federal entities.

Cultural councils were established to safeguard the interests of the Francophone and Flemish communities, and regional councils were founded to legislate in policy areas of direct concern to the regions of Flanders, Wallonia and Brussels. The plan was implemented in 1981 and appears to have begun to nudge linguistic conflict from the national political arena. The ingenious flexibility of the party system and of the political infrastructure therefore mitigated the tendency to growth of separatist terrorism, while the political and social force of the linguistic conflict served to co-opt other radical political expressions, thus preserving Belgium from ideological terrorism. Without the conditions that gave birth to similar terrorist groups in Italy, West Germany and France, then, whence did the CCC emerge?

THE IDEOLOGICAL DEVELOPMENT OF THE CCC

There are many speculations and allegations regarding the origins of the CCC, but concrete knowledge is so far limited by several factors, not least of which is that it is such a recent and, at the time of writing, short-lived phenomenon. Attacks began on 2 October 1984 and the last occurred ten days before the 16 December 1985 arrests of four leading members. Documents found in CCC hide-outs have not yet been released; those arrested have not yet come to trial, and Belgian law stipulates that details of an investigation cannot be revealed until the case comes to court; the police and the alleged terrorists have been quite tight-lipped (a 'repentant' terrorist policy would not behove either party, in any case); and there has evidently been little police penetration into the outer ranks of the group. Nonetheless, on the basis of evidence currently available, the CCC is apparently the result of a relatively small group of people determined to plagiarise the experiences of Red Army Faction, Red Brigades and *Action Directe* terrorists, and graft these on to the social and political tissue of Belgium. Indeed, the CCC itself implies that such is the case in the first words of its very first communiqué: 'Today, through our action against the multinational Litton, the CCC *imposes* a practical organisation of armed politico-military struggle on this country until now, too little affected by the armed struggle for communism' (emphasis added).

Pierre Carette, arrested in Namur, Belgium on 16 December 1985 with three 'colleagues', is the man without whom the CCC never would have existed. Carette's activities alone, however, were not a sufficient cause for the development of the terrorist group. After all, he had been interested in forming such an organisation for about five years prior to the public emergence of the CCC. The development of the CCC was catalysed by several factors which largely did not exist before 1980: mass opposition to and deployment of NATO cruise missiles in Belgium; a worsening of the country's economic problems, and rising unemployment; and Carette's personal ties with the founders of *Action Directe,* Jean Marc Rouillan and Nathalie Menigon, who were, and quite possibly remain, refugees in Belgium.

In analysing the formation of terrorist groups in Italy, della Porta posits several variables which affect the mobilisation of violence: ideology and political beliefs; the existence of mass social movements; the adequacy of political institutions in dealing with such protest; the repressive and violent nature of the socio-political milieu; and, critically, the presence in the social environment of ideological and strategic resources that make clandestineness feasible.[20] Although della Porta does not suggest that the model has universal applications, it is instructive to analyse the genesis of the CCC in its light. To begin with ideology and political beliefs, it is necessary to sketch the 'career' of the founder of the CCC.[21]

Pierre Carette, born in Charleroi, Belgium in 1952, is not an original political thinker. His ideology is based on classic Marxist-Leninist revolutionary dogma coloured by a political appreciation of the global political situation as enunciated by Baader-Meinhof and the Red Brigades. Carette had been a militant of sorts since the early 1970s, when his training as a printer brought him into contact with ultra-left groups in Brussels, Mons and Charleroi. In 1975 he was instrumental in the organisation of a Belgian committee in solidarity with the RAF prisoners held in Stammhein, West Germany. Evidently alone among the extreme left in wanting to duplicate the actions of the RAF, Carette announced his anger with the Belgian ultra-left in 1977 and openly broke with it. To Carette, only violent action led by the urban guerilla could give direction to extreme leftist movements. In 1978, he was among a group which occupied the Dutch embassy in Brussels and the offices of the German magazine, *Der Spiegel* in support of RAF hunger strikers. In the summer of that year Carette was arrested in Switzerland for attempting to purchase automatic weapons. His speedy release by the authorities added to the suspicion with which he was already viewed among Belgian ultra-left militants.

On 25 June 1979 three extremist groups (Vengeance and Liberty, the Julien Lahaut Brigade and the Commando Andreas Baader) claimed responsibility for an assassination attempt on General Alexander Haig, then NATO's Supreme Allied Commander Europe. In its communiqué, the Lahaut Brigade said Haig was 'the most visible representative of the United States' aggressive and military policy'. Carette was questioned in connection with the attempt, but was not indicted. Indeed, he must have known something about it because he published an account of the attack and an analysis of the reasons for its failure in a 1982 issue of his journal, *Subversion. Subversion* was founded in 1979 when Carette set up the *Ligne rouge* 'collective' printing establishment dedicated to the propagation of 'progressive' ideas. Two alleged CCC members who were arrested with Carette in Namur on 16 December 1985, Pascale Vandegeerde and Didier Chevolet, were part of the original *Ligne rouge* collective.

By 1980, Carette had decided to realise his grand project: the creation of a Belgian urban guerilla movement. Unfortunately, he was still isolated from the bulk of the Belgian extreme left. which regarded him as a *provocateur*. Even the ultra leftist Internationalist Communist Group (GCI), which preached revolutionary violence, refused to work with Carette, who instead joined a GCI splinter group, the Internationalist Communist Front (FCI). It appears that Carette tried to form the CCC from the ranks of the FCI and his own *Ligne rouge* community. The decisive point in the genesis of the CCC, however, occurred early in 1982 when Carette met the French militant theorist Frederic Oriach, then a refugee in Belgium.

Oriach, known as an independent, pro-Palestinian theorist, agreed to collaborate with Carette in editing *Subversion*. Oriach succeeded in honing the ill-formed revolutionary ideas of Carette, and in the short period of the cooperation (Oriach was re-arrested in October 1982[22]), he was instrumental in defining what was to become the political-strategic platform of the CCC. Under the influence of Oriach, Carette realised that revolutionary struggles in the industrialised countries did not have to be subordinated to those in the Third World, but should complement them, and that the priority of an urban guerilla in the West should be to foment workers' revolutions in their own countries. Instead of exerting pressure on the developed countries from the outside, this strategy seeks to exert pressure from within. Oriach was merely introducing an idea which Ulrike Meinhof advanced almost a decade earlier, but to Carette it seemed no less anachronistic.[23] Thus in the communiqué claiming the 8 October 1984 bomb attack on the offices of Honeywell, the CCC claims that the global process of world proletarian revolution is advanced through 'conquering political power in one or several capitalist countries . . . Striking the bourgeoisie in the capitalist countries . . . deals a decisive blow against imperialism'.

Oriach also played a critical role in the structural organisation of the CCC by introducing Carette to two founders of *Action Directe* (AD) then hiding in Belgium: Jean Marc Rouillan and Nathalie Menigon. In 1977 Rouillan and Oriach fused the remnants of their former terrorist groups, GARI (*Groupe d'Action Revolutionnaire Internationaliste*) and NAPAP (*Noyaux Armes pour l'Autonomie Populaire*); thus AD emerged by 1979. Rouillan had created GARI in 1973 ostensibly to overthrow the Franco regime in Spain. Groups were created in France, Belgium and Italy in the hope that bank robberies and other attacks would pressure these governments into imposing sanctions on Franco. It is therefore reasonable to assume that Rouillan retained some Belgian contacts with clandestine resources which were used to help Carette launch the CCC.

The CCC's first activity was the establishment of a 'war treasury' to finance future terrorist operations. This was accomplished as always through robbery. In one communiqué, the CCC fixes its date of birth as 1982, with the 'creation of logistical unity with other foreign groups and organisations'. Perhaps in return for this organisational and strategic help, Carette used the *Ligne rouge* facilities to print AD and Lebanese Armed Revolutionary Factions (LARF) tracts and communiqués, including one claiming responsibility by LARF for the 22 April 1982 assassination of the Israeli diplomat Yacob Barsimantov in Paris.

Evidence that the ties between Carette and AD were strong certainly is not lacking. Carette and Menigon were in a car accident on 27 May 1982; both escaped, but 15,000 AD tracts denouncing President Reagan on his visit to Paris were discovered in their car. In August 1982 police discovered the *Ligne rouge* printing presses and realised they were the source of many AD tracts. Carette was arrested after the discovery, but was later released. On 13 March 1984, Rouillan and Menigon took a Brussels inspector hostage to avoid arrest and they also stole his notebook, thereby harming the investigation into the bank robberies; his identification card was later discovered in a CCC hide-out. On 23 August 1984, the fingerprints of Carette, Menigon and Rouillan were found in an apartment in Uccle, along with those of Chantal Paternostre, later arrested for alleged involvement with another transient Belgian terrorist group, FRAP (Proletarian Revolutionary Action Front).[24] The most significant sign of cooperation, however, was the division of an 816-kilo haul of F-15 dynamite stolen from a quarry in Ecaussines, Belgium on 3 June 1984. Two months later, 23 and 25kg of these explosives turned up in AD and RAF bombs in Paris and Oberrammergau, respectively; both bombs were defused. The division of the dynamite signalled the waning of contact between the CCC and AD. The Honeywell communiqué made a specific effort to refute any idea of continuing strategic ties between the two groups: 'The CCC and AD are totally separate from political orientation to structural autonomy'. Two weeks later AD issued its own denial of organisational links with the CCC.

Differences over revolutionary ideology and guerilla tactics led to the possibly bitter split. Whereas Carette firmly believed in the historic role of the revolutionary avant-garde, Rouillan was more 'democratic' in approach, more willing to encompass a variety of groups under his revolutionary umbrella. AD was also more murderous in intent, as was the RAF. Carette rightly felt that assassination was too big a step for the embryonic CCC, although the tactic was not ruled out for the future. Therefore the CCC did not sign the RAF-AD pact of 15 January 1985 dedicated to establishing a European revolutionary guerilla, and sealed in the next two weeks by the assassinations of General René Audran in Paris, and arms merchant Ernst Zimmermann in Munich. In view of the RAF-AD pact and much terrorist rhetoric about the need to unite the revolutionary avant-gardes to create an international revolutionary organisation, much has been made of 'Euro-terrorism'. However, the groups are jealous of their operational independence. Unity exists primarily in opposition to NATO and Western targets. Cooperation between groups is *ad hoc* and only extended when expedient.

THE GEOPOLITICAL PERCEPTIONS OF THE CCC

The RAF-AD communiqué advanced a global political scenario very similar to that which the CCC enunciated several months earlier during their first attacks. The gist of the perspective of the modern, West European urban guerilla movements is that Western Europe is the stage upon which the global conflict between the international proletariat and imperialist bourgeoisie is played out. It is in this context that the Baader-Meinhof strategy of striking the institutions of the bourgeoisie in their own strongholds assumes such importance. Moreover, the Western powers, deemed to be controlled politically and militarily by the United States and economically by multinational corporations, are perceived to be in the final stages of preparation for a new imperialist war. To the guerilla, the assumed unification and integration of this imperialist strategy is manifest through NATO, which therefore becomes an important terrorist target. For the CCC, this outlook is firmly rooted in Marxist-Leninist assumptions. In their first communiqué, they claim, 'Imperialist war is absolutely indissociable from the capitalist mode of production'. The development of this particular perspective can be traced directly to themes which recurred in *Subversion: imperialism and unemployment.*

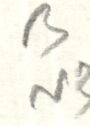

It is significant that coinciding with this period in the development of the CCC (early 1980s), Belgium was in the throes of a cruise missile deployment debate which generated the largest protests in the country's post-war history, and was also experiencing perhaps the worst economic crisis since post-war reconstruction. To Carette and the CCC, deployment and unemployment are intimately related: the instalment of a new generation of NATO missiles in Europe is seen as the prelude to the next capitalist war, which would be fought to make money for the bourgeoisie and to reduce unemployment, thereby stifling the proletarian revolution and consolidating the neo-imperialist position. In the verbose and clumsy style of the CCC, the Litton communiqué claims that

The imperialist war (which is permanently waged against the people of the entire world) is, in its global quality, the only adequate solution for the capitalist powers in crisis . . . It is the 'abc' of marxist economics that the economic crisis which plagues the whole world is not an 'accident' of the free-market . . . but the very product of the nature of the system of exploitation which can only right itself through war.

In the Honeywell communiqué, the CCC makes 'the positions of the Red Brigades' PCC [Combatant Communist

Party] our own': in effect reiterating that the capitalist system exploits and oppresses workers in the worst way by making them pay the price for recurring wars. Having relied on the Red Brigades (BR) for a diagnosis of the problem, the CCC also turns to them for the prescribed solution: the creation of a new International Communist Organisation, spearheaded by revolutionary urban guerilla structures which can articulate the political/military needs of the class revolution. The principal task of the armed avant-garde, 'which the Combatant Communist Cells have had the honor of initiating in this country', is to usher in a phase of civil war (very much a BR concept). The Litton communiqué closes by saying that 'it is no longer a matter of avoiding war, but of realising social revolution through following the motto of Lenin: "AGAINST IMPERIALIST WAR, CIVIL WAR"!'. All communiqués close with this exhortation, which is followed by numerous slogans 'popularised' by BR, such as: 'Forward toward the construction of a fighting proletarian organisation! Forward toward communist revolution! All power to the workers!'. Finally, the CCC 'signs-off' with what sounds like an advertising slogan: 'Communist Combatant Cells: for the construction of the fighting Proletarian Organisation'. This attack has been brought to you by . . .

THE CAMPAIGN OF THE CCC

Armed with revolutionary conviction and compelled by the momentum of historical determinism, the CCC had only to choose its targets, and make its attacks appear specific to the Belgian socio-political context. It attempted to do both in demagogic fashion by riding the wave of popular disapproval of deployment and the anti-NATO sentiment the movement engendered, and by seeking to place itself within the history of worker militancy in Belgium. The overriding importance of NATO as a target for European terrorists during the 1980s is by no means coincidental. All are trying to harness a popular sentiment (as expressed through the mass demonstrations in the early 1980s) to regenerate the ostensible momentum and support terrorists enjoyed during the 1970s. NATO is also an attractive target because its supranationality makes it a common enemy to all European terrorist groups; thus the struggle of each one immediately assumes a wider dimension.

For the CCC, the anti-NATO theme could be applied with particular relevance since Belgium is the seat of the treaty organisation: 'Belgium is a node of imperialism and one of the main centres of NATO', they observed. In the first four months of the CCC campaign, eight targets were attacked because of a perceived or an obvious connection to NATO. Whether the target was a NATO defence contractor, political party offices or NATO infrastructure, the CCC went to great lengths to describe the alleged connection of the target, the pernicious nature of NATO and the place of that attack within the overall context of the wider anti-NATO campaign of all European guerillas.[25] Litton was accused of designing and producing cruise missile guidance systems; MAN of making Pershing II carriers and launchers; and Honeywell of fabricating part of the cruise electronics systems, B-52 bomber navigation systems and elements for the United States' MX missile. Offices of the Liberal *Centre Paul Hymans* and of the Christian Social Party (CVP)—the two parties in the ruling government coalition—were attacked for backing deployment and for being the 'instruments of capitalist domination in this country'. NATO airport transmission antennae, fuel pipelines and the SHAPE (Supreme Headquarters Allied Powers Europe) building were attacked for obvious reasons. The pipelines attacks on 11 December 1984 were particularly disturbing because explosions occurred almost simultaneously at five different sites. The attacks reflected a good deal of organisational and logistical sophistication, and raised troubling questions about the actual size of the CCC and how they acquired strategic NATO intelligence.

The communiqués accompanying these attacks made clear that the CCC felt 'NATO is the most obvious expression of the highest stage of capitalism: imperialism', and that 'NATO is at the same time a function of permanent social domination and the last rampart of the capitalist mode of production'. They posit 'the installation of cruise and Pershing missiles in Europe, the rupture in East-West negotiations, the increase in military conflicts in recent years and their qualities (political, geographical and economic), the arms race and crusading chauvinism [*sic*] . . .' as evidence of the inexorable advance towards imperialist war. Proof that 'the true decisions concerning our future are taken in supranational bodies [such as] the multinationals, the IMF, EEC, OECD, NATO, the World Bank etc . . .' is allegedly contained in the fact that deployment occurred against the manifest wishes of the masses.

In face of the conspiracy of these external forces, the Belgian government is portrayed as an impotent talking shop: 'The bourgeoisie which reigns in this country [is the] valet of US imperialism and the mercenary of the *Société Generale* [*de Banque*], throwing hundreds of thousands of workers into unemployment'. That statement in the first commmuniqué forecast the nature of the CCC's future attacks. The group later struck the offices of the Federation of Belgian Businesses (in which two firemen were accidentally killed); Sibelgaz, a gas and electricity company; and Fabrimètal, the metalworking industries association, all with the motive of attacking the pillars of the Belgian bourgeois imperialists who profit from war. In November 1985 the CCC launched its 'Karl Marx' campaign against Belgian and US banks (which, CCC argues, finance imperialism), before returning to a more directly anti-NATO theme with their last two attacks on 6 December 1985.

Throughout the entire campaign, the CCC wanted to depict itself as being on the side of the working man; to portray itself as a populist, if not popular movement. The CCC was careful to present itself as attuned to 'the millions of workers in North America and Western Europe who say "NO" to the bellicose choices of "their" governments'. The group continuously reiterated that it attacked only enemies of the working class, and that it had the interests of the people at heart. In most of the attacks it gave at least thirty minutes warning and repeatedly advised people to evacuate the premises, stay away from windows etc. Bombs were said to be calculated not to incur damage to innocent, adjacent premises. This 'protection' of the people and the issuing of communiqués designed to convince and explain would, they hoped, win the confidence of the public. Later, the CCC hoped they could lead the people in 'sabotage and desertion of the institutions which exploit us'.

To win this confidence, the CCC had to demonstrate they were part of the history of worker militancy in Belgium: 'The economic crisis affects workers in Belgium as in other countries. [Since] we live in a country where the working class has more than once demonstrated great militancy, today this can only manifest itself in a radicalisation of the revolutionary struggle'. The CCC is often found accusing the government of harsh repression during the periods of greatest worker agitation such as 1960-61 and 1981, then offering itself as the means whereby the worker can 'tear away from the claws of the bourgeoisie, which impose on him the methods of dictatorship: police, gendarmerie, prisons, the army etc . . .'.

THE SOCIAL EVOLUTION AND ORGANISATION OF THE CCC

It is clear how the Marxist-Leninist ideology of the CCC was to be used to justify a terrorist campaign, but ideology is only one of della Porta's variables which affect the mobilisation of violence, and perhaps it is the least important. Ideology, della Porta concludes, is only a 'facilitating factor', not a cause of a certain behaviour.[26] By relating the evolution of Carette's political beliefs to della Porta's second variable (the existence of periods of mass social mobilisation, in this case the anti-deployment movement), I have attempted to show how, once armed with ideology, the CCC gained its motive. Ideology becomes the paint, and social mobilisation the brush with which terrorism can be applied to the canvas of society. But such a bloody picture cannot be created without a painter, so other factors must come into play. Della Porta's third variable suggests that institutional 'blockage' plays a role in the development of political violence.

At first glance, one may say that this could not have been a factor in the Belgian instance, where political structures are flexible and accustomed to resolving conflicts much more deeply rooted in society. But upon closer inspection, this may not have been the case with the deployment issue. There was never any question about the essentially Atlanticist orientation of all Belgium's major political parties. Throughout the post-war era, efforts at improving collective security among European countries have been spearheaded by Belgium.[27] Indeed, NATO was built on the foundation of the five-nation Brussels Treaty (Benelux, France and the United Kingdom) which constitutes a regional security pact. European military cooperation, security policy integration and arms standardisation have always been planks of Belgian foreign policy. Even the Communist Party, although critical of NATO, does not explicitly call for withdrawal. During the deployment debate, the Socialist Party was the only major party to support the anti-missile movement. But even if anti-NATO sentiments received little forum in the political establishment, they certainly could be vented in the legitimate, non-violent 'peace' movement.

To the CCC, however, this movement was not and never would be a useful tool in opposing the entrenched powers. In the CCC communiqué claiming the 26 November 1984 attack on the NATO antennae, the CCC berated the anti-war movement (in which it claimed to count some of its own activists) for its pacifism and its reformism, which it felt were both signs of the movement's infestation with bourgeois values. 'Non-violence is nothing but desertion in the face of an enemy . . . .. Legalism, parliamentarism and non-violence are counter-revolutionary because they confine the anti-war and anti-missile movements within a circus controlled by bourgeois power'. To be successful, 'the movement must link war to imperialism and place itself within a revolutionary proletarian perspective'. The CCC 'analysis' of the reasons for the failure of the peace movement to prevent deployment relies heavily on

a more sophisticated work published by the German Revolutionary Cells (RZ).RZ's conclusion that revolution was not only not wanted, but increasingly rejected by the radical left itself led it to reduce its terrorist operations. The CCC, however, ignores RZ's experience and concludes that violence is the only way to galvanise a proletarian consciousness and revolutionary movement.

The CCC also may have distrusted the peace movement because it was generally Flemish in character (perhaps because of close proximity to the strong Dutch peace movement) and, as in the Netherlands, it was supported by the Church. Not least of all, however, there was the traditional alienation between Carette and the Belgian radical left which was influential in the peace movement. Indeed, the CCC held the left in such contempt that it attempted to blow up the car of Pierre Galand, a leading Belgian pacifist. The feeling was mutual, however. The extreme left *Parti du Travail de Belgique* claimed the CCC was a CIA plot to discredit the left and the peace movement. The radical left felt that terrorism placed the cart before the horse by using armed violence prior to the political development of a revolutionary consciousness among workers, and only served to reinforce the powers of the state.[28] Obviously, the CCC felt class awareness could be forged through violence, and stated that all other forms of resistance, 'mass demonstrations, violent or not; strikes, general or not; union activity, progressive or reactionary; voting by left or right have only brought costly defeat and demoralisation to the anti-capitalist anti-war movement'. Had the CCC felt more comfortable with the radical left, the tendency towards violence might have been mitigated. But for the CCC, there could be no political compromise and no coalition with the radical left, and thus no political resolution of its demands. As long as the extreme left worked within the system, it was part of the structure the CCC wanted to destroy.

To what degree CCC activists had been acclimatised to and conditioned by violence or repressiveness in the socio-political milieu is the fourth variable which della Porta suggests affects the resort to terrorist violence. This is perhaps the weakest factor in applying the della Porta model to the growth of Belgian terrorism. Indeed, in the 1970s and early 1980s Belgium was not immune to international terrorism: terrorists from the Provisional IRA, ETA, Armenian, Ukrainian, Palestinian and Islamic groups exploded bombs and assassinated many people. Violence was not an unknown factor in linguistic or labour disputes in Belgium, and the people were used to a good deal of confrontation. But the clashes among groups and with the police rarely assumed the proportions of the tribal fights in Northern Ireland and the Basque region, or of the workers' struggles in Italy and West Germany. Yet in spite of CCC allegations about the huge machinery of state repression, many concrete manifestations of such machinery were sorely lacking in Belgium. For instance, Justice Minister Gol has clamoured for years for the establishment of a GSG-9 type anti-terrorist force. In fact, it was the ineptitude of the existing security forces and the laxity of certain laws which helped to create a climate suitable for violence. The one concrete security development to which the CCC does refer (instead of levelling the usual vague accusations) is the creation in 1983 of the GIA (*Groupe Interforces Antiterroriste*). The GIA, however, does not represent a formidable, repressive security apparatus. Its first success occurred two years later with, ironically, the arrest of Carette and his three colleagues.

It is della Porta's fifth and final variable that is the most important in the evolution of a terrorist group, and the one that is perhaps the most disturbing omen for the future: the ability of a group to go underground. Della Porta concludes that

The presence in society of emerging (or sometimes declining) interests not institutionally channelled and the diffusion of violent ideologies and strategies are the environmental facilitating factors for the rise of terrorism . . . .. For the formation of an armed organisation it is also necessary that networks of militants socialised to violent repertoires rise and that a collective actor decides to use these resources by founding a clandestine group.[29]

In other words, Carette and the three people arrested with him, while they may have founded the CCC, could not have constituted the group alone. Most European terrorist organisations are made up of a hard core, a second layer of 'active supporters' and an outer ring of sympathisers. The RAF, for instance, is currently constituted of about fifteen to twenty hard-core terrorists, 200 supporters and 2,000 to 3,000 sympathisers. At its peak strength, the Red Brigades probably had tens of thousands of sympathisers. The CCC hard core probably comprises about ten people, but it may have almost double that many supporters and as many as several hundred sympathisers. The number of CCC hide-outs and arms caches which have been discovered confirms that it had more than marginal support.

The four members arrested in Namur were most likely the leading propaganda/intellectual cell of the group. It is less probable that Carette himself made and planted the bombs. This role was allegedly fulfilled by a fifth person arrested, Luc Van Acker. He could very well have been the maker of the FRAP bombs as well, but it is doubtful that he was the movement's only 'artisan'. Van Acker allegedly lost his nerve after the death of two firemen in the 1 May 1985 attack and distanced himself from the group.

The 'professionalism' of the CCC attacks—the planning and coordination of the attacks (some of which occurred in daytime), and the sophistication of the devices (some of which involved gelignite fuses and propane gas canisters)—adds strength to the theory that the group was organised by a division of labour based on expertise: action, support and propaganda. If the CCC is organised along traditional 'cellular' lines, it has a politico-military executive made up of the heads of each 'column'. The column is divided into 'brigades', each with a specific function such as intelligence gathering, propaganda or fund raising (robbery). Brigades are in turn composed of cells. The CCC may be too small to have as many divisions, but its attacks suggest that a similar structure was used. That the CCC enjoyed enough support within the society to sustain an underground operation for fourteen months will have to be addressed by the government. Until it does so, the government has only cut the weeds while leaving the roots intact.

THE RESPONSE OF THE BELGIAN GOVERNMENT TO TERRORISM

The issue of security almost brought down the last Martens-led government coalition, and has plagued the current one. The catastrophic riot which occurred at Heysel soccer stadium on 28 May 1985 which left thirty-nine dead and was blamed partly on errors in security organisation and police coordination; the (still) unsolved massacres of sixteen people in three late 1985 robberies of Delhaize supermarket stores (bringing the total number of dead to twenty-nine since 1983 when the attacks began); the rise in both petty crime and violent armed robbery in recent years and the activities of the CCC all contributed to virtual public hysteria over security matters and police incompetence.

Manpower is not the problem: on a *per capita* basis, Belgium is the most highly policed country in the EEC.[30] Unfortunately, the police forces are decentralised, over-bureaucratised and poorly coordinated. The *gendarmerie* is a national force organised over five regions. It is part of the armed forces and is responsible to the Minister of National Defence on military matters, to the Minister of Justice on matters of judiciary police work and internal security, and to the Minister of the Interior on matters of general police work. This is a poor rationalisation of function and responsibility in itself. Then there is the judicial police (PJ), which is organised into twenty-seven precincts and reports to the Minister of Justice via the Procurator General. It is a centralised force composed of civil servants who carry out criminal investigations. Finally, there are the communal police forces which are usually under the control of municipal authorities and whose jurisdiction does not extend beyond communal boundaries. Belgium is composed of 589 communes.[31] Coordinating a national investigation, therefore, becomes a nightmare, and is only exacerbated by linguistic problems and intercommunal rivalry. Communication between these municipal forces is chaotic, at best. Nor are they funded, trained, equipped or organised to take a more active role in the fight against crime and terrorism.

The activities of the communal police are often badly coordinated with those of the *gendarmerie* and the judicial police; not least of all because one investigation could involve both PG and BSR (the judiciary investigation wing of the gendarmerie) with both reporting to different precincts. It is not surprising that, at 22 per cent, the rate of overall crime solution in Belgium is among the lowest in the EEC.

Even at the upper levels of the police hierarchy there is substantial decentralisation. There are five 'anti-terrorist' groups: ESI (special intervention squad), CNAT (college of the anti-terrorist struggle), GRT (group for the repression of terrorism), GSO (surveillance and observation group) and finally the GIA which is supposed to coordinate all their activities. However, not until 6 November 1985, thirteen months after the first CCC attacks, was the investigation placed in the hands of a single magistrate. Not until 10 November 1985 did the government decide to convene a crisis committee. Justice Minister Jean Gol was well aware of these problems when he declared that the anti-terrorist fight was hampered by bureaucratic resistance, security force lethargy, police rivalries, lack of funds, public anti-police prejudice and the necessity of protecting the rights of the individual in a democratic society.[32]

One possible reason for Gol's sensitivity to the balance between the need for security and the need to protect the rights of the individual may reside in the fact that Belgium has come under internal and external criticism for abuses within the judiciary system. One human rights group estimated that, in 1984, one third of Belgium's prison population was being held in 'preventative detention'.[33] Another study found on average a wait of seventeen months before a case comes to trial.[34] For any infraction which would draw a sentence of more than three months, this has meant the possibility of 'preventative' incarceration for over a year. The system allows for someone to be held without being charged for a period up to twenty-four hours. In that time, a judge must grant a warrant of arrest if police wish to detain the suspect. Within five days a judicial council must approve the warrant, and then must review it on a monthly basis. The criterion which the judge must accept to grant preventative detention is one of 'grave and exceptional circumstances which jeopardise public security'. This has obviously been too easily accepted, and the system abused. The study also found that 51.8 per cent of convicted criminals serve over half their term, and 29 per cent serve two thirds of their sentence. Such rigour is partly due to the fact that prisoners cannot petition for parole; prison wardens must propose it for them. Taken together, these factors suggest that, abuse aside, the judiciary system itself can already be used as one effective element in the struggle against terrorism in Belgium.[35]

Judicial matters aside, the government rightly felt that active measures designed to prevent and repress terrorism were sorely needed.

In a package approved by the government, the Council of Ministers proposed several measures designed to improve public security.[36] The most important proposals are the allocation of increased resources to and the rationalisation of the security forces; arms law reform; legislation allowing electronic surveillance and modification of the doctrine defining the proper use of deadly force by the police. Eight billion francs (over £100 million) are to be allocated to the various police forces over the next three years. Much of the money is destined to modernise communications equipment, scientific forensic equipment, support equipment and weaponry, and will also be spent on improving training and increasing pay. Other measures concern greater coordination among the forces and improved rationalisation of their various responsibilities.

On arms and munitions, the government proposes several reforms to a 1933 law. It will establish a commission on arms composed of government officials and representatives from the arms industry, hunters' and collectors' associations to advise the government on arms issues. A central registry would be created to record information on all arms transactions. Most importantly, arms and munitions would be classified into three categories and restricted, depending on the danger presented to public safety. The three categories are outright prohibition, arms which need prior authorisation, and arms which merely have to registered. For instance, a fully-automatic carbine is prohibited, whereas a semi-automatic must be authorised; hunting weapons only need to be registered. Two additional innovations are that responsibility for authorisations will be nationally centralised, and specific authorisations can be revoked.

Belgium is the only one of the Council of Europe countries not to employ means of electronic intelligence gathering in police work. The proposals on electronic surveillance create a legal machinery to enable police to exploit this means of investigation. Many safeguards are written into the propositions in order to guarantee the respect of individual privacy. Telephone taps and the like can only be installed by order of a judge with the prior approval from the court, and the order must be reviewed in fifteen days. 'Grave and exceptional circumstances' must be proven and written into the order, which cannot be issued for crimes punishable by less than five years. Orders can only be executed by the judicial police, and evidence obtained not specified in the order will not be allowed in court. Finally, the district attorney is empowered to warn the suspect that he is being observed in this manner. To ensure that there is a minimum of abuse, a commission on the protection of privacy will report to the Minister of Justice.

The package of proposals also modified the doctrine governing the use of arms by the police, replacing 'legitimate defence' with 'absolute necessity'. The distinction revolves around subtle differences in a policeman's perception of threat. Before, the use of deadly force was only justifiable if an officer felt personally endangered. The new doctrine enables the officer to use his weapon if he perceives a deadly threat to third parties.

That the bulk of these proposals will pass through Parliament with little problem signifies that Belgium realises it has entered a phase in which it is no longer immune to the ravages of terrorism.

The absence of a serious terrorist threat has not only affected the readiness of the security forces, but has also created a certain intransigence in the Belgian attitude towards extradition. Just as the former is now changing, so is the latter. The almost arrogant attitude toward extradition can be summed up in the remarks made by a Belgian jurist in 1973: 'Belgium does not have as much to fear from terrorism as those states in which terrorism finds its source and thrives. Therefore, Belgium must be very prudent about changing its own laws to suit the purposes of these states rather than its own'.[37] Developments over the next fifteen years did much to change this appraisal, but during this period any European effort to achieve a coordinated, unified extradition policy was to founder in Belgium on the rocks of its constitutional commitment to protect the rights of asylum. Although the government signed the 1977 European Convention on Suppression of Terrorism, it has been painfully slow in ratifying the treaty. Indeed, since the postulation of the Belgian *clause d'attentat* in 1856, which prohibited a political consideration for attacks on heads of foreign governments or members of their families, there has been, until recently, little Belgian legislation concerning extradition.

Justice Minister Gol, however, has pressed for greater domestic movement on this front and for a greater internationalisation of effort in the anti-terrorist fight. Due in part to his pressure, a law came into effect on 17 December 1985 bringing Belgian legislation on extradition more into line with the standards of the European conventions on extradition.[38] Extradition will now be based on the 'elimination' system, which compares the punishments mandated for a specific crime in the two countries. Also written into the new law are safeguard clauses guaranteeing the respect of the rights and fundamental freedoms of the individual: extradition is prohibited if the request is based on reasons of race, religion, nationality, political opinion, or if 'there is a risk of aggravating the situation of the individual for one or another of these reasons'. Gol has also been instrumental in Belgium's ready support for the European Community's recently imposed diplomatic sanctions on Libya, to which end the country quickly expelled nine Libyans.

These efforts signal Belgium's determination to combat terrorism and reflect its realisation that the struggle against terrorism within any one country must be supplemented by—indeed would be ineffective without—a concerted anti-terrorist effort from all European states. As Gol has said, the internationalisation of terrorism demands an international-isation of response.

THE POTENTIAL FOR THE RESURGENCE OF BELGIAN TERRORISM

Given what is now known about the history of domestic terrorism in Belgium, the government's appreciation of the need for concerted international action against terrorism is critical. Although four self-professed CCC terrorists and at least two suspected terrorists are now imprisoned, Belgium surely has not seen the last of domestic terrorism. In fact, the CCC may have merely broken the ice and been the prelude to more violence. As we have seen, the CCC must have enjoyed enough support to sustain a clandestine operation, and indeed in the weeks after the Namur arrests, a group claiming to be the CCC threatened to commit new attacks (none occurred). Numerous 'pro-CCC' tracts have been found in Brussels, and on 27 February 1986 a small demonstration was held outside the *Palais de Justice* in solidarity with Chantal Paternostre, an alleged FRAP member. On 2 May 1986, the four CCC prisoners, true to terrorist precedent, declared they would go on an indefinite hunger strike to protest against their prison conditions. Doubtless, they hope to generate the support and publicity gained by RAF and Provisional IRA hunger strikers. The results remain to be seen.

Even more troubling was the discovery in a CCC hide-out of a 'hit-list' of prominent Belgian businessmen, judges and political figures. In its final attacks the CCC was becoming more bold, attacking in daylight and attacking a NATO target in Versailles, France in cooperation with a 'group of internationalist communists in France'—notably not AD.

Perhaps a resuscitated 'rump' CCC will pick up where the founders left off. This tendency could only be augmented by renewed contacts with other internationalist groups which have demonstrated a proclivity for assassination. That Carette had at least some contact with LARF in 1982 is certain; now it appears that Jean-Paul Mazurier, an attorney for one of LARF's members, is in Belgium to defend the CCC terrorists. What is most disturbing in all this is that if the CCC was able to exploit objective conditions in society, what is to prevent a possibly more experienced group from recreating a Belgian terrorist organisation?

The soil is now fertile for the growth of such a group. The apparent youth of the CCC is not insignificant: Carette, 34; Didier Chevolet, 30; Pascale Vandegeerde, 28; Bertrand Sassoye, 22; Luc Van Acker, 24. Add to this that most of a 10 per cent rise in crime between 1984 and 1985 can be accounted for by an increase in juvenile crime.[39] Add the fact that about 10 per cent of Belgium's inhabitants are immigrants and that crime among second-generation immigrant youths is also increasing. In fact, several ethnic youth groups are assuming an openly militant character, as the children of immigrants feel increasingly alienated from their foster society.[40] Add persistent unemployment, and one has a sizeable pool of potential terrorist recruits. It is also interesting to note that the developments of the CCC coincided with a decline in linguistic/ethnic tensions as the devolution plans were implemented. Perhaps latent extreme-left sentiments which I suggested had been bottled up in the linguistic movements could finally express themselves because of the increasing resolution of the ethnic problem. Perhaps violent impulses deprived of a vent in the linguistic dispute found expression in the radical left. It is too early to test the validity of these postulates; I merely point out a correlation which, if valid, indicates a greater potential for terrorism in Belgium in the future.

Just because domestic terrorism is a latent phenomenon in Belgium does not mean that it is an aberration. What Belgian society must do to prevent a recurrence of such terrorism is to

apply the political ingenuity with which it has defused religious
and ethnic tensions to the domestic problems which could
foster the resurgence of terrorism. It would be a costly error for
the country to content itself with bolstered security measures,
and mistake temporary victory in the battle against the CCC
for ultimate victory in the war on terrorism.

APPENDIX A: CHRONOLOGY OF CCC ATTACKS

Date	Location	Target
2 Oct. 84	Brussels	Litton Business Systems
3 Oct. 84	Groot-Bijgaarden	MAN
8 Oct. 84	Brussels	Honeywell
15 Oct. 84	Brussels	Centre Paul Hymans
17 Oct. 84	Ghent	Christian Democratic Party (CVP)
26 Nov. 84	Bierset	NATO transmission antennae
11 Dec. 84	Ittre, Ensival, Glons, Archennes, Ath	NATO fuel pipelines
10 Jan. 85	Brussels	SHAPE building
1 May 85	Brussels	Federation of Belgian Businesses (2 killed)
8 Oct. 85	Brussels	Sibelgaz
12 Oct. 85	Charleroi	Fabrimétal
19 Oct. 85	Namur	Army Information office
4 Nov. 85	Brussels	Banque Bruxelles Lambert
	Charleroi	Société de Banque
5 Nov. 85	Charleroi	Manufacturers Hanover Bank
	Leuven	Kredietbank
21 Nov. 85	Brussels	Motorola
4 Dec. 85	Antwerp	Bank of America
6 Dec. 85	Oudenaarde	NATO fuel pipeline

6 Dec. 85   Versailles, France   Managing office of the
                                     5-nation NATO pipeline
                                     system

NOTES

1. J. Polasky, 'Liberalism and Biculturism', in A. Lijphart (ed.) *Conflict and Coexistence in Belgium,* Berkeley: University of California, 1980, p. 34.
2. *La Dernière Heure,* Brussels, 28 April 1986.
3. G. Thayer, *The War Business: The International Trade in Armaments,* London: Weidenfeld & Nicholson, 1969, p. 294.
4. *Ibid.,* p. 114.
5. A Molitor, 'The Reform of the Belgian Constitution', in Lijphart, *op. cit.,* p. 134.
6. R.E.M. Irving, *The Flemings and the Walloons of Belgium,* London: Minority Rights Group, 1980. p. 6.
7. See A. Lijphart, 'The Belgian Experience of Cultural Coexistence in Comparative Perspective', in Lijphart, *op. cit.*
8. The habit of consulting numerous interest groups and of allowing virtually unlimited time for parliamentary debate has forced the previous and present Martens government to seek the power to rule by decree in the economic arena, thus bypassing Parliament.
9. 'Belgian Survey', *The Economist,* 22 Feb. 1986, p. 4.
10. Irving, *op. cit.,* p. 7.
11. *The Economist, op. cit.,* p. 4.
12. D. Urwin, 'Social Cleavages and Political Parties in Belgium: Problems of Institutionalisation', *Political Studies,* Vol. 18, No. 3 (Sept. 1970), p. 321.
13. Contemporary labour disputes roughly reflect this pattern of support as well.
14. *The Economist, op. cit.,* p. 13-14.
15. J. Fitzmaurice, *The Politics of Belgium: Crisis and Compromise in a Plural Society,* London: C. Hurst, 1983, p. 208.
16. In contrast to the VMO, the quasi-fascist Flemish nationalist organisation which was proscribed in 1981.
17. A Lijphart, 'Political Theories and the Explanation of Ethnic Conflict in the Western World', in M.J. Esman (ed.) *Ethnic Conflict in the Western World,* Ithaca: Cornell University Press, 1977, pp. 61-2.
18. L. Huyse, 'Political Conflict in Bicultural Belgium', in Lijphart, *op. cit.,* pp. 115-16.
19. As quoted in *Le Monde,* 8 Jan. 1986.
20. D. della Porta. 'Left-wing Political Violence in Italy During the

Seventies: the Formation of Terrorists Organizations', a paper prepared for the International Political Science Association World Congress, Paris, July 1985.

21. Much of the following history of Pierre Carette is derived from articles in the Belgian newspaper *Le Soir,* and magazines *Pourquoi Pas?* and *Le Vif-Express,* and from the French newspapers *Le Monde* and *Liberation.*

22. Convicted in November 1983 in France for conspiracy and sentenced to five years, Oriach was released on 11 April 1986.

23. For a brief sketch of the ideology and evolution of fighting communist parties, see X. Raufer, *Terrorisme: Maintenant la France?: La Guerre des Partis Communistes Combattants,* Paris: Garniers Frères, 1982, pp. 180-93.

24. FRAP exploded only two bombs between April and June of 1985: at AEG-Telefunken and at the NATO assembly building. It claimed to be a 'revolutionary anti-imperialist organisation (acting) against everything which directly or indirectly works at preparing the imperialist war'. FRAP may have been founded by AD after its rift with the CCC, or it may have operated in conjunction with the CCC. In any case, FRAP will not be treated separately as it did not constitute a distinct phenomenon.

25. Euroterrorism should not be taken to mean that any degree of structural integration exists between any two European terrorist groups; it does not.

26. Della Porta, *loc. cit.,* p. 5.

27. For a detailed history of the relationship between Belgium and NATO, see H. Simonet, *Belgium in the Post-war Period: Partner and Ally,* Washington, DC: Georgetown University, 1981.

28. For an analysis of the left's view on terrorism, see R. Lallemand, *Terrorisme et Democratie,* Brussels: Institut Emile Vandervelde, 1979.

29. Della Porta, *loc. cit.,* pp. 14-15.

30. *Le Soir,* 17 April 1986.

31. J. Andrade, *World Police and Paramilitary Forces,* London: Macmillan, 1985, pp. 20-1.

32. *Le Soir,* 6 May 1985.

33. Report of the Belgian League for the Defence of Human Rights, in *La Cité,* 8 March 1985.

34. *Le Soir,* 14 May 1985.

35. Although legal definitions for what constitutes a terrorist act have been proposed for insurance purposes, terrorist activities, charges or criteria for defining crimes of a barbarous nature (e.g. an odious act against humanity, directed against innocent victims etc.) do not exist in Belgian law. The arrested CCC members have been charged with conspiracy, possession of illegal arms, forgery and possession of false papers.

36. Le Conseil des Ministres, *Projet de loi portant diverses mesures visant à renforcer la sécurité des citoyens,* Brussels, 30 Jan. 1986.

37. Centre de Droit Internationale et Association Belge des Juristes Démocrates, *Réflexions sur la Definition et la Repression du Terrorisme: Actes du Colloque,* Brussels: Université de Bruxelles, 1974, p. 228.
38. *La Lanterne,* 16 Sept. 1985.
39. *Pourquoi Pas?,* 9 April 1986.
40. Belgian society does not cultivate a 'melting pot' mentality, thus reinforcing this trend. For a study of this problem, see E. Roosens, 'The Multicultural Nature of Contemporary Belgian Society: the Immigrant Community', in Lijphart, *op. cit.*

8 Terrorism in France

Edward Moxon-Browne

BACKGROUND

Incidents attributable to terrorist groups have remained at a fairly constant level in France during the past ten years. Between 1976 and 1985, about 100 people have died as a result of terrorism. Fatalities are not the only reflection of terrorist activity. A government report on terrorism published in 1984[1] mentions over 700 people injured and around 4,600 attacks on property during the preceding nine years, making a grand total of some 6,000 terrorist incidents. The fact that much of this terrorism involves aliens (in fact, over half the fatalities in the past ten years) has caused the French government to be under some pressure not only from its own citizens but also from foreign governments to take a sterner hand with 'unwanted guests' on French territory. The attitude of successive French governments has appeared to some observers to be somewhat lackadaisical, and this may well be explained by the ambivalent connotations of the concept of 'terror' in the French political psyche.

Historically, it has to be remembered that the terror weapon has, to some extent, been perceived as synonymous with acts of heroism and indeed patriotism. The Republic itself was born in a violent revolution whose immediate aftermath was the eponymous terror of the Jacobins; and in the resistance to the Nazi occupation, acts of terroristic heroism have coloured the attitudes of French governments to similar resistance

movements in other countries. This, in turn, makes it difficult for the French state to denouce all 'freedom fighters'
as terrorists, with the consequence that the French have
been more prone to offer hospitality to political refugees,
and to refuse extradition, than is the case with their neighbours.

France itself is home to about a million foreigners who have
taken French citizenship since 1945; and there are about
150,000 political refugees, most of whom observe the
condition that political asylum excludes political activism. The
influx of other races is a legacy of France's colonial role in
Africa and the Far East. The racial mingling in France's cities
makes it easier for the would-be terrorist to blend in with his
surroundings, and harder for the police to find him. The
French tradition of welcoming political refugees creates a
constant fermentation of political activity in French cities. The
young and disillusioned urban intelligentsia from Italy, West
Germany, Spain and elsewhere find a fertile milieu in Paris and
other cities for the propagation of idealistic and even fantastic
dreams of creating a new society in Western Europe. Nor are
all the dreams fantastic: many groups are genuinely aggrieved
at the 'colonial' status of their homelands and only wish to
achieve some sort of autonomy or independence for their
territories. Paris acts as a refuge for exiles from a wide variety
of political regimes; its atmosphere of free political debate and
its long tradition of nurturing radical points of view make it a
natural home for disaffected groups from almost every
continent.

If France's role as a *terre d'asile,* and the tolerant
atmosphere of French political debate, provide a fertile seed
bed for terrorism, it is also true that France's geographical
location enables it to be an effective magnet for political
dissidents from other countries. With seven other countries
bordering on its long frontiers, France is especially vulnerable
to the international terrorist who takes easy advantage of the
relatively free movement afforded by the European
Community. All this is greatly facilitated by France's position
at the hub of Western Europe and its direct transport links to

the rest of the continent. Highly developed media networks in France and a tradition of free thought in the French press combine to provide the terrorist with the oxygen of publicity that his campaign inevitably requires.

The categorisation of terrorist groups in France is not easy nor can one pinpoint strategies or goals in the same way that is possible for more familiar groups in other countries. French terror groups defy a facile left-right classification, and even the autonomist groups whose goals mirror those of analogous groups in other parts of the world adopt ideological slogans and declared 'aims' that appear to place them on the left-right spectrum. The problems of classification are further complicated by the appearance of splits within movements (with one wing typically adopting an ideological stance and the other a more pragmatic position). Groups with differing aims will adopt similar tactics (three British commercial targets attacked in France in 1981 and 1982 were in fact claimed by three different groups: two extreme left groups antipathetic to business interests and IRA sympathisers demonstrating solidarity with the Northern Ireland hunger striker Bobby Sands); or one group will change its tactics over a period of time; all this makes it difficult (sometime impossible) to attribute particular incidents to particular groups. Moreover, groups have been known to claim credit for the action of other groups (six different groups claimed credit for the bombing of the International Hotel in Paris in August 1981) but, on the contrary, others have been anxious to make it appear that another group has performed some action lest the public outcry following an exceptionally grisly piece of carnage should prove counter-productive in terms of the group's image (for example the shooting dead of six people in a Jewish restaurant in Paris 1982 was thought to be the work of Arab terrorists but may well have been the work of a neo-Nazi group). Some incidents (e.g. the bombing of the Paris-Toulouse express, in March 1982, with five deaths) are claimed by no one.

A final background factor that has to be considered when highlighting the incidence of terrorism in France is the policies of governments towards the phenomenon. The response of the French state is dealt with in more detail at the end of the chapter. Suffice it for now to mention a major constraint under which French governments have to operate. In tackling terrorism, French administrations have to walk a precarious tightrope between safeguarding individual liberties of citizens, and responding effectively to the threats that terrorism clearly poses to a democratic society. This choice is not, of course, peculiar to France, but the issues at stake are clearly linked to the central political values born in 1789 and embodied in successive French Constitutions. The debate on the death penalty epitomises this dilemma. Abolished by the previous Socialist government there are now calls for its restoration. The tightening up carried out by the previous Socialist government in 1982 was a response to public outcry at what was clearly an increase in terrorism in the French capital in the summer months of that year. Being a left-wing government made it vulnerable to charges that it was trampling on the civil liberties of citizens whereas if it had remained inactive it would have been charged (as it had already been) with being 'soft on terrorism'. More recently, in May 1985, the new French government introduced a wide range of measures to combat terrorism in the wake of the Libyan crisis. Again public opinion seems to be ambivalent. On the one hand a poll shows that 87 per cent of French people believe that terrorism constitutes a 'serious threat' to France but, on the other hand, there has been some opposition to the new measures on the grounds that they pose a serious threat to individual liberties.[2]

TERRORIST GROUPS

We turn now to consider some of the principal groups engaged in terrorism in France over the past ten years. With each group we consider the frequency and character of their attacks, the targets selected, and the ideological arguments used to 'justify' the group's campaign of violence. In the spring of 1986, the headlines of French newspapers began to reflect an upsurge in terrorist activity after a relative lull during 1985. In particular, the attack by *Action Directe* (AD) on the Interpol headquarters, in May 1986, emphasised that this extreme left group was far from beaten despite the arrest of one of its leading figures, André Olivier, the previous day. AD first came to public notice in 1979 as a result of the merger between GARI (*Groupe d'action Revolutionnaire Internationale*) and NAPAP (*Noyaux Armes pour l'Autonomie Populaire*). GARI had been working for the overthrow of the Franco regime in Spain, while NAPAP was a small group of urban guerillas with Maoist sympathies sharing both tactics and aims with the Red Brigades in Italy. Since 1979 AD has claimed responsibility for about fifty attacks mainly in the Paris area. Its targets have included businesses (especially those concerned with computers), government buildings, and both Jewish and American institutions. In April 1980 there were two attacks on computer firms in Toulouse. In one case, an attack on Philips, the firm's computers had been scientifically neutralised; in the other, an attack on CII-Honeywell-Bull Co, the firm's offices were destroyed in an arson attack. In March 1980, the Ministry of Overseas Cooperation in Paris was attacked with automatic weapons, and leaflets explaining AD policy were distributed. In early 1982, the Israeli mission was attacked and an Israeli diplomat had his car machine-gunned later the same year. Both attacks were part of a wider AD campaign connected with the group's support of the Arab cause in the Middle East. Closely linked with this campaign was one against American targets. An American school at St Cloud was bombed in the summer of 1982 following an earlier attack on the Bank of America. The forces of law and order are an obvious target for AD. There are two aims here: one is to secure the release of AD prisoners, and the other is to demonstrate that the group is still alive and well after a particular victory by the police. For example, a police station in Toulouse was attacked in 1980 just two days after twenty-eight AD suspects had been rounded up by the police. An attack on the Intercontinental Hotel in August 1981 in which ten people were injured was designed to intimidate the police into releasing AD suspects who had not benefitted from a recently announced government amnesty. The attack on the Interpol headquarters, mentioned earlier, was a clear reprisal for recent police successes against the group. Interpol had been particularly successful at passing information across frontiers about the increasingly international character of AD's membership and links (including the merging of West German RAF cells and the AD group in January 1985).

The tracts and leaflets of AD make it possible to piece together the ideological sub-structure of the group's activities. Firstly there has obviously been an anti-colonial ingredient in their operations. The attack on the Overseas Cooperation Ministry was accompanied by leaflets that condemned France's neo-colonial involvement in Africa in general, and in Tunisia, Chad, Djibouti and the Central African Republic in particular. The leaflets argued that the 'struggle against French imperialist politics in Africa' was part of the 'struggle against the French state in its world institutions' and that now was the time to 'take up arms against the slave-making state'. Secondly, we have seen that there has been a strong concern with the Middle East situation. This has manifested itself in the attacks on American and Jewish buildings. After the attack on the car of the Israeli diplomat, an AD communiqué deplored the 'genocide of Palestinians by Israeli troops' and asserted that AD could not 'allow the Palestinian people to be exterminated in West Beirut'. The attacks on computer firms provide a third strand in AD thinking. Computers are perceived as epitomising the materialist, profit-oriented and dehumanising ethos of Western capitalism. Here we note a close affinity to the thinking of the Baader-Meinhof group, whose attacks on capitalist institutions and symbolic individuals (e.g. the killing of Hans Martin Schleyer) are redolent of the same alienation. After the attack on the computer firms in Toulouse AD explained that computers were 'the favoured tool of people who dominate. They serve to exploit, to document, to control, and to punish'. AD ideology then links together a variety of concerns associated with the extreme left: anti-colonialism, anti-Americanism, anti-capitalism and anti-militarism. These themes are reflected, albeit clumsily, in the communiqué released after the attack on the Interpol headquarters. In part, and in translation, AD aims are alleged to be; 'to hit at central installations which link their political, economic and military strategy, and at the heart of which are found the strongest antagonisms of the international proletariat/imperialist bourgeoisie; to concretise the qualitative leap of all antagonisms of the masses and develop them toward a global revolutionary strategy'.

Structurally, AD can best be seen as a network of groups working in loose cooperation with each other and having absorbed the remnants of similarly-minded groups in other countries. AD is unusual in having a high proportion of non-French members working within it (and, incidentally, a high proportion of women). Many of the earlier constituent groups under the AD 'umbrella' adopted exotic *noms de guerre* such as *Jeune Taupe* (Young Mole) and *Moutons Enragés* (Angry Sheep), names that spoke eloquently for the movement's clandestine and anarchical activities. In January 1985, AD split into two wings with the more aggressive faction merging with the Red Army Faction (RAF) from West Germany and the *Cellules Communistes Combattantes* (CCC) from Belgium. Since then, AD has maintained a higher profile, bombing business premises in Paris, and attempting to murder Guy Brana, the vice-president of the French employers' organisation, in April 1986.

As we have already seen, the Middle East situation provides a background against which much terrorism in France takes place. This can be accounted for by the historic links that France has with the Lebanon and by the fact that there are a considerable number of Arabs living in France. When one adds to that the hospitality that France offers to political refugees one clearly has a potentially explosive situation.

Terrorism arising from the Middle East situation is in a category by itself in the sense that it is 'imported terrorism'. As the Interior Minister, M. Defferre, said in 1982, 'we will discourage them from coming to settle their scores on our territory'. In fact, that discouragement has not been very successful and there are a number of groups at work in the

Paris area who have Middle Eastern connections. One of the most recent to appear (in February 1986) was the *Comité de Solidarité aux Prisonniers Politiques Arabes et du Proche Orient* (Committee of Solidarity with Arab and Middle Eastern Political Prisoners) or CSPPA. This group has specialised in bombing stores in Paris, and many people have been injured. In March 1986, the group bombed the Galerie Point show on the Champs Elysées killing two people and injuring twenty-eight. Three days earlier the same group had bombed the Paris-Lyon express, injuring ten.

The Arab-Israeli conflict has been the central theme for Middle Eastern terrorism in France. In 1978 four people were killed at Orly airport by a group calling itself the Sons of Southern Lebanon. In July 1982, Fadl Dani, deputy at the PLO office in Paris, was killed in a bomb explosion, becoming the seventh PLO victim in France in ten years. In the same year, the second secretary at the Israeli embassy was shot dead as he returned home.

Iranian politics have provided another rationale for violence in France, especially since the fall of the Shah. A former Prime Minister of the Shah, Shahpour Bahktiar, living in exile in Neuilly, narrowly escaped assassination outside his home in early 1979, and two people were killed in the subsequent shoot out. Tension between France and Iran was heightened in 1981 when the French government decided to give political asylum to the Iranian ex-president Bani Sadr. Street clashes led to one death. In 1982 an Iranian was arrested at Orly airport while trying to smuggle in explosives allegedly for an attempt on Bani Sadr's life.

Armenian terrorism has also used French soil for some of its operations. The main group is The Armenian Secret Army for the Liberation of Armenia (ASALA). In 1979 the director of the Turkish tourist office was assassinated. A Turkish labour attaché was gunned down in the street in 1981. Hostages were taken at the Turkish cultural centre in September 1981 and although all were released unharmed, a guard was shot dead. The most serious incident, and one of the most serious of any recent terrorist incidents in France, was the bombing of the

Turkish Airlines counter at Orly airport on 7 July 1983 when seven people died and fifty-five were injured. Since then ASALA has been fairly quiescent following the arrest and life imprisonment of the group's leader, Varodjian Garbidjian. ASALA's *raison d'être* is the sense of grievance felt by Armenians in many parts of the world at the treatment meted out to their countrymen by the Turkish government between 1915 and 1922, when it is claimed that one million Armenians were virtually massacred. Today ASALA fights for Armenian autonomy despite the demographic complexities of the Armenian community being divided between three different countries (Turkey, the USSR and Iran).

In May 1986, an attack by the *Front de la Libération Nationale de la Corse* (FLNC) reminded French public opinion that the violent struggle for autonomy on the island of Corsica was still very much alive. A gang of about thirteen FLNC members entered a tourist complex at Cargese, took thirty people hostage, and then placed explosive charges in several different places in the complex. Later the owner of the complex and a policeman were killed when they tried to defuse the devices. The attack came ten years after the founding of the FLNC in January 1976, when two separatist organisations, *Giustizia Paolina* and the *Fronte Parisann Corsu di Liberazione* (FPLC) merged to form the new organisation. Since that date the FLNC has proved to be the most violent of all terrorist groups in France, although it does not seek to take life but merely to destroy property, particularly targets that relate to the French occupation of the island.

In late 1976 bombs destroyed a chemist shop, a bank, and business offices in Porto Vecchio. The most serious incident of the year was the blowing up of an Air France airliner at Ajaccio airport just after 181 passengers were forced to disembark. In 1977, a holiday village was partly destroyed at Cargese, and a TV transmitter was blown up, depriving the island of television programmes for several weeks. In 1978 a radar mast at the Solenzara air base was destroyed; and later the same year public utility offices were destroyed in Ajaccio. In the summer of the year a visit to the island by President Giscard d'Estaing sparked protests; in July the FLNC claimed responsibility for thirty-three bombings in one night. From 1979 onwards violence increased and spread to the mainland. The Ministry of Finance in Paris was bombed; and the following year FLNC bombs affected both Paris and Nice. In early 1981 violence escalated further: forty-six bombs went off in one night in January after prison sentences had been handed down to some FLNC members; and at Ajaccio airport a bomb went off killing one person just a few minutes after Giscard d'Estaing arrived from Paris for an offical visit. A truce was declared in April when the new government of President Mitterand took office, although this was later suspended. Violence has not been serious recently except for the renewal in early 1986 after the attack at Cargese mentioned above.

Having assessed the incidence of FLNC violence in the past ten years, we have to consider the ideology that lies behind it. Basically the FLNC believes that Corsica should be an independent country and that France exploits the Corsican people in a number of ways. Economically, the tourist industry is resented because it brings profits to the French companies that own most of the holiday complexes (*Club Mediterranée* is especially detested) and there is a strand of thought that argues that Corsica is being environmentally damaged by insensitive commercial tourist development. At a clandestine press conference in 1979 the FLNC argued that 'land is being surrendered to property speculators supported in their depredations by the colonial administration'. The loans given by French banks to settlers to operate their businesses are resented and this explains the FLNC attacks on banks in the island and in mainland France. French culture is seen as assaulting the native Corsican language and culture. Hence school teachers are the targets of threats in their mail, and their homes are attacked. Likewise the attack on the TV mast was a symbolic attack on the transmission of French culture to the island. At his trial for alleged complicity in the explosion, one of the defendants said that television 'transmits throughout our country, all of French culture, all that alienates and destroys the language and culture of Corsica, the collective memory of our people'. Targets of FLNC attacks also include police stations, since the police represent most obviously the French state and French law in the island. Likewise the military presence at the Solenzara base is singled out by the FLNC as an insult because it suggests that Corsica has colonial status and requires a military occupation force (Solenzara is the biggest French air base outside mainland France). After the attack on Solenzara (in January 1978) an FLNC message pointed out the wider implications of the base, calling it

an instrument of under-development imposed on Corsica . . . Solenzara allows western imperialism to threaten the free and progressive countries of the Mediterranean . . . a base for intervention and aggression against the Palestinian people in 1967, hand in glove with fascist and bloody regimes in Iran and South Africa who send their pilots to train at Solenzara . . .. The Front will continue the political and military struggle which is the only way the Corsican people can throw off colonialism.

There is undoubtedly a great deal of support for autonomy among Corsicans within France: possibly half the Corsican population support more autonomy and renounce violence to achieve it. The small minority that espouses violence has been able however to count on a fairly passive population that understands, even if it does not support, the methods of the younger extremists. Admiral Sanguinetti (a moderate Corsican nationalist) put this view in an interview for the *Irish Times*[3]: 'Today's violence is a direct result of successive denials of our national and cultural rights by the most centralised, industrialised, state in the world . . .. Repression instead of a political solution provides further solidarity among Corsicans, and above all pushes them all further towards a radical stand'. The moderate politician Dr Simeoni echoed this view in an interview for *El Pais* when he said:

Violence is inevitable because of a block of the situation maintained by Paris with growing repression . . .. Repressions of every kind are exercised by Paris, a public repression under the pretext of fighting the FLNC . . .. We're besieged by police and soldiers . . . the FLNC is not exploited by foreigners, I know them, they are patriots helped by Corsicans.[4]

In response to such sentiments, the French government set up an assembly in the island to give the politicians a chance to outflank the men of violence by taking control of some decisions away from Paris. The assembly, elected in August 1982, boosted the moderate autonomous parties but has not been particularly successful in stemming the violence on the island. What it has done is to drive a wedge between the FLNC and the moderate autonomists, and it is now more difficult for the FLNC to count on popular support from the indigenous population. All through its ten-year existence the FLNC has zigzagged between being a 'fish in the water' of popular autonomist sentiment, and being 'patriots in a citadel' besieged by anti-nationalist antagonism. It is in the latter phase now. During the last two years, the 'third world, anti-colonial' element has deserted the movement and it has been left in the hands of the 'hard men' whose current attacks on tourist targets are particularly unpopular as they reduce employment on an island where jobs are already scarce. The new tough tactics are a sign of weakness and the Interior Minister put his finger on this when he said, after the May 1986 attack at Cargese, 'We are not dealing with nationalists but with gangsters . . .. When a minority tries to impose its own law by force it becomes a fascist minority'.[5]

Although Corsica has been the cause of most of France's terrorism rooted in separatist aspirations, something must be said about the Breton separatist movement which, although now quiescent, was until recently the origin of spasmodic violence. Most of the terrorism in the Brittany region occurred in the late 1970s and was mostly the responsibility of a group calling itself *Front de la Libération de la Bretagne-Armée Republicaine Bretonne* (FLB-ARB) which was outlawed in 1974. The ARB represented the more extreme Marxist-oriented wing of the movement, but both wings were committed to violence. At the start of the campaign, the main targets were buildings and property connected with the forces of law and order. Lawyers' offices were damaged by a bomb in 1976 in Quimper; a court-house in St Malo and police vehicles in St Brieuc were destroyed by explosives the following year. In late 1977 five explosions in a single night were aimed against targets connected with governmental authority in the region, including military installations and a tax office. In 1978 the FLB-ARB campaign reached its peak and was extended outside Brittany. Police buildings were once again a favourite target for attack. The climax of the campaign came on 26 June when a huge bomb exploded inside the Palace of Versailles in the middle of the night. About half-a-million pounds worth of damage was done and some valuable paintings were destroyed. After the Versailles attack the impetus of militant Breton separatism began to wane as leading members of the FLB-ARB found themselves arrested and tried. Except for a bomb in Paris and a handful of attacks in 1979 in Brittany itself, the violence had virtually ceased by 1980.

The attack on Versailles represented the climax of the campaign in the sense that it struck at a leading repository of French culture. As President Giscard d'Estaing observed, this was 'lamentable damage to part of France's heritage'. Perhaps intentionally, the terrorists had struck at an exhibition of Napoleonic painting—and Napoleon represents the very centralisation that the Breton separatists and all separatists were so much opposed to. After the Versailles attack the FLB-ARB left a message for police which said: 'The Breton people is oppressed; the land of Brittany is occupied by French military camps; the Breton language and culture are denied and destroyed by the imperialist French power'. That message encapsulates the aspirations of Breton separatists to assert the cultural and political independence of the Brittany region, a region that was only subsumed into the French state in 1532 and which shares a Celtic culture with Cornwall, Wales and Ireland. The cultural distinctiveness of the region was reinforced by its economic underdevelopment, its declining population and its dying industries. However, in the last ten years new investment in the region, better transport links with the rest of France and a token recognition of the Breton language have contributed to a reduction in the extent of the region's economic dependence, and a defusing of cultural grievances.

THE RESPONSE OF THE STATE

The political flavour of recent French governments has been a crucial factor in determining their response to terrorism. In 1981, for example, following a period of relative calm, the Mitterrand government made some important changes to what were perceived as excessively harsh measures instituted by the previous regime. The State Security Court was abolished after eighteen years of operation; hundreds of prisoners were granted an amnesty which effectively put many potential terrorists back into circulation; and the death penalty was abolished. The government reiterated its policy of welcoming political refugees to France and thereby discouraged any speculation that extradition of suspects for 'politically motivated' offences might become the rule rather than the exception. In the summer of 1982, as the death toll from terrorism reached fifteen within a four-month period, the government was forced to tighten up its policies once again although it is debatable whether these measures were more than cosmetic. A Secretary of State for Public Security was appointed; laws on the sale of certain weapons were revised; *Action Directe* was banned; and within the government a 'council of terrorism' was established to keep a watching brief on the situation. It was announced that there would be a stricter control on foreigners entering France. As a sign of its seriousness the government expelled two Syrian diplomats, the first expulsions of Arab diplomats for ten years.

More recently under the 'cohabiting' (but essentially right-wing) Chirac government, there has been increased reaction against what are seen as the lax policies of the previous administration. Following a number of incidents, attributable partly to *Action Directe,* the government announced new measures at the end of May 1986. Terrorist suspects could now be held for four days instead of forty-eight hours; twenty-year jail terms could be stipulated for the most serious offences carrying a life sentence; the police may now stop anyone and ask for identification, and if not satisfied detain the person for questioning; and convicted terrorists would be given incentives to inform on their colleagues. Calls for the death penalty to be reinstated have been resisted, however. On September 1986, in the wake of a number of deaths in Paris from terrorist bombs, the government required visas from all persons entering France except those from the EEC and Switzerland.

Greater police powers are a response to widespread public concern over the violent crimes that now seem to be more prevalent—especially in Paris. Nevertheless, the conduct of the police has itself become a political issue. After the 'Les Halles incident' in early 1986 (in which eight teenagers were held overnight by the police without charge, and without their parents being informed), and more recently after the shooting dead by police of a motorist, there is concern about the apparent lack of control and accountability in the French police.

Public opinion, according to a poll taken in France in February 1986, should prove receptive to the government's latest measures. Most respondents consider imported terrorism to be more serious than the indigenous variety, with Iran, Libya and the PLO seen as the prime instigators. Fifty-nine per cent felt that the government should 'do more' against international terrorism, with 'stricter security at airports' being the most popular option (69 per cent) and 'economic sanctions against governments that support terrorists' (48 per cent) also commanding support. There is however a reluctance to counter terrorism with violence. Twenty-seven per cent felt that military action by the USA against those perpetrating acts of terrorism against Americans would 'reduce international terrorism' but 44 per cent said it 'would make things worse'. There is strong support for international cooperation against terrorism in Western Europe, 86 per cent agreeing that it is 'the only way to reduce the number of international terrorist attacks'.[6]

The time may be ripe therefore for greater cooperation between France and her EEC neighbours on the subject of terrorism. France's lukewarm attitude towards the European Convention on the Suppression of Terrorism can be explained by an ideological attachment to its role as a haven for political refugees, a low incidence of terrorism in France at the time the Convention was negotiated, and adequate domestic legislation for coping with most anticipated incidents of violence. The environment has changed; the transition of Spain to democracy and its later entry to the EEC make France's reluctance to extradite Basque terrorist suspects to Madrid more difficult to justify (although the exile of an ETA leader in July 1986 to Gabon rather than Spain must rank as a curious response to the new circumstance).[7] In the aftermath of the American air raid on Libya, France has not been slow to fall in with collective actions endorsed within the framework of the EEC. Links between *Action Directe* and groups in West Germany have also compelled the French police to work very closely with their counterparts in other parts of Western Europe.

NOTES

1. *Rapport du Senat sur le Terrorisme,* Paris: Imprimerie du Senat, 1984, appendix 6, p. 217.
2. *The Times,* 27 May 1986.
3. *Irish Times,* 16 Jan. 1980.
4. *El Pais,* 5 Sept. 1979.
5. *Le Monde,* 17 May 1986.
6. MORI poll, Feb. 1986 (carried out in France on behalf of MORI by Institut de Sondages Lavialle).
7. *The Guardian,* 16 July 1986.

9 The European Community and Terrorism: From Principles to Concerted Action

Juliet Lodge

INTRODUCTION

In 1986 members of the European Community were to take unprecedented steps to augment their capacity to act in concert in the attempt to combat terrorism. There can be little doubt that extraneous factors, not least among which was the US military action against Libya in April, conspired to produce a sense of urgency among the majority of—but not all—EC states for a recognisable and enforceable Community response to terrorist threats. At the same time, the internal context within which the member states were to consider taking measures that could be construed as a further limitation upon their individual sovereignties were significant, and should not be overlooked.

Pressure had been growing for several years, for example, for the states to improve the effectiveness of the operation of the political cooperation machinery established in the early 1970s for the purpose of facilitating cooperation of a non-binding sort among member states in the sphere of foreign policy. For over a decade, the artificial distinctions between external policy and foreign policy had been assiduously cultivated. The latter was deemed the pre-eminent and inviolable preserve of the individual member states, the former subject to supranational regulation. Thus, external policy was loosely construed as a technical area and as one where the European Community had jurisdiction. External policy was seen to be concerned principally with commerce and external trade. It was linked to the creation of a common market and hence to the establishment of a common external tariff, the Common Agricultural Policy, relations with the Lomé country signatories, and so on.

The confluence of several factors in the wake of the first direct elections to the European Parliament in June 1979 was to heighten the imperative for the member states to tighten up and improve their endeavours, if not to enable the Community to 'speak with one voice' then to minimise the chances of its members simultaneously speaking with several, often embarrassingly contradictory, voices in the face of major international events. Whether or not the then Nine member states were ready or willing to compromise their autonomy in the ever-increasing interactions over a range of matters not foreseen, or at least not mentioned, in the Treaty of Rome was of less consequence perhaps than the fact that the international community at large increasingly expected the European Community to have if not a unified position on international issues (which by definition could not be limited to trade) then complementary ones.

Furthermore, it became obvious that the political dimensions and conflicts over aspects of external relations could not be ignored or surreptitiously subsumed under the rubric of external trade when national interests within the Community diverged—as, for example, in respect of US-EC quarrels over steel and agriculture. Divisions simply gave non-Community states an opportunity to exploit an issue, possibly to the overall longer-term detriment of the Community's general interest. Moreover, whether disputes arose over matters linked to the establishment of a new policy *vis-à-vis* developing countries that were to become signatories to the Lomé conventions or whether they surfaced as it became manifest that member states' national interests converged—however imperfectly—more than they diverged, the effect was to hasten a hesitant rethink on the implications of political cooperation in foreign policy matters. This was, moreover, expedited by growing recognition among EC members that national foreign policy objectives could be pursued and reinforced by their 'Europeanisation' and concerted Community backing; that increasingly on key issues the member states' foreign policies—in spite of differences of opinion—had more in common with each other than with the United States; and that as a Community, EC states' international interests were not always coterminous with those of the United States.[1]

This realisation was not exactly novel. It had been identified before the European Community's creation. However, for many years it had been construed largely in military terms—the notion of the two pillars of the Atlantic Alliance being a case in point. By the 1970s, however, there was increasing dissatisfaction with the compartmentalisation of military and Atlantic Alliance matters when security problems had very clear ramifications of a non-military kind.

The idea that such compartmentalisation was necessary to avoid compromising neutral states or those not fully integrated into the Atlantic Alliance was also losing credibility. Irish politicians were increasingly to acknowledge the extent to which Irish foreign policy interests coincided with those of its EC partners. It is true that Ireland appended an annex to its ratification of the Single European Act in late 1986, but this was not inspired simply by a desire to highlight its neutral status in view of greater cooperation in EPC (European Political Cooperation). Rather, an overriding consideration was insistence upon due recognition being paid to the promotion of social and economic convergence in tandem with the realisation of the internal market. The oil crisis and efforts to apprehend terrorists were, moreover, to highlight the drawbacks of compartmentalisation and to underline the obvious point that security could not be treated simply and strictly as a military matter when external threats assumed economic or other non-military forms.

However, the logical consequences of this for the way in which member states worked together in the Community—notably in respect of international events—and more so in EPC were slow to be realised. Not until the 1980s was real progress to be made on institutionalising cooperation on foreign affairs among member states, the aim being to enhance the credibility of any Community responses, to limit the chances for others to exploit internal rifts, and to augment efficiency in EPC, for example by means of the Troika arrangements and the setting up—under the provisions of the Single European Act—of a secretariat to assist the EC Presidency. International developments hastened this, as did the pressure for institutional rationalisation from within the Community. To the forefront of this was pressure for integrating the EPC into the EC and for allowing the Community to discuss matters with security (and also defence) implications. Divisions between the US and the Community in view of the Arab-Israeli conflict, the export of high-technology goods to the East bloc, and finally the determination of an appropriate response to state-sponsored terrorism, accentuated the need for the Community to make clear its own position and to devise appropriate machinery to facilitate speedy decision-making. This was not to herald a proactive rather than reactive foreign policy style on the Community's part in international arena. But it was designed to remedy decision-making deficiencies.

The need to improve the Community's general decision-making capacity, to augment its international competitiveness and to redress economic recession produced in both supranational and national political elites a readiness, if not an anxiousness, to stimulate changes in the Community: changes that would significantly increase its capability to act appropriately and promptly, and that would enhance the member states' ability to meet their goals. This was coupled with the desire of many Members of the European Parliament (MEPs) to increase the power of the European Parliament effectively to control, supervise and hold accountable the Council of Ministers as well as the Commission. The question of creating an effective EC capable of action was therefore inextricably linked to the underlying idea that efficiency should not be purchased at the expense of democracy; and that, if anything, the Community's democratic deficit should be redressed by dint of enabling the European Parliament to play a truly legislative role (both on internal and external policy matters).

In the event, it was to be the European Parliament that was to galvanise the member states into action. It cannot be denied that MEPs were partly motivated by self-interest—by a desire to increase their own power. Nor can it be denied that divisions existed over the appropriate way to address the problem of increasing the European Parliament's influence in the Community. However, even those who favoured the policy of small steps and gradual institutional change were largely to be swayed in favour of a more direct approach. Thus, consensus was achieved on institutional and policy reforms and on encouraging the Community to cross the Rubicon from a trade pact to a European Union.[2] The result was the Draft Treaty establishing the European Union (EUT) that MEPs adopted on 14 February 1984.[3]

The detail of this draft treaty need not detain us.[4] Suffice it to say that member governments were sufficiently seized of the imperative of institutional and policy reform to consider it seriously[5] and to seek an intergovernmental alternative to it embodying some of its recommendations: the Single European Act (SEA). Approved in essence by the European Council meeting in Luxembourg in December 1985, the SEA was presented for ratification during 1986 and is due to come into force on 1 July 1987.

One of its most notable features from the point of view of this discussion was its attempt to fudge the issue of the distinction between the EC and EPC. While political cooperation was not brought under the rubric of the EC completely, it was significant that it should be mentioned in the same document (the SEA) as the EC and the completion of the Community's internal market.[6] Moreover, the member states were pledged to greater cooperation on a range of foreign policy issues that eroded the barriers which had previously separated fundamentally inseparable elements of international relations.

The SEA went further still in advancing, but not in so many

words, the creation of a European judicial area. Henceforth, cooperation against terrorism and drug trafficking was to be promoted overtly within the context of the Community. Although cooperation in these matters had previously been pursued within TREVI, Interpol and among national police and security forces, the aim of completing the internal market by the early 1990s had implications for criminal law.

The European Parliament was instrumental in exploiting the climate of opinion (born possibly of desperation in the face of recession) in favour of reform. The EUT, coupled with MEPs' increasing preoccupations during the European Parliament's plenary sessions with matters of 'high politics' and international affairs stimulated steps that were eventually to commit the EC's members formally to concert action in foreign policy matters including the attempt to confound terrorism.

In practice, however, it was to be an issue of international terrorism that was to test the new agreements (which were only in the process of being ratified—often amid stiff internal opposition). The response to the Libyan terrorist incidents and more especially to the US retaliatory moves highlighted the complex problems involved in formulating and implementing concerted Community action on foreign and security issues. It was also to reveal the limited ability of essentially intergovernmental arrangements (such as those in EPC) to persuade the member states first to construct and then comply with a common line when one new Community state (Greece) distanced itself repeatedly from Community views while others appeared to ignore them temporarily: concerted Community efforts could be frustrated by outsiders (including as powerful an ally as the USA) if but one member could be persuaded to demur from the common line. Thus, in the Libyan case, vacillation by the British led to some bitter exchanges among EC states, with complaints that the British government had either simply insisted that British interests in this matter were virtually identical to those of the USA, or had seriously underestimated the validity of other member states' views on the matter.

It was hardly surprising then that some EC states should

consider in what forum—EC, EPC, NATO, WEU, London and Bonn summits, TREVI or the Council of Europe—more extensive anti-terrorist measures could be most effectively pursued and should see a possibility for revitalising WEU. The chance of realising EC states' Europeanised national foreign policy goals could be enhanced by parallel action in several bodies. The European Community and EPC were, however, to remain foremost among these not least because of the binding nature of Community agreements. The extent of overlap in the context of a new European and Community response to terrorism between various fora is quite marked: recurrent themes emerged during 1985-86 in EPC, the European Parliament and the NATO and WEU assemblies. The following overview of the response to Libyan terrorist incidents will show how the Community, in default of military intentions or means, belatedly opted for a range of politico-economic and legal measures designed to deter and curtail terrorism. It will also reveal the EC's multi-faceted approach to combatting terrorism. This combines politico-economic and diplomatic offensives with legal sanctions and increased internal security cooperation.

THE CATALYST—LIBYA

1986 was to mark a turning point in EC states' reaction to terrorism. In the past, member states had been reticent to name officially countries as either practitioners, sponsors or sympathisers of terrorism. Attempts by some states to exclude from Lomé or from the enjoyment of Lomé arrangements and funds, or from Community benefits, those states guilty either of covertly sponsoring, or committing terrorist acts, or of providing safe havens for fugitive terrorists had foundered on the rock of non-intervention in the internal affairs of other states. The Libyan débâcle in 1986 was to end such wariness; the Community was to name publicly those states which its members broadly considered to be sponsors of terrorism.

That the Community was able to make such a move was no

mean feat given both the reservations expressed by Greece, Spain and Italy and intra-EC differences in perception of the seriousness of the threat of terrorism and the appropriateness of new Community-based anti-terrorist action. There can be no doubt that reservations hinged on to what extent the Community's 'civilian power' image might be compromised by action that some states in the international arena might have construed as having been taken at the behest of the United States. Given the Community's hopes of maintaining its independent line, notably on Middle East conflicts, this was no small consideration. Moreover, the reconciliation of differing viewpoints on such a sensitive issue was facilitated by the new Troika arrangements (providing for close association between the immediate past, present and future EC Council Presidencies).

Important as the step to name states sponsoring terrorism was for the Community, this was to be but one element in an anti-terrorism package that embraced both punitive and defensive measures. While Libya was the specific target, general principles in respect of counter-terrorist responses were enunciated. As will be shown below, these reflected a more widespread view among Western democratic states that the 1980s had witnessed a qualitative change in the nature and ambit of terrorism to which appropriate responses had to be developed. Moreover, the Community's commitment to the completion of the internal market (which implied the removal of intra-Community frontier controls) had implications for EC states' efforts to combat terrorism.

Douglas Hurd, echoing the views of Members of the European Parliament, pointed out that relaxing internal barriers demanded a concomitant strengthening of the Community's external frontiers, and increased cooperation and information-sharing among member states. While the EC states did not contemplate developing a military response to terrorism, partly for logistical, political and moral reasons, 1986 was to be the first occasion on which one of the Western targets of international terrorism was to retaliate militarily. EC states openly doubted the wisdom and utility of such a response. Few believed it would curb terrorism, which many felt had to be seen in the context of Arab efforts to defeat Israel.

The problem for the European Community lay in preserving in theory and practice its independence from the US on Middle East issues while broadly condoning tighter anti-terrorist measures. For the Community this meant scrutiny of a range of diplomatic, legal and economic but not military sanctions that the states could invoke in concert. The deteriorating situation in the Lebanon and the Middle East generally, coupled with the spate of terrorist attacks against Western targets there and elsewhere, and the covert deals with terrorists (often conducted by intermediaries) to secure the release of hostages meant that the timing of further anti-terrorist measures was a highly sensitive matter.

Irrespective of mounting US pressure, some EC member governments were unwilling to jeopardise their own positions through the imposition of new Community measures at delicate moments. Thus, on an individual basis, member states' responses continued to reflect past practice. Terrorism had been treated primarily as a domestic problem requiring first and foremost domestic political and legal responses. International endeavours to counter and frustrate terrorism were adjuncts to these. During 1984 and 1985 in particular the inadequacy of existing national and international responses was underlined. This meant that the drawbacks of rather tentative agreements on European cooperation against terrorism—whether within the context of the Council of Europe or of the European Community—were accentuated.

The Community's first response to this was to try and ensure that all its members ratified and applied existing conventions and agreements (such as the European Convention on the Suppression of Terrorism). Then attention turned to making each state's provisions as compatible as possible with the others. Progress was arduous, to say the least. US pressure on the Community to supplement such legal responses with additional measures, principally wide-ranging economic sanctions—was not well-received and failed to elicit prompt compliance. Member states were wary of damaging national interests, contracts and bilateral links and loath to invoke measures that might be construed as hostile particularly when sensitive secret talks were under way. However, they were equally tardy in producing a prompt and decisive alternative anti-terrorism package.

One of the most important factors determining the content and timing of further Community responses was the intention of preserving the credibility of its carefully cultivated 'independent' image in respect of the Middle East. EC members were more aware of linkages in international affairs and less willing to contemplate military retaliation than was the United States. These considerations coloured their response. Even so, US-Libyan confrontations on Europe's doorstep were to prove the catalyst in producing the more extensive and concerted response to terrorism by the Community that several states and their politicians had long been advocating and threatening. Prior to analysing this response in some detail, it will be useful to outline briefly the genesis of the crisis.

The crisis

A spate of anti-NATO bombings in 1984 and 1985 was followed by the hijack of the Italian cruise liner, the *Achille Lauro,* in October 1985 and the ensuing escalation in US-Libyan confrontation that culminated in the US military raid on Libya. Many commentators felt that Libya had got its just deserts: Libya was perhaps foremost among a group of Middle East states including Syria and Iran that sponsored terrorism. State sponsorship was seen to be fundamental to the rise in international terrorism.[7] Its beneficiaries encompassed not only indigenous terrorist groups like Abu Nidal's Black September but also the Italian Red Brigades and the Provisional IRA who derived support from Libya.[8]

While Libya was not the sole dispenser of such aid, it was certainly the most vociferous. Moreover, once the US had acted against Libya, it could not maintain its credibility without both taking steps both to discourage Americans from supporting the IRA and to review its own views on the extradition to Britain of fugitives, and espousing the view that the USSR—by dint of military aid provided to Middle East states including Libya – profited indirectly from terrorism.[9]

A brief survey of the background to the US-Libyan confrontation shows that relations had not been cordial for many years.[10] Since the unsuccessful attempted intervention in Libya by the US and British secret services in 1969 when a group of army officers had seized power from King Idris, relations had deteriorated progressively.[11] The Middle East wars and Gadaffi's vociferous offensive against Israel and those he deemed to be its supporters led him not only to sponsor terrorism but ultimately to do so publicly while issuing direct threats against the US President.[12]

From the time of the US-Iranian embassy siege and the car-bombing of the US embassy in Tripoli in December 1979, the situation grew worse. Between 1979 and 1981, President Reagan stressed his commitment to combatting international terrorism. His allegations of Soviet complicity became more muted under Gorbachev, but evidence of Libyan subversion against other states in the Middle East that were, unlike Libya, prepared to tolerate Israel's existence (e.g. Egypt, Sudan, Tunisia and Lebanon) grew. Libyan troops intervened in Chad in 1980 and 1983 and Libya announced its determination to undermine US interests throughout the world. As Hubel argues, Reagan was especially annoyed by the export of Libyan arms to Nicaragua in April 1983[13] and by incidents against the Sixth Fleet. Anxiety was also apparent over Libyan activities in the South Pacific.

US allegations of Libyan sponsorship of terrorism against the US and Atlantic Alliance were not unfounded. In 1981, maintaining that Libyan assassination squads were operating in the USA, the American government expelled Libyan diplomats and closed the Libyan People's Bureau in Washington. US concern did not abate, so the authorities contemplated afresh alternative responses. By 1986 the US had banned economic cooperation with Libya and in the interim had increased pressure on the European Community for an effective economic boycott.

Although several EC states had been somewhat sceptical of the evidence the US adduced to prove Libyan complicity in terrorist incidents in Europe, incontrovertible signs of Libyan involvement grew and were confirmed with the murder of British policewoman Yvonne Fletcher outside the People's Bureau in London in April 1984. The anniversary of her death saw US military retaliation for the spate of terrorist attacks against US targets that reached a climax in spring 1986.

Gadaffi's call in March 1985 for suicide missions to oust moderate Middle East governments reinforced the US view of Libyan sponsorship of terrorism: in July President Reagan referred to twenty-five incidents over the past year implicating Libya. He argued that Libya had committed 'acts of war' against the US and stressed that 'under international law any state which is the victim of acts of war had the right to defend itself'.[14] This statement was not just part of the rhetoric of brinkmanship but had implications too for members of the Atlantic Alliance. They, too, were to debate appropriate new and more integrated anti-terrorist measures and to probe the issue of what types of action NATO could legitimately engage in.

The Europeans were worried lest their professed solidarity with the US occasion economic and political penalties for themselves. If they had to choose, then it was doubtful that the former would be purchased at the expense of the latter in the Middle East. However, in 1984 and 1985, as pressure grew in the European Parliament for concrete measures, they had taken steps to advance Community cooperation against terrorism. In September 1984 they agreed on a set of principles to combat terrorism, including the need for a joint response in the event of a serious attack involving the abuse of diplomatic immunity. In June 1985, Ministers of the Interior and of Justice adopted recommendations on the hijacking of aircraft; and in July 1985 there was agreement on increased cooperation in aviation security—fears persisting that some airports had lax security precautions. 1986 was to see principles being translated into action. At their EPC meeting of 27 January 1986, EC Foreign Ministers adopted a declaration strongly condemning states supporting terrorism (though Greece and Spain bitterly opposed any reference to Libya); noting their intention to ban the export of arms or military equipment to such states, and to explore national measures to prevent such exports being diverted to terrorists; and committing themselves to deterring their citizens and industries from seeking commercial advantage from others' (i.e. the US's) retaliatory anti-terrorist measures.[15] They also set up a permanent working body with a precise mandate within EPC to monitor and promote the implementation of these measures.

What was particularly worrying about the 1980s spate of terrorism against US targets was that the target had shifted from diplomatic and military personnel to the public. Whereas the 1979 US Iranian embassy siege involved diplomats, and the car-bombing of the US barracks in 1983 in Beirut involved servicemen, subsequent attacks were less discriminating. As a result, US citizens withdrew from sports tournaments such as the Italian Open tennis tournament in Rome in May 1986; trade delegations cancelled projected trips to Europe; the number of US tourists to Europe fell dramatically;[16] TWA closed its Cairo-Athens and Cairo-Rome connections, and Pan Am cancelled planned new European routes to Frankfurt and Paris. It seems to have been the shift to the public domain (and with it the assault on Westerners in the Middle East where their governments were immediately at a disadvantage) that was to be the last straw for the US. Libya seemed to be spearheading increased provocation.

In March 1986, Libya used anti-aircraft missiles against US force exercises in the Gulf of Sidra to which Libya (seemingly breach of international law) laid claim as part of its territorial waters. This direct attack on the US triggered the switch to a military response to terrorism. Even if the European Community had supported the US earlier by invoking political and economic sanctions against Libya it seems unlikely that the US retaliatory strike would have been averted. A catalogue of attacks, since the summer of 1985, including those clearly implicating Abu Nidal, seemed to have convinced the US that force was warranted in the endeavour to counter international terrorism against the US and her Allies.

Among such attacks were: the June hijacking of TWA 847; the July bombing of the British Airways and Alia offices in Spain; the August bombing of the Café de Paris in Rome injuring thirty-eight, the bombing of BA offices in Rome injuring fifteen, and the further bomb attack on an Athens hotel. Aircraft over the Mediterranean proved vulnerable to hijackings. In October, the *Achille Lauro* was hijacked between Egyptian ports of call. One US citizen was murdered, 194 passengers and 189 crew were held hostage. Italy allegedly gave guarantees to the hijackers in return for the release of the hostages. However, US airforce planes intercepted the aeroplane carrying the apprehended terrorists to Sicily and forced it to land at a European US base. This was followed by the November Valetta hijack with fifty-seven fatalities and the bomb attacks against Rome and Vienna airports in December. Attacks against US citizens intensified in early 1986.

On 5 April, a disco in West Berlin frequented by US soldiers was attacked and several people were injured or killed. US intelligence agents traced the incident to Libyan agents in East Berlin[17] and others found evidence of Syrian complicity. On 15 April the US bombed Tripoli. Many EC member states publicly deplored this action. Privately, however, several supported the move either directly with logistical assistance, or indirectly. Moreover, this military response was to galvanise Community leaders into publicly identifying Libya as a terrorist state. On 21 April EC ministers agreed to intensify Community cooperation against terrorism and to impose sanctions on Libya.

The European Community's response to the US strike

The European Community's response was elaborated in the face of a rapidly worsening situation in the Middle East, notably in Lebanon, where Westerners increasingly were frequent targets. Anxiety had grown among EC states about the rise in terrorism during 1985 and efforts had been made, as noted above, to increase cooperation against it. In particular, the Community came under pressure to act against states believed to be sponsors of terrorism. When the EC's Foreign Ministers met on 27 January 1986 to discuss terrorism, they set up an *ad hoc* committee on terrorism. This was to prepare EC positions and to elaborate possible additional measures to be taken to combat international terrorism. The group's third meeting was held shortly before the US raid on Libya. Immediately before this, several EC states had backed the US in contesting Libya's claims *vis-à-vis* the Gulf of Sitre. The Community wanted to see the crisis defused, but on the surface it seemed paralysed. Member states reacted differently, partly because the US had failed to keep its allies sufficiently informed of its intentions.[18] As a group, however, they made clear their intention to take punitive measures against state sponsors of terrorism. Their declaration seemed like a warning shot across the bows when the immediate enforcement of new measures in view of the escalating situation seemed warranted.

Community concord proving elusive, in March 1986 the Dutch Foreign Ministry (while holding the EC presidency) issued a statement on its own behalf deploring Libya's action and arguing that it was not justified historically or under maritime law. Libya launched missiles against the US Sixth Fleet exercising in the Gulf, and Mr Weinberger confirmed the sinking of four Libyan warships. Libya called on 'the Arab nation to rise up' against the US, arguing that the latter had violated its airspace, and lodged a protest with the UN stating that the US represented a threat to world peace.

The deteriorating situation was well appreciated by EC ministers who realised that Europe, because of its geographical proximity to the Middle East, could take the brunt of further terrorist attacks. Mr Andreotti cancelled his official visit to Hungary at the end of March in order to keep an eye on the situation. Meanwhile, it was officially denied that any manoeuvres or alerts were under way at Comiso, NATO's Italian cruise missile base.[19]

Moreover, EC member states were very mindful of the damage that could be wrought to their carefully cultivated policy of independence from the US in respect of the Middle East. Numerous intensive talks took place and statements were made indicating the long-held belief that the roots of terrorism were located in the Arab-Israeli conflict and that a political solution to that was essential both in itself and to denying terrorism a *raison d'être*.[20] Herr Genscher argued both in February and at the emergency meeting of EC Foreign Ministers in The Hague on the eve of the US raid that the European Troika and representatives from the Arab League should meet to examine joint measures against terrorism.

Declaratory action but little else seemed feasible. This was not just because the member states diverged over what additional measures would be desirable and warranted, but because such measures inevitably involved action outside the Treaty of Rome and impinged further on states' national sovereignties. Even the imposition of economic sanctions against third states is a far from simple measure in view of the European Community's jurisdiction.

Much as many people believed any military retaliation by the US to be politically unwise and potentially counter-productive, they secretly shared the belief that something had to be done to curb someone like Gadaffi who had personally indicated willingness to train, organise and help terrorist actions against US interests and those of its Allies. The editor of *Europe* argued that since terrorists aim to limit and modify the range of political choices open to people, and since Europe had experienced in the 1930s the dangers of capitulation at the time of the Munich settlement, state terrorism must not be accepted simply in order to avoid tension. He called upon the international community to combat terrorism, a call that many reiterated both then and now.[21]

EC Foreign Ministers were to meet three times in April to discuss terrorism and the crisis in the Mediterranean. Meeting in emergency session within the framework of Political Cooperation on 14 April, they confirmed their January decision to cease the export of arms to countries suspected of supporting terrorism, but this time went further and named

Libya. However, they were anxious to avoid creating the impression that Libya was the sole perpetrator of state-sponsored terrorism in the Arab world and elsewhere. Consequently, their reference to Libya was placed in the context of threats issued by Gadaffi against Spain and Italy.

It was these threats that had led Spain and Italy jointly to request an emergency EPC meeting. On 9 April President Reagan said in a speech that the US would take reprisals against any state guilty of terrorism and indicated that Libya was under suspicion. It was rumoured that he had approached Mrs Thatcher with a view to using F-111s stationed in Britain for a raid on Libya. On 10 April Libya announced a counter-attack plan embracing all southern European towns, having interpreted President Reagan's speech as implying that Libya was threatened not just by the US but by the whole of NATO.

Intense bilateral discussions took place among EC states at this stage. The Italian-Spanish request for the emergency meeting was tabled with France's signature, and the Dutch Presidency announced on 11 April that it was to be convened on 16 April. Exchanges via the COREU network resulted in it being brought forward to 14 April. On 12 April, at Malta's request the UN Security Council examined the situation, and it was rumoured that the Kremlin had initiated a hot-line conversation with Washington.[22] Indeed, some sources claim that although the Kremlin wanted to avoid direct confrontation with the US in the Middle East and while it was anxious to uphold the principle of the freedom of the high seas, it had indirectly strengthened Libya's position through its provision of military advisers and modern weapons systems.[23]

As is typical in crises, things were moving rapidly, with a maximum of secrecy. Thus also on 12 April, a US mission led by Mr Vernon Walters met British leaders, and Mrs Thatcher announced that she did not think that it would be appropriate for F-111s stationed in Britain to be used in any possible action.[24] Mr Walters then went on to Bonn, Paris and Rome for further talks. At 2 a.m. on 15 April, the US bombed Tripoli and Bengazi using aircraft from the Six Fleet and 18 F-111 bombers stationed in Britain and refuelled in flight, as France and Spain had refused transit permission in their airspace. No NATO Mediterranean base was used; the USSR was informed of the raid; and EC states were informed of the possibility of such an action by the President's Special Envoy, General Walters.[25]

Speculation in the US and Europe had been growing during the preceding few months over if and when the US might resort to military action against terrorism. Many observers believed it to be a real option. Nevertheless, few in Europe seemed to have anticipated the strike. EC member governments had painfully inched their way towards measures supporting earlier US demands during the spring. They had indicated in January that if terrorism continued they would act against its perpetrators. Unanimity on firmer EC reprisals remained elusive, however, though measures against the abuse of diplomatic immunity were being taken.

Member governments reacted to the raid with barely concealed anger. The day before they had urged caution and moderation. Their Ad Hoc Committee was due to submit a report to the Twelve the following week, and their Interior and Justice Ministers were also to meet to discuss terrorism. The Twelve held an extraordinary meeting in Paris on 17 April and reaffirmed their decisions of 14 April which had been taken in ignorance of US intentions. Before meeting again on 21 April, the Dutch Presidency had further contacts with the US, Arab countries, the Warsaw Pact and non-aligned countries to seek agreement on joint action against terrorism. Some EC member governments vented their anger on Britain, and Mr Tindemans, as well as some MEPs, accused Sir Geoffrey Howe of complicity. The Community was divided on the issue of the raid but united in the demand for a political solution. Sir Geoffrey explained that he did not know of the US decision to effect military action until after his return from the Hague where the EC Foreign Ministers had reached agreement, and had issued a declaration on international terrorism and the crisis in the Mediterranean.[26] This statement is in sharp contrast to the US position.

THE HAGUE DECLARATION ON TERRORISM

The Foreign Ministers' declaration went beyond condemnation of terrorism and a commitment to concert common action against terrorism. The Twelve, calling on states believed to sponsor terrorism to renounce such support and to respect the rule of international law, requested Libya to act accordingly. Promising a 'vigorous response' to state-sponsored terrorism, the Twelve announced a series of measures against such states and Libya, including:

—restricting the freedom of movement of diplomatic and consular personnel; (note that Libya had already at the beginning of the year made such restrictions on foreign personnel in Libya);
—cutting the size of diplomatic and consular missions in EC states;
—stricter visa requirements and procedures;
—an export ban on arms and other military equipment to Libya as per their declaration of 27 January;
—increased intelligence cooperation by the Twelve with other states to improve security and combat terrorism;
—joint pressure by the Twelve, and in conjunction with other states, on Libya;
—inviting Arab states and the Arab League to analyse jointly and urgently the matter of international terrorism.

In addition, the Twelve urged caution to avoid military escalation, and to facilitate a political solution. They decided to implement measures agreed on 14 April and to invoke additional measures against Libya. They also agreed to increase cooperation with other states in intelligence matters; to improve security measures; and to combat terrorism. To this end they instructed experts to identify appropriate measures to be taken by the Twelve including tightened security, the application of international conventions on diplomatic and consular privileges and immunities and on the safety of civil aviation. Countries abusing privileges and supporting terrorism were given notice that normal relations between them and EC states were in danger of being severed.

What this meant in practice was that TREVI cooperation was intensified, and the member states immediately began ordering Libya to reduce its staff in their capitals while simultaneously reducing their own representation there and in Syria. Libyan terrorist suspects expelled from one member state were to be denied entry to another. Tripoli then expelled several Western journalists but by the end of April, with intenser Community cooperation by ministers of the Interior and Justice as well, there were signs that Libya was worried by EC sanctions (the Community ceased to sell intervention butter benefitting from special refunds to Libya) and particularly by signs that it could no longer rely on Italy, Greece and Spain for sympathy. (Spain had, for example, backed Community sanctions and had allowed six of the US air tankers that participated in the raid on Libya to be transferred from the US Spanish base only days before the raid, according to *El Pais*.)[27] However, Greece's refusal to comply with sanctions against Libya resulted in a Community reprimand to the Greek government that insisted that it would delay sanctions until presented with 'tangible evidence' of Libyan complicity in acts of terrorism.[28] When Libya expelled thirty-six West European envoys in mid-May, in retaliation for recent expulsions and restrictions on Libyan diplomats, Greece—which had not expelled any Libyans—was excluded.

European governments were under American pressure to adopt a more forceful line against terrorism. As a result of their Hague deliberations and the raid, they expedited measures already under consideration, including the drafting of a diplomatic blacklist (under which diplomats expelled from one state would not be readmitted to another) agreed by the Twelve and pressed for by Mrs Thatcher at the Tokyo summit. Libyan action and US pressure probably also led to the leak of the Twelve's 'blacklist' of countries believed to be sympathetic to terrorism. This had been drafted by European police chiefs and security experts. They identified Libya, Syria, Iran, Iraq and the Lebanon as operating bases; Libya, Syria, Iran and Iraq as offering logistical support; Libya and Iran as offering

ideological backing; Libya, Syria, Iran, Iraq, the Lebanon and
South Yemen as providing terrorist bases; Tunisia, Jordan,
Algeria, Sudan and North Yemen as giving homes but not
direct support to terrorist bases.[29]

Simultaneously, discussions proceeded along very similar
lines in other European bodies. The President of the WEU
Assembly, Mr Caro, proposed the creation of a 'European
Group to Coordinate the Fight Against Terrorism'(GECLAT)
to centralise intelligence information and coordinate measures
to prevent terrorists evading prosecution. This matter was one
that keenly preoccupied EC Ministers, who were acutely aware
of the potential security risks that might be posed by the policy
to which they were committed of realising the customs union
and eliminating barriers (including border controls). Mr Caro
also advocated the creation of a multinational operational unit
to coordinate all relevant services and police forces and, if
necessary, the armed forces. He was not alone in interpreting
commitments of mutual support in the event of armed attack
in international organisations to include support in the event of
terrorist attack.[30] However, while no Euro-equivalent of
GSG-9 or the SAS was accepted, the need for effective and
timely exchange of information and concerted European-wide
action was.

Not until the late summer, after the spate of terrorist
attacks in France, was real progress noted. In the interim, it
became clear that several states—foremost among which was
perhaps France—had paid lip service to previous agreements
to cooperate in combatting terrorism but had then forsaken
international cooperation against terrorism in favour of
national action: action which, it was alleged, involved
negotiation with terrorists. The terrorist bombing campaign in
France during August and September was widely interpreted as
a reprisal by terrorists against France for failing to deliver on a
previous deal. New visa requirements introduced by France
against all non-EC nationals resulted in a swift response from
five of the six members of the European Free Trade
Association (EFTA) requesting that they be waived for their
nationals.

THE EUROPEAN COMMUNITY'S RESPONSE IN CONTEXT

Pressure for the European Community to reinforce its own attempts to formulate and enforce anti-terrorist measures on a Community-wide basis intensified during the first half of 1986. Indeed, even before the spate of terrorist bombings in France in September, steps had been taken to increase EC cooperation against terrorism. However, as late as July, the Council's January decision to deny support or refuge to terrorists was weakened by the lack of a decision on what form cooperation in this matter with third countries would take.[31]

Meanwhile, numerous preparatory meetings indicated not only the depth of Community concern at terrorism and at intimations of a renewed military response by the US but also presaged firmer action when the Foreign Ministers met in September. Indeed, although the June European Council meeting in the Hague had been overshadowed by the problems of determining the nature and scope of any economic sanctions to be taken against South Africa, by late summer it was clear that the Community intended to accord priority to the elaboration of more stringent anti-terrorist measures.

It was also apparent that efforts were being made among the Western Allies as a group to take more coherent and coordinated measures against terrorism. The EC states, however, were keen to maintain a position that was recognisably independent from that of the US. They also remained reluctant to accept the stationing of forward bases for US Delta Force counter-terrorist teams and other US special operations forces (the Navy SEALS, army Ranger battalions and US air force 1st Special Operations Wing) in Europe.[32] However, they agreed in principle with the Americans on the need for greater exchange of information and concerted action among the Western Allies.

At the beginning of September, the US Permanent Representative at the UN, Mr Walters, had a series of talks with the NATO Deputy Secretary General Mr Guidi, several EC Foreign and Defence Ministers, Prime Ministers and

President Mitterrand. Mr Walters invited the Europeans to 'continue the process of economic and political dissuasion already underway against terrorism'.[33] He also discussed with them the implementation of measures against Tripoli that had already been determined earlier in the year and indicated that the US hoped that the French would not participate in the maintenance of two Airbuses sold to Libya in August by a Hong Kong-based company.[34]

While Mr Walters desisted from requesting additional measures against Tripoli by the Europeans, he insisted that any new Libyan assault be countered by a united NATO response. Italy immediately opposed any military initiatives, stressing that the EC response should be to exploit remedies at international law. Simultaneously, however, several terrorist attacks occurred: a Pan Am jet was hijacked in Karachi; the Munich industrialist Karl Heinz Beckurts was murdered in July and the German Red Army Faction launched a new bombing campaign—bombs were hurled at the Office for the Protection of the Constitution in Germany; twenty-three were killed in the Istambul synagogue; the British base at Akrotiri was attacked in August; and a series of bomb attacks occurred in Paris and elsewhere in Europe. Kidnappings of Westerners rose both within Europe and in the Middle East, and the Council of Europe reported that over 3,000 terrorist incidents had occurred between 1970 and 1985.[35]

When the twelve Foreign Ministers met informally at Brocket Hall, they underlined the need for concerted international action to combat terrorism. Sir Geoffrey Howe argued for greater exchange of information among member states and for reducing the presence of bodies like the Libyan People's Bureaux. Similar arguments were echoed by Members of the European Parliament.

In a compromise resolution adopted by 193 to 11 with one abstention, MEPs called for more effective cooperation between the security services of democratic states, strict application of extradition regulations (which continued to be bedevilled by national caveats) and the creation of a Community bureau for the fight against terrorism. Arab leaders were asked to combat terrorism and to suppress terrorist bases. As in the past, this compromise resolution embraced many (but not all) of the demands tabled in individual resolutions from six different groups. (The European Right did not sign the compromise text and a separate vote was taken on its draft resolution.) All agreed on the need for international cooperation, notably with UN agencies, and well-coordinated action to combat terrorism. M. Planas (Soc./Spain) called for the holding of a European conference on terrorism, and M. Coste-Floret (EARD/France) for the creation of a European Prosecuting Office.

Meanwhile, Belgian Justice Minister Gol took up the invitation by US officials concerned with terrorism to visit Washington to discuss the issue with them. On his return, he noted his intention to start negotiations aimed at the conclusion of a bilateral convention for extraditing terrorists. The significance of his visit should not be underestimated since Belgium was to take up the Presidency in January 1987, and the fight against terrorism remained a Community priority. Moreover, TREVI meetings had continued throughout the summer, and counter-terrorist experts from EC states' security services met to exchange information and to improve intelligence and police cooperation.

In September, following the TREVI meeting of Interior Ministers, work began on compiling a blacklist of the most dangerous terrorists, assassins and arms dealers. Intelligence information, it was decided, would be sent to all EC states' police forces via a secure, coded facsimile service.[36] This agreement was a breakthrough given the known reluctance of the French security forces—the DST (equivalent to MI5) and the DGSE (similar to MI6)[37]—to pool information.[38]

By the autumn, however, it was clear that whereas progress on internal security cooperation was possible, securing Community agreement on appropriate political and diplomatic responses to terrorism was far from straightforward. The British adopted the most consistent approach when the government broke off diplomatic relations with Syria following the submission of evidence implicating

Syrian representatives in the Hindawi case. The other member governments did not follow the British line, and only through sustained pressure was Britain able to secure agreement from them to chastise Syria. Even then, Greece demurred, as expected. However, Members of the European Parliament backed Britain's stand by approving an amendment to the Community's budget freezing aid to Syria.[39]

When Ministers of the Interior met in London on 20 October to discuss immigration and means of combatting drug trafficking and terrorism, the deliberations had to be seen against the context of the plans to advance the completion of the internal market. A major consideration for the European Community is the creation of a system of relaxed internal border controls that cannot be easily abused. To this end, consideration is being given to the coordination of visa policies; improved information-sharing between immigration and passport services; and measures to promote a common policy to eliminate the abuse of the right of asylum (Germany's very liberal policy has come in for close scrutiny).

The ministers set up a high-level *ad hoc* working group comprising ministers' immigration policy advisers and EC Commission representatives to examine all these issues as well as the role and effectiveness of border controls at internal frontiers in the fight against terrorism, drugs, crime and illegal immigration. In addition, the group is to investigate ways of easing intra-EC travel without opening the system to abuse by terrorists and criminals. It is also scrutinizing measures to develop a common policy to prevent the abuse of political asylum in consultation with the Council of Europe and the UN High Commission for Refugees. It is interesting that these deliberations coincided with the production of new internal frontier signs combining twelve gold stars on a royal blue background which are supposed to appear at the Community's internal borders in future; and that the group's work is to be coordinated with advances on the internal market. Clearly, one of the greatest dilemmas for the Community lies in how to reconcile two aims: first, the creation of the internal market and with it the realisation of a People's Europe (with all it implies for freedom of movement across national frontiers); and second, the containment—in the absence of a supranational system of criminal jurisdiction—of the threat posed by anyone seeking to abuse the former in order to engage in trans-frontier criminal activities.

CONCLUSION

The problems of defining a European Community response to terrorism in the mid-1980s were exacerbated by the erosion of the interface between strictly national, member-state areas of jurisdiction and the steady expansion of Community competence. To some extent this was furthered by the adoption of the Single European Act. However, Mediterranean enlargement and external factors including growing EC-US friction over other issues also played an important role in increasing member states' readiness to contemplate action which would impinge on their national sovereignty. There can be little doubt that the European Community is seen as a proper arena for member states to pursue shared aims on international policy matters. Naturally, the tendency is for high political issues to be pursued within the context of European Political Cooperation. The British government certainly favours the conclusion of international conventions over supranational action, and like others welcomes parallel moves to combat terrorism within the Council of Europe where Interior and Justice Ministers have begun to study states' different penalties for terrorism, and political and legal steps that could be taken to combat terrorism; ways of harmonising legislation on terrorism; improving coordination among anti-terrorist services; formulating a common European definition of terrorism; and examining emergency measures against terrorism. The problem seems to be that neither the Council of Europe nor EPC is able to ensure prompt and uniform compliance with agreements reached not least in such a sensitive area as terrorism. However, the Community's concern with the completion of the internal market and the realisation of a

People's Europe has shown both the limits of EPC action and the potential need for increased coordination between EPC and EC goals, and for promoting a common legal space, possibly by means of variable geometry.

This is one reason why emphasis seems to have been put on the pursuit of complementary action in different European bodies ranging from the Council of Europe and the WEU to NATO. It also helps to account for the shift in views on the type of action that might be contemplated to combat terrorism. By the autumn of 1986, it was clear that EC member states were considering seriously new measures to supplement their existing anti-terrorist provisions based on extradition arrangements.

This implied both realisation of the limitations of those provisions but also acceptance of the implications of other, apparently discrete, policies—such as those relating to immigration, visa controls, and rules governing diplomats from non-Community states. Indeed, it was recognised that useful as the exchange of information, for example among EC police forces, might be, this needed to be translated into action if it was to mean more than a data-gathering exercise. This is borne out by TREVI-related developments, including the creation of a small permanent body to enhance continuity; improved relations with third states; and better coordination of the work of specialised internal groups dealing with drugs, crime, police training, harmonising the right to asylum and immigration policies.

Other ideas have also been revived. The Belgian government has indicated interest in promoting cooperation on legal matters among member states whereby existing conventions (such as those on extradition, and on child custody) might form the starting point for new measures.

In 1987, the Belgian Presidency could claim the credit for finalising three initiatives, taken in early 1985 by the Italian presidency, to encourage the creation of a European legal area (the *espace judiciare européen*). In May 1987 ten member states signed the Council of Europe's Convention on the Transfer of Sentenced Persons which is designed to allow people sentenced to imprisonment in an EC state other than their own to choose to serve their sentence in the home prison. In addition, seven member states signed a Convention between the EC's members on double jeopardy, and eight signed the Convention abolishing the legalisation of documents in the EC's states. These agreements were all signed in the presence of Commissioner Sutherland who also heard the Twelve's Justice Ministers affirm the need to increase international legal cooperation in criminal and civil matters in order to realise the *espace judiciare européen* which is seen as basic to achieving free movement within the EC as laid down in the Single European Act.

The member states have recently reconsidered the usefulness of the Dublin Agreement as an appropriate framework for *close* judicial cooperation in combatting terrorism. The possibility of opening it to all member states and of removing earlier reservations has also been scrutinised and sent to experts for detailed examination.

In May 1987, consideration was given to the Belgian draft agreement on simplifying and modernising extradition procedures. Further investigation of these matters will take place during late 1987 under the Danish Presidency. A key issue to be examined concerns the use of modern communication techniques such as facsimile machines. EC Ministers and others involved in parallel discussions in other international bodies are also contemplating the recurrent question of creating an international or a European Court for terrorist activities (modelled on the European Court of Human Rights).

Given EC states' underlying commitment to achieving political solutions to difficult and threatening occurrences by resorting to legal sanctions, the idea of Europeanising still further the legal process and legal measures is gaining ground even though formidable barriers, in the shape of national legal and political traditions, exist. Yet, the Italian government is not alone in thinking that such a process would enhance each member state's ability to withstand terrorism and retaliation by terrorists.

However, if Europeanisation of legal responses to terrorism and international crime is to be effective, then many of the unspoken ground rules concerning the fight against terrorism will have to be honoured by all concerned. Abandoning, for example, the 'political defence' argument in extradition proceedings has implications for fugitives and reinforces the commitment to the *aut dedere aut judicare* principle. Increased kidnappings and hostage-taking also have implications for the policy of non-negotiation with terrorists. Governments may have to reappraise any activities leading to secret deals whether these are elaborated through government agents or non-governmental intermediaries.[40] Moreover, they will have to try and be consistent and, whenever possible, ensure correspondence between what they say publicly and what they do privately in the fight against terrorism.

In the short term, however, EC member states have to deal with the external implications of their commitment to realise an internal goal: completing the market. The Single European Act recognises the inevitability of security matters becoming properly subject to common scrutiny and action either within the context of EPC, the EC or international organisations where EC states will expect to act in concert. More exchange of views may be expected among the groups concerned with counter-terrorist measures in such bodies as TREVI, EPC, WEU, NATO, economic summits and the Council of Europe. The elaboration of a common set of counter-terrorist measures by West European states is clearly a desirable goal in its own right. However, the European Community has now to consider another side to the coin which the completion of the internal market highlights.

So far, the implications of the internal market for the Community's internal border controls have been commented upon. Much thought has gone into refining police coordination and cooperation and coordination of intelligence work, using TREVI, for example. At this level, however, the member states are operating very largely within the parameters of past policy: the principle of extraditing and trying fugitive terrorists remains a cornerstone of this policy.[41] The creation of a European legal space similarly relates to this principle and to the formulation and implementation of a range of linked principles based on the premise that common penalties for terrorism and international crimes should obtain. Terrorism will continue to be defined as a crime and increasingly the 'political defence' will not be allowed.

The completion of the internal market also suggests the need for the European Community to take on board other facets of the fight against terrorism. Indeed, certain additional measures might be said to complement both the realisation of the internal market and the Community's more recent steps to counter state-sponsored terrorism. Tougher scrutiny of foreign diplomats and their activities; refusal to allow diplomatic personnel expelled from one EC state to enter another; ceasing arms sales to states known to sponsor terrorism by whatever means, and refusing to trade hostages and negotiate with terrorists, have counterpoints in commercial policy as well as in member states' broader foreign policy dealings. This means that EC states will seriously have to contemplate the introduction of measures to stop, rather than simply to deter, companies from trading with states sponsoring terrorism. If diplomatic ties are severed or very strained, political pressure needs to be bolstered by real economic sanctions—notably where sensitive military and high-technology goods are involved. However, achieving consistency remains problematic. It makes little sense for one EC state to stop trading in such an instance, if the gap is to be filled by either an EC or a US competitor.

While in theory it may seem simple to suggest common sanctions policies, this would be difficult to achieve and not just because of the limits of the Treaty of Rome. The European Community itself has but a rudimentary industrial policy, and the notion that defence equipment may be legitimately considered by EC institutions is a highly sensitive matter on which progress is only beginning to be made. It is clearly very difficult for the diverse membership of the Community to agree on contentious principles let alone on ones which may result in lost contracts.

The question of combatting terrorism effectively by resorting to legal sanctions available at national and international law is becoming increasingly complex. The kinds of response that might be deemed desirable on the Community's part are both hard to elaborate and problematic to enforce. This is partly because the member states have different legal and political traditions and overseas trading patterns and political ties, but also because the legal basis for EC action in this area is very narrow and, to an extent, an unknown quantity. The member states are, moreover, very wary of relinquishing sovereignty in both existing and new policy sectors. Criminal law matters were not originally seen as falling under the European Community's jurisdiction. Measures to combat terrorism may continue to be agreed within EPC but their enforcement depends on member states' compliance and approved links between judicial and foreign policy cooperation officials involved in EPC itself and in TREVI and the EC. The creation of the *espace judiciare européen* is no easy matter.

The type of response expected from the European Community far exceeds its ability to deliver: it is not a state. It does not have similar state apparatus at its command to conduct foreign policy. Nor does it have agreement among its members that would enable it to implement a far-reaching anti-terrorist policy even assuming that consensus on its contents could be secured. It has to rely on each of its members to honour agreements. This is both a weakness and a source of strength: a weakness in that the Community's diversity can be exploited by others; a strength in that the closure of channels of communication between an adversary and one or more member states does not mean the blocking of all communication, since an EC partner can keep a friendly eye on developments and can explore the chances of renewing severed links at an opportune moment. This is an important consideration if embassies and diplomatic missions are closed. But care must be taken to discourage third states from exploiting any intra-EC divisions.[42] In the case of fractured links with both Libya and Syria, Italy seemed to test diplomatic overtures.[43]

However, it is equally apparent that the real scope of EC states' cooperation within the context of both judicial and foreign policy cooperation in EPC is probably greater than the Single European Act would suggest. Informal links are significant and the potential for joint action especially important given the known failings and limitations of possible action under WEU.[44]

Moreover, while this discussion has focused on Community-level action, it must be remembered that this complements rather than supplants national provisions. However, national and Community measures must be made compatible with one another if they are not to cancel each other out. This is one of the Community's major preoccupations at present. A further dimension to the problem concerns their relationship to other commitments in organisations like the Council of Europe, WEU and NATO (witness the series of parallel discussions in WEU during 1986 on terrorism) and the compatibility and effectiveness of domestic, provincial arrangements. If Community level action is to be effective, then steps must also be taken to ensure that the various police and security forces are well-briefed and equipped to implement any action that is foreseen.

It is at this level that responsibility for the policy once more devolves to national and regional levels and accentuates the need for common standards and procedures. It is also at this level that the general issue is once more raised as to how to ensure that measures introduced designed to deter and to apprehend criminals (terrorists) do not curtail individuals' freedoms and endanger liberal democracy. For legal measures to be effective, however, there must be consistency, cooperation, coordination and consultation. Standard operating procedures and contingency measures must be devised in the knowledge that they can be implemented swiftly, when circumstances demand, at all appropriate levels.

This means that the European Community has moved (and indeed is endeavouring to move) from a phase where the issuing of declarations and statements of principle was the main hallmark of the Community response, to a phase where enforcing those principles becomes a realistic, attainable and expected response. Inevitably, there will be instances where the Community has to act by a majority decision rather than unanimity among its member states on certain issues. Greece has repeatedly demurred from a generally agreed line. It is debatable whether Greece will, in the longer term, find it in its interests to be isolated from its partners.

What Community responses to terrorism reveal is the continuing commitment of its member states (even after the Community's enlargement) to countering terrorist offensives by the resort to legal remedies. By the mid-1980s, EC policy had moved from the notion of isolating state sponsors of terrorism and exerting verbal and moral diplomatic pressure, to the introduction of measures designed to inhibit the activities of their personnel in the Community. At the same time, there remained a distrust of a policy based on negative sanctions—whatever form they might take—and a real interest in promoting dialogue, notably in the Middle East, to find a peaceful solution to the current problems.

For the European Community to stand any chance of making a credible input in the attempt to render the climate of opinion favourable to talks, it had to distance itself as much as possible from US actions. Bilateral links with Middle East figures therefore remain important and, in a sense, a part of EC states' arsenal of measures aimed at averting terrorism.[45] Indeed, Community anti-terrorist measures increasingly are fashioned in the light of external terrorism emanating from the Middle East rather than in the light of indigenous terrorism, ethnic nationalism or European terrorism.

While based on a continuing commitment to legal remedies, the Community's response to terrorism brings into sharp relief the limitations of the Community in time of crisis and the acute difficulties it has in making any EC policy towards the Middle East credible. The commitment to legal remedies remains, nonetheless, important. It has helped to shape measures designed to prevent the abuse of political asylum, to coordinate action to combat organised crime, harmonise extradition agreements, promote the rapid exchange of information and regular exchanges of personnel between police and security forces, and encourage member governments to name publicly those states responsible for sponsoring terrorism. It has also helped to fashion consensus over appropriate responses having the broad support of most Community governments and major political parties, as is shown by the plethora of resolutions tabled over the years in the European Parliament in favour of concerted Community action.

Resolutions may differ in the emphasis accorded particular points or in the stress placed on the need to maintain civil liberties, but the drift is the same. More recently, there have been calls for the establishment of procedures for common anti-terrorist laws to be administered by a common court dispensing uniform penalties and possibly imprisonment in a Euro-prison. Extreme as some of the measures advocated (but not implemented) may seem, they are not simply demanded by the far right but enjoy some support in other quarters. Indeed, an international court authorised to deal with terrorism may exist by the 1990s.

The difficulty for member governments is to reconcile their commitment to firm, consistent Community anti-terrorist principles with practice. In crises, political expediency may lead them to engage in clandestine deals or to pursue policies producing contradictory messages to state sponsors of terrorism and others. The credibility of both national and Community anti-terrorist policies may then be shaken.

Member states' and Community measures to combat terrorism highlight the complex moral and political issues that anti-terrorist measures involve. However, a realistic gradualistic policy based on the rule of law commands Community-wide consent. Such a policy is rooted not simply in the Community's distrust of the long-term effectiveness of military action, nor in its own civilian power image, but in a belief that concerted action based on the rule of law (and having a demonstration effect to the rest of the world) is the proper course for liberal democracies wishing to balance counter-terrorist measures and liberal democratic values in the pursuit of peaceful political solutions to pressing potentially destabilising domestic and international problems.

NOTES

1. See P. Taylor, *When Europe Speaks with One Voice,* London: Aldwych Press, 1979; D. Allen, A. Pijpers *et al., European Policymaking and the Arab-Israeli Conflict,* The Hague: Nijhoff, 1984; and D. Allen, R. Rummel, *et al., European Political Cooperation,* London: Butterworth, 1982.
2. See J. Lodge, 'European Union and the first elected Parliament: the Spinelli Initiative', *JCMS* 22(1984)377-402.
3. See text of the EUT (draft treaty establishing the European Union) in J. Lodge, *European Union: the EEC in Search of a Future,* London: Macmillan, 1986.
4. R. Bieber and J. Weiler, *An Ever Closer Union,* Luxembourg, 1985.
5. See House of Lords Select Committee on the European Communities, *European Union,* HL226, 1984-85; and R. Corbett, *The 1985 Intergovernmental Conference,* Hull: European Community Research Unit, 1986.
6. See *Completing the Internal Market,* White Paper from the Commission to the European Council, Brussels, 1985; and J. Lodge, 'The Single European Act: Towards a new Euro-Dynamism'? *JCMS* 24(1986)203-23.
7. *NATO Assembly,* May 1986, p. 7.
8. Also accused by President Reagan of sponsoring terrorism are N. Korea, Cuba, Iran and Nicaragua. *Ibid.,* p. 10.
9. See *Official Journal of the European Communities* (hereinafter *OJ*) C104, 16 April 1984, 44; R. Goren, *The Soviet Union and Terrorism,* London: Allen & Unwin, 1984; *NATO Assembly, op. cit.,* p. 10.
10. See *WEU document 1057* on the report submitted on behalf of the General Affairs Committee by Mr van der Werff (rapporteur) to the Assembly of Western European Union, 32nd Ordinary Session on 29 April 1986. This was devoted to the topic of 'Security and terrorism: the implications for Europe of crises in other parts of the world'.
11. H. Hubel, 'Der Hintergrund der Libyen-Krise', *Europa-Archiv* 18(1986) 541-50, 543.
12. *Ibid.*
13. *Ibid.,* 544.
14. *NATO Assembly, op. cit.,* p. 10.
15. See *Bulletin of the European Communities,* 1/86, pt.2.4.1 for text of declaration. For MEPs' earlier demands see *OJ* C141, 10 June 1985, 455; C122, 20 May 1985, 109; C72, 18 March 1985, 92.
16. 'USA-Europa: Das absolute Katastrophenjahr', *Der Spiegel,* No.22

(1986), 122-3.

17. *Christian Science Monitor,* 21-27 June 1986, B1.
18. *WEU document 1057, op. cit.,* p. 13.
19. *Europe,* 26 March 1986.
20. *Europe,* 27 March 1986. For earlier remarks to same effect see *OJ* C343, 31 Dec. 1985, 86; C342, 19 Dec. 1983, 49-50; C267, 10 Oct. 1982, 45.
21. *Europe,* 14-15 April 1986.
22. *Ibid.,* and *Europe,* 16 April 1986.
23. Hubel, *loc. cit.,* 545.
24. *Europe,* 14-15 April 1986.
25. *Europe,* 16 April 1986.
26. *Ibid.*
27. *The Times,* 28 April 1986.
28. *The Times,* 25 and 28 April 1986.
29. *The Sunday Times,* 27 April 1986.
30. *Ibid.*
31. Reply by Sir Geoffrey Howe to T.J. Maher in the European Parliament, 8 July 1986.
32. *The Guardian,* 9 Sept. 1986.
33. *Europe,* 3 Sept. 1986.
34. *Europe,* 4 Sept. 1986.
35. *Europe,* 9 Jan. 1987.
36. *The Times,* 27 Sept. 1986.
37. *The Times,* 24 Sept. 1986.
38. For the summary of active units see *The Times,* 24 Sept. 1986.
39. *EP News,* Nov. 1968.
40. When two French hostages were returned to the French embassy in Damascus, French Premier Chirac sincerely thanked the Syrian authorities, Saudi Arabia and Algeria at the very time when many of his Community partners and the US were taking measures against Syria to penalise it for complicity in terrorism. *Europe,* 12 Nov. 1986. Simultaneously, King Hussein of Jordan had contacts with EC states to explore the possibility of reducing differences between the US and USSR on calling a Middle East peace conference. *Europe,* 5 Nov. 1986.
41. See *OJ* C267, 11 Oct. 1982 44; C238 13 Sept. 1982. 83; also C. Fletcher-Cooke, *Terrorism and the European Community,* London: European Conservative Group, 1979.
42. Before the EPC meeting on 10 Nov. 1986 the Syrian Foreign Minister met ambassadors from the FRG, Italy, France, Spain, Belgium, Greece and the Netherlands. *Europe,* 7 Nov. 1986.
43. Bilateral exchanges also resulted in Andreotti explaining to Libya's Foreign Minister that Italy did not harbour hostility towards Libya and would like to restore normal relations. He noted the UN condemnation of the US raid. *Europe* 20 Nov. 1986.
44. *WEU document 1057, op. cit.,* p. 7.
45. Italy's statements may be relevant here. See n. 43.

Select Bibliography

There is voluminous primary and secondary literature on terrorism and many of the EC's member states, especially the Federal Republic of Germany, Italy and the United Kingdom, which is too extensive to list in the limited space available. Much official documentation is very useful. Many of the general works already listed in the chapter notes contain relevant chapters, and much of Paul Wilkinson's work gives details about terrorism in the UK and government responses to it. For the other states examined, the secondary source literature varies extensively in quantity and quality.

There is fairly extensive primary source material on the European Community and terrorism to be found in the Community's *Official Journal* and in the *Working Documents* of the European Parliament. Primary source material from other European organisations is often a rich source of information.

Alexander, Y., Carlton, D. and Wilkinson, P., *Terrorism: Theory and Practice,* Boulder, Colorado: Westview Press, 1979.

Alexander, Y. and Ebinger C., *Political Terrorism and Energy: The Threat and Response,* New York: Praeger, 1981.

Alexander, Y. and Finger, S.M. (eds) *Terrorism: Interdisciplinary Perspectives,* New York: John Jay Press, 1977.

Alexander, Y. and Finger, S.M., 'Terrorism and the Media', *Terrorism* 2 (1979) 55-137.

Alexander, Y. and Gleason, C. (eds) *Behavioral and Quantitative*

Perspectives on Terrorism, New York: Pergamon, 1981.

Alexander, Y. and Myers, K. (eds) *Terrorism in Europe,* New York: St Martin's, 1982.

Alexander, Y. and Nanes, A.S. (eds) *Legislative Responses to Terrorism,* Dordrecht: Nijhoff, 1986.

Amersfoort, J.M.M. van, *De Sociale positie van der Molukkers in Nederland,* The Hague: Staatsuitgeverij, 1971.

Assersohn, R., *The Biggest Deal: Bankers, Politics and the Hostages of Iran,* London: Methuen, 1982.

Aston. C.C., *A Contemporary Political Crisis: Hostage taking and the Experience of Western Europe,* Westport, CT: Greenwood Press, 1982.

Backes, U. and Jesse, E., *Totalitarismus, Extremismus, Terrorismus,* Opladen: Leske & Budrich, 1984.

Becker, G., *Hitler's Children,* London: Michael Joseph, 1977.

Bell, J.B., *Transnational Terror,* Washington DC: AEI, 1975.

Bell, J.B., 'Trends on Terror: the Analysis of Political Violence', *World Politics* 29 (1977) 446-88.

Benjamin, G. (ed.) *The Communications Revolution in Politics,* New York: Academy of Political Science, 1982.

Bowyer Bell, J., *A Time of Terror,* New York: Basic Books, 1978.

— *Transnational Terror,* Washington: AEI, 1975.

Boyle, K. *et al., Law and State: The Case of Northern Ireland,* London: Martin Robertson, 1975.

Bundesministerium des Inneren (ed.) *Gewalt von rechts,* Bonn: BMI, 1982.

— *Terroristen im Kampf gegen Recht und Menschenwürde,* (2nd edn) Bonn: BMI, 1985.

— *Der Terrorismus. Eine Akute Bedrohung des Menschenrechte,* Bonn: BMI, 1985.

Bundeszentrale für Politische Bildung (ed.) *Freiheit und Sicherheit. Die Demokratie wehrt sich gegen Terrorismus,* Bonn: BZPB, 1979.

Burton, A., *Urban Terrorism—Theory, Practice and Response,* New York: The Free Press, 1975.

Burton, J., *Deviance, Terrorism, and War,* Oxford: Martin Robertson, 1979.

Carlton, D. and Shaerf, C. (eds) *International Terrorism and World Security,* London: Croom Helm, 1975.

— *Arms Control and Technological Innovation,* London: Croom

Helm, 1977.
— *Contemporary Terror: Studies in Sub-State Violence*, London: Macmillan, 1981.
Carr, R. and Fusi, J.P., *Spain, Dictatorship to Democracy*, London: Allen & Unwin, 1981.
Cerny, P.G., 'France: Non-Terrorism and the Politics of Repressive Tolerance', in J. Lodge (ed.) *Terrorism: A Challenge to the State*, Oxford: Martin Robertson, 1981.
Chachet, A., 'De Molukse Minderheid in Nederland', *Sociale Wetenschappen*, 20(1977)124-37.
Cline, R.S. and Alexander, Y., *Terrorism: the Soviet Connection*, Centre for Strategic and International Studies, Georgetown: Georgetown UP, 1984.
Clutterbuck, R., *Kidnap and Ransom: The Response*, London: Faber, 1978.
— *Guerillas and Terrorists*, London: Faber, 1977.
— *Living with Terrorism*, London: Faber, 1975.
— 'Terrorism and Urban Violence', in G. Benjamin (ed.) *The Communications Revolution in Politics*, New York: Academy of Political Science, 1982.
Colectivo Herria Eliza, *Autodeterminacion de los pueblos: un reto para Euzkadi y Europe*, Bilbao: Herria 2000 Eliza, 1985.
Council of Europe, *Explanatory Report on the ECST*, Strasbourg: Council of Europe, 1977.
Crelinsten, R. *et al.*, *Terrorism and Criminal Justice*, Lexington, Mass: Lexington Books, 1978.
Crozier, B., *Strategy for Survival*, London: Temple Smith, 1978.

Dobson, C. and Payne, R., *The Weapons of Terror*, London: Macmillan, 1979.
— *Terror! The West Fights Back*, London: Macmillan, 1982.

Evans, A.E. and Murphy, J.F. (eds) *Legal Aspects of International Terrorism*, Lexington, Mass: Lexington Books, 1978.
Evelegh, R., *Peacekeeping in Democratic Society*, London: Hurst, 1978.

Fitzmaurice, J., *The Politics of Belgium: Crisis and Compromise in a Plural Society*, London: Hurst & Co., 1983.
Freedman, L., *et al.*, *Terrorism and International Order*, London: Routledge and Kegan Paul, 1986.
Friedlander, R., *Terrorism: Documents of International and Local*

Control, (3 Vols) New York: Oceana, 1979.

Fromkin, D., 'The Strategy of Terrorism', *Foreign Affairs,* 53 (1975) 683-98.

Funke, M., (ed.) *Terrorismus,* Düsseldorf: Droste Verlag, 1977.

Gal-Or, N., *International Cooperation to Suppress Terrorism,* London: Croom Helm, 1985.

Gaucher, R., *The Terrorists: From Tsarist Russia to the OAS,* London: Secker & Warburg, 1968.

Glaser, H., *Jugend zwischen Aggression und Apathie. Diagnose der Terrorismus—Diskussion,* Heidelberg: Muller, 1980.

Goren, R., *The Soviet Union and Terrorism,* London: Allen & Unwin, 1984.

Groom, A.J.R., 'Coming to Terms with Terrorism', *British Journal of International Studies* 4 (1978) 62-77.

Gurr, T., *Why Men Rebel,* Princeton: Princeton UP, 1970.

Harris, D.R., *Cases and Materials in International Law,* London: Sweet & Maxwell, 1979.

Horn, J., 'Terrorismebestrijding in Nederland', *Intermediaire,* 22 (1986) 35-9.

Horn, M., *Sozialpsychologie des Terrorismus,* Frankfurt: Campus, 1982.

Hoveyda, F., 'The Problem of International Terrorism at the United nations', *Terrorism,* 1 (1977) 71-84.

Hyams, E., *Terrorists and Terrorism,* London: Dent, 1975.

Jacobs, F.G., *The European Convention on Human Rights,* Oxford: OUP, 1975.

Janke, P., *Guerilla and Terrorist Organisations: A World Directory and Bibliography,* Brighton: Harvester Press, 1983.

— *Spanish Separatism: ETA's Threat to Basque Democracy,* London: Institute for the Study of Conflict, 1980.

Jenkins, B., *International Terrorism: A New Mode of Conflict,* Los Angeles, CA: Crescent, 1975.

Jenkins, B.M., 'International Terrorism: Trends and Potentialities', *Journal of International Affairs* 32 (1978) 115-23.

Kupperman, R.H., 'Treating the Symptoms of Terrorism: Some Principles of Good Hygiene', *Terrorism,* 1 (1977) 35-50.

Kupperman, R.H. and Trent, D.M., *Terrorism: Threat, Reality and Response,* Stanford: Hoover Institution Press, 1979.

Lacquer, W. (ed.) *The Terrorism Reader: A Historical Anthology,* Philadelphia, PA: Temple UP, 1978.

— *Terrorism,* London: Weidenfeld & Nicolson, 1977.

Lijphart, A. (ed.) *Conflict and Coexistence in Belgium,* Berkeley: Univ. of California Press, 1980.

Lipset, S.M. and Albach, P.G., *Students in Revolt,* Boston: Houghton-Mifflin, 1969.

Livingstone, N.C., *The War Against Terrorism,* Farnborough: D.C. Heath, 1982.

Lodge, J. (ed.) *Terrorism: A Challenge to the State,* Oxford: Martin Robertson, 1981.

Martin, L.J., 'The Media's Role in International Terrorism', *Terrorism,* 8 (1985) 127-46.

Medhurst, K., *The Basques and Catalans,* London: Minority Rights Group, 1982.

Meny. Y. and Wright, V. (eds) *Centre-Periphery Relations in Western Europe,* London: Allen & Unwin, 1985.

Merari, A., 'A Classification of Terrorist Groups', *Terrorism,* 1 (1978) 331-46.

Merari, A. and Friedland, N., 'Social Psychological Aspects of Political Terrorism', in S. Oskamp (ed.) *International Conflict and National Public Policy Issues,* special issue of *Applied Social Psychology Annual,* 6 (1985) 185-206.

Merkl, P.H. (ed.) *Political Violence and Terror: Motifs and Motivations,* Berkeley, CA: Univ. of California Press, 1986.

Norton, A. and Greenberg, M.H., *International Terrorism: An Annotated Bibliography and Research Guide,* Boulder, Colorado: Westview, 1980.

O'Brien, C.C., *States of Ireland,* London: Panther, 1974.

O'Connell, D.P., *International Law,* London: Stevens, 1970.

O'Sullivan, N. (ed.) *Terrorism, Ideology and Revolution: The Origins of Modern Political Violence,* Brighton: Wheatsheaf Books, 1986.

Parry, A., *Terrorism: From Robespierre to Arafat,* New York: Vanguard, 1976.

Pisano, V., *The Red Brigades: A Challenge to Italian Democracy,* Conflict Studies, No. 120, London: ISC, 1980.

Plascov, A., 'The Palestinian Gap between Israel and Egypt', *Survival*, 22 (1980) 50-8.

Rapoport, D. and Alexander, Y. (eds) *The Morality of Terrorism: Religious and Secular Justifications*, Oxford: Pergamon, 1982.
Raufer, X., *Terrorisme, Maintenant la France? La Guerre des Partis Communistes Combattants*, Paris: Ed Garniers Frères, 1982.

Schmid, A.P., *Political Terrorism: A Research Guide to Concepts, Theories, Data Bases and Literature*, Amsterdam: North Holland, 1983.
— and de Graaf, J., *Violence and Communication: Insurgent Terrorism and the Western News Media*, Beverly Hills, CA: Sage, 1982.
Shearer, I.A., *Extradition in International Law*, Manchester: Manchester UP, 1971.
Sobel, L.S. (ed.) *Political Terrorism*, New York: Facts on File, 1975.
Sterling, C., *The Terror Network*, London: Weidenfeld & Nicolson, 1982.
Stohl, M. (ed.) *The Politics of Terrorism*, New York: Marcel Dekker, 1979.

Townshend, C., *Britain's Civil Wars*, London: Faber, 1986.

Urwin, R.E.M., *The Flemings and the Walloons of Belgium*, London: Minority Rights Group, 1980.
US Department of State, *Patterns of International Terrorism: 1982*, Washington, DC: Government Printing Office, 1983.

Wardlaw, G., *Political Terrorism: Theory, Tactics, and Counter-measures*, Cambridge: Cambridge UP, 1982.
Weiler, J.H.H., 'Eurocracy and Distrust: Some Questions concerning the Role of the European Court of Justice in the Protection of Fundamental Human Rights within the Legal Order of the European Communities', *Washington Law Review* 61 (1986) 1103-42.
Wilkinson, P., 'Three Questions on Terrorism', *Government & Opposition* 8 (1973) 290-312.
— *Political Terrorism*, London: Macmillan, 1974.
— *Terrorism and the Liberal State* (2nd edn) London: Macmillan, 1986.

— 'Terrorism: International Dimensions', *Conflict Studies,* No. 67, London: Institute for the Study of Conflict, 1979.

— (ed.) *British Perspectives on Terrorism,* London: Allen & Unwin, 1981.

— 'After Tehran', *Conflict Quarterly,* 1 (1981) 5-14.

— 'Can a state be "terrorist"?', *International Affairs,* 57 (1981) 467-72.

Wittke, T., *Terrorismusbekämpfung als rationale politische Entscheidung,* Frankfurt: Peter Lang, 1983.

Index

Abasolo, Domingo Iturbe,
    139-40
Abu Nidal, 48, 171, 238, 241
Achille Lauro, 113, 238, 242
Action Directe, 70, 109, 186,
    187, 189-91, 217-19, 226,
    228
Aden, 32
Agca, Ali, 113
Aid to imprisoned terrorists,
    79-80
Aktion Widerstand, 71
Alessandrini, Emilio, 99
Algeria, 249
Andreotti, G., 243
Anglo-Irish Agreement, 51
Animal Liberation Front, 156
Anti-apartheid movement,
    163-5
Anti-colonialism, 218
Anti-fascism, 161-2
Anti-Imperialist Front in
    Western Europe, 70
Anti-militarism, 165-8
Anti-nuclear protest, 151, 152,
    154-6, 165-8, 192, 194-5
    see also Peace movement
Anti-terrorist measures, 6, 52-3
    in Spain, 130-7
    see also Government

response, Legal remedies,
    Military solutions
Arab terrorists, 113
    see also Libya, Middle East,
    State-sponsored terrorism
Argentina, 108
Argov, Shlomo, 48
Army *see* Military solutions
Arrest, powers of, 46
Arrogui, Jesús Mariía Zabarte,
    131
ASALA, 220-1
Audran, General René, 191
Austria, 21
Autonomia Operaia, 102, 107
Avanguardia Nazionale, 92-3
Azcárra, Joseba, 137

Baader-Meinhof Group, 11,
    60-1, 187, 192, 218
Bachelet, Vittorio, 99
Bakunin, M., 29
Bandrés, Juan Maria, 136
Barsimantov, Yacob, 190
Basques, 2, 120-3
    parties of, 128-9
Belgium, 179-209, 255
    arms industry, 180-1, 203
Bergarache, Moreno, 127-8
Biagi, Enzo, 94

Black Orchestra, 108, 111
Black terrorism, 89, 92-5, 101
Blanco, Admiral Carrero, 124
Bolivia, 108
Böll, Heinrich, 66
Bombings
   in Belgium, 179, 194-6, 208-9
   in Britain, 44-5
   in France, 215, 220-3
   in Germany, 62-3, 72-3
   in Italy, 89
   by Libya, 242
   in Netherlands, 158, 171-2
Brana, Guy, 219
Brigate Rosse, 95-101, 102,
      106-7, 110-12, 186, 193,
      238
Britain, 29-54
   bombings in, 44-5
   and the IRA 31-2, 36, 38-47
   policy principles, 50-1
   see also Thatcher, Margaret
Brittany, 224-5
Bruyn, Dr W.J., 162
Buscetta, Tommaso, 113
Byford, Sir Laurence, 52-3

Calogero, Pietro, 107
Camorra terrorism, 112-13
Capitanchik, D., 5
Carette, Pierre, 187-92, 196,
      198-200, 207
Carlos, 69
Caro, Mr., 249
Casalengo, Carlo, 106
Casardi, Admiral Mario, 105
Cattin, Marco Donat, 97, 99
      111
CCC (Belgium), 179, 181, 183
      186-202, 206-9, 219
Chevolet, Didier, 188, 207
CIA, 7
Ciolini, Elio, 111

Cirillo, Ciro, 89, 100
Civil war as terrorist aim, 193
Claessens, D., 69
Coco, Francesco, 96, 106
Commercial interests, 53, 258
Compartmentalisation in EC,
      231
Computer firms, attacks on,
      217, 218
Conspiracy theories, 3
Contest protest methods, 147
Convention on the Transfer of
      Sentenced Persons, 255-6
Cooperation between nations,
      9-10, 16-17, 53, 133-5,
      231-2, 235, 252
   see also Dublin Agreement,
      European Community
Corsica, 221-4
Costa, Pietro, 97
Coste-Floret, M., 252
Council of Europe, 14, 16-19
      20-1, 253-7
Craxi, Bettino, 98, 99, 109,
      112
Crime, terrorism as, 6, 64
Curcio, Renato, 95-6, 99, 102,
      103
Cutolo, Raffaela, 100
Cyprus, 32
Czechoslovakia, 108

Dalla Chiesa, Carlo Alberto,
      104-5, 111, 112
Dani, Fadl, 220
Defferre, M., 219
de Jonge, Hans, 155
delle Chiaie, Stefano, 92, 93,
      94-5, 108
della Porta, D., 187, 196, 198-9
Demonstrations, 84-5
Denmark, 23
d'Estaing, Giscard, 221-2, 225

Diplomatic bags, 22
Diplomatic personnel, 258
Disguise, 84-5
Downes, Sean, 41
Dozier, General James Lee,
    89, 100-1, 105, 109
Dublin Agreement, 21-4, 256
D'Urso, Giovanni, 89, 99-100,
    107
Dutschke, Rudi, 65

Easter Rising, 1916, 30-1
Electronic passports, 84
Employment, 77-8
Environment movement, 154-6
ETA, 119-42
    deaths due to, 124-6
    fragmentation of, 127-30,
    140
Ethnic nationalism, 2-3, 7, 42,
    119-21, 179-80
    see also CCC, ETA
European Community, 6-7,
    229-63
    disputes within, 230
European Convention on the
    Suppression of Terrorism,
    14, 16, 18-21, 53, 175, 205,
    227, 237
European Political
    Cooperation, 9-10, 15, 23,
    25, 231-5, 240-1, 254-5,
    257
European Union Treaty,
    233-4
Evola, Julius, 101
Extradition, 109, 205
    agreements, 18-20, 22-3,
    175, 255, 256
Extra-parliamentary
    movements, 58-9, 66, 146

Feltrinelli, Giangiacomo, 102,
    108
Fenians, 30
Finland, 170
Fiorini, Carlo, 111
Firearms control, 22
FLB-ARB, 224-5
Fletcher, Yvonne, 48, 240
FLNC, 221-4
France, 109, 213-28, 249
    and ECST, 19, 20,23
    and ETA, 134-5, 137, 141
Franke, Herman, 172
Freda, Franco, 93, 101, 108
Friedland, N., 11
FUAN (Italy), 93

Gaddafi, Colonel, 69, 237,
    238, 244-5
GAL (Spain), 141
Galand, Pierre, 198
Galvaligi, Enrico, 99
Galvin, Martin, 41
Garbidjian, Varodjian, 221
Gelli, Licio, 94-5, 108
Geneva Convention on the
    High Seas, 16
Genscher, H.D., 244
German Revolutionary Cells,
    198
Germany, 6, 21, 57-86
    left-wing terrorism, 60-70,
    75-7
    right-wing terrorism, 71-80
Gianettini, Guido, 93, 108
Godschalk, J.J., 151
Gol, Jean, 180, 199, 202,
    205-6, 252
Gordon riots, 1780, 29
Government response to
    terrorism, 11-13
    in Belgium, 199, 201-6
    in France, 212-13, 216,
    220, 222, 224-8

in Germany, 80-6
in Italy, 97-8, 99, 103-6
in Netherlands, 173-5
in Spain, 121, 124, 128
    131-41
in UK, 34-8, 45-7
Grassini, General, 105
Greece, 108, 234, 236, 241,
    248, 253, 261
Greenpeace, 155

Hague Convention, 1970, 16
Hague Declaration on
    terrorism, 247-9
Haig, General Alexander, 188
Herri Batasuna, 128, 136, 138
Hijacking, 240, 242
Holland *see* Netherlands
Hostage taking, 8-9, 47, 53,
    237
Howe, Sir Geoffrey, 246,
    251
Hubel, H., 239
Hunger strikes, 67, 70
Hunter, Graham, 119-42
Hurd, Douglas, 236

Ideology, 196
Imagery of terrorism, 3
India, 32
Intellectuals, 101-3
Intelligence gathering, 34,
    37-8, 50, 51-2, 174-5, 204
Intelligence services, 105-6
International Committee for
    the Defence of Political
    Prisoners in Western
    Europe, 70
International terrorism, 5,
    7-8, 47-9, 69
  and Belgium, 199
  and France, 218-22
  and Germany, 65, 67,

    69-70
  and Italy, 107-14
  and Netherlands, 168-71
  and Spain, 133-5
  and UK, 47-50
Internment, 39
IRA, 7, 31-2, 36, 38-47,
    120, 133, 238
Iran, 220-1, 227, 248-9
Iranian Embassy siege, 47-8
Ireland, 231
  British Army in, 34-41
  and ECST, 19, 21, 23
  partition of, 30-2
Iraq, 248-9
Islamic terrorism, 5
  see also Iran
Italy, 4, 20, 23, 89-114,
    236, 245, 248, 251, 259

Jaimaya, Zabarte, 131
Janmaat, J., 162
Jenkins, Roy, 45
Jordan, 249
Joxe, Pierre, 135
Judiciary system in Belgium,
    202-3
Jurisdiction *see* Legal
    remedies

KAS programme (Spain),
    138-9
Kema Keur Korps, 156
Kidnapping, 89, 97-100, 132
Koebben, A.J.F., 151, 162
Kok, Hans, 159
Kolinsky, Eva, 57-86

Lahaut Brigade, 188
Laqueur, W., 65
League of Nations, 16
Lebanese Armed Revolutionary
    Factions, 190

Lebanon, 248-9
Left-wing terrorism
  in Germany, 60-70, 75-7
  in Italy, 90-1, 95-103
Legal remedies against
  terrorism, 6, 13-25, 82-6,
  256-7, 259, 261-2
  in Italy, 103-4, 106-7
  in Spain, 132-3
Leisure time terorrists, 68
Les Halles incident, 227
Liberal democratic values, 1,
  9
Libya, 48-9, 53, 69, 205,
  227, 247-9, 251
  US bombing of, 228, 229,
  234-46
Liera, Savasta and Emilio, 111
Lodge, Juliet, 1-25, 229-63
Lomé Conventions, 24, 230,
  235
Luxembourg, 21

Mafia, 112-13
Malayan Emergency, 33-4
Malta, 21, 245
Maraval, J.M., 122
Marx, Karl, 29
Mazurier, Jean-Paul, 207
Media, 10-11, 13, 152
Meinhof, Ulrike, 70, 189
  see also Baader-Meinhof
  Group
Meins, Holger, 69
Menigon, Nathalie, 187,
  189-90
Merari, A., 11
Merkl, P.H., 2, 4
Meza, Garcia, 108
Miceli, General Vito, 93,
  94, 105
Middle East
  factions, 47

situation, 218, 219-20
  see also Libya
Military solutions, xiii-xiv
  in Britain, 32-41
  dangers in, 35
  and police, 51-2
Montreal Convention, 1971, 16
Moretti, Mario, 96, 97, 110,
  111
Moro, Aldo, 89, 97-8, 104,
  106-7
Moxon-Browne, Edward,
  213-28
Musumeci, Pietro, 94-5, 100,
  106

Nationalism *see* Ethnic
  nationalism
NATO, 10, 64, 109, 150,
  164, 166, 192, 193-7,
  250-1, 255, 257
Negotiation
  in Belgium, 181-2
  with ETA, 137-41
Negri, A., 103, 107, 111
Neo-nazism in Germany, 71-80
Netherlands, 7, 145-75, 243
  its politics, 150-1
New Left in Belgium, 185
Newman, Sir Kenneth, 40
Niedhart, F., 75-7
Non-violent action, 146-7
North Yemen, 249
Norway, 20, 170
Nuclear energy, 151
Nuclei Armati Proletari, 95-6
Nuclei Armati Rivoluzionari,
  93

OAS, 4
Occorsio, Victor, 93
Oldfield, Sir Maurice, 51-2
Olivier, André, 217

Onaindia, Mario, 136
Onkruit (Netherlands), 166-8
Oppressed groups, 2-3
Ordine Nuovo, 92-3
Oriach, Frederic, 189

Pagliai, Pierluigi, 94, 108
Paisley, Ian, 32, 42
Palestine, 32, 51, 69
Paternostre, Chantal, 190, 206
Peace movement, 58, 63, 66, 165-8, 197-8
Pearse, Patrick, 30-1
Peci, Patrizio, 111
Peci, Roberto, 112
Pelosi, Walter, 105
Pertur, 127-8
Phoenix Park murders, 30
Piccoli, Flaminio, 100
Pillarisation, 148
Planas, M., 252
PLO, 69, 74, 80, 109, 146, 220, 227
Police
  in Belgium, 201-2
  in Italy, 104-5
  power, 45-6, 132
  in Spain, 131-3
Political violence, 4,
  in Netherlands, 149, 153-68, 173
Pollack, Benny, 119-42
Potere Operaio, 102
Pozzan, Marco, 92
Prevention of Terrorism Act, 44-6
Prima Linea, 96-7
Propaganda Due (Italy), 94
Proscription of IRA, 45
Protestant Action Force, 40
Public responses to terrorism, 3, 5, 10-13, 106-7, 140, 227

Racism, 160-2
Rauti, Pino, 92, 108
Reagan, President, 239-40, 245
Reale, Oronzo, 103
Red Aid, 70
Red Army Faction, 2, 5, 7, 66-70, 108-9, 153, 171, 186, 190-1, 200, 219, 251
Red Brigades *see Brigate Rosse*
Red Help, 146, 153
Red Resistance Front, 146, 153, 171
Red terrorism, 90-1, 95-103
Red Youth, 146, 153, 175
Rees, Merlyn, 39
Refugees in France, 214
Right-wing terrorism
  in Germany, 71-80
  in Italy, 89-95, 101
  in Netherlands, 160-2
Rosón, Juan José, 136
Rossa, Guido, 110
Rossanda, Rossana, 106
Rouillan, Jean Marc, 187, 189-91
Royal Ulster Constabulary, 40-1, 51

Sabotage, 154-5
Sandalo, Roberto, 111
Sandrucci, Renzo, 100
Sanguinetti, Admiral, 223
Santillo, Emilio, 104
Santovito, General, 105
Sassoye, Bertrand, 207
Savasta, Antonio, 100-1
Schleyer, Hans-Martin, 218
Schmid, A.P., 6-7, 145-75
Search powers, 46
Secret services, 52
Security police in Ireland, 40-1
Senzani, Giovanni, 100-1,

110-11
Seton-Watson, Christopher,
    89-114
SID (Italy), 92-3, 94, 105
Signorelli, Paolo, 93, 95
Simeoni, Dr., 223
Single European Act, 10, 25,
    231, 232, 233, 254, 256,
    257, 260
Social composition of German
    terrorism, 75
Social movements, 58, 153-4
Social reinsertion, 135-7
Sossi, Mario, 96, 106
South Moluccan protests,
    145-6, 173-4
South Yemen, 249
Spain, 108, 109, 119-42, 236,
    241, 245, 248
    change to democracy, 124-6
Spiral of conflict (ETA), 123-4,
    129-30, 139
Squatters' movement, 156-60
State-sponsored terrorism, 4, 8,
    12-13, 16, 17, 22, 232,
    238-40, 248-9
    see also Libya
Stohl, M., 12
Student movements
    in Belgium, 184-5
    in Germany, 58-9, 64
Subversion, 188-9, 192
Sudan, 249
Sunningdale Agreement, 39
Supergrasses, 47, 111-12, 113
Surinam Liberation Council,
    169
Sweden, 20, 21, 170
Switzerland, 170
Syria, 248-9, 252-3

Taliercio, Giuseppe   100
Tejero, Antonio, 129

Terrorism
    decline of, in Italy, 109-10,
        113-14
    definition of, 1-13, 72, 145
    limitations of, 42
    and political violence, 4, 68,
        71, 149, 153-68, 173
    potential, 206-8
    state-sponsored, 4, 8, 12-13,
        16, 17, 22, 232, 238-40,
        248-9
    as strategy, 12
    targets of, 63
Terrorists
    attempts to categorise, 3-4,
        75-6, 215
    'leisure time', 68
Terza Posizioni, 93
Thatcher, Margaret, 53, 245,
    248
Third World solidarity, 162-5,
    167
Thompson, Sir Robert, 34
TIGER committee, 52
Tokyo Convention, 1963, 16
Tolerance of dissent, 175, 214
Trade unions
    in Belgium, 183
    in Italy, 90, 91, 110
Transnational terrorism, 7
    see also International
        Terrorism
TREVI system of consultation,
    22, 50, 175, 234, 248, 252,
    255, 257
Troika arrangements, 232, 236,
    244
Tunisia, 249
Tupamaros, 5
Tuti, Mario, 94
Txomin, 139-40

UK, 21

see also Britain
Ulster Freedom Fighters, 40
Ulster Volunteer Force, 40
Unemployment, 77-8
    in Netherlands, 151-2
United Nations, 16
Urban guerillas, 65
US attack on Libya, 234-46

Van Acker, Luc, 200, 207
Vandegeerde, Pascale, 188, 207
Van der Loo, H., 147
Van Thijn, Ed, 159-60
Ventura, A., 108
Vietnam war, 34
Viking Youth, 161
Violence, acceptability of, 68,
    71

see also Political violence

Walloons, 184-6
Walters, Vernon, 245-6, 250-1
Weinberger, Caspar, 243
West Germany *see* Germany
WEU, 10, 249, 255, 257, 260
Wiersma, B.Y., 161
Wilkinson, P., 4, 7, 9, 10,
    17, 29-54
Women, 75, 77, 165, 219

Xenophobia, 152, 160

Zimmermann, Ernst, 191